English Unlimited

B1+ Intermediate
Coursebook with e-Portfolio

David Rea & Theresa Clementson with Alex Tilbury & Leslie Anne Hendra
Course consultant: Adrian Doff

CAMBRIDGE
UNIVERSITY PRESS

Contents

Contents

How to use this coursebook

Every unit of this book is divided into sections, with clear, practical **goals** for learning.

The first four pages of the unit help you build your language skills and knowledge. These pages include speaking, listening, reading, writing, grammar, vocabulary and pronunciation activities. They are followed by a **Target activity** which will help you put together what you have learned.

The **Explore** section of the unit begins with either a **Keyword** page, which looks at one or two of the most common and useful words in English, or an **Across cultures** page, and then an **Explore speaking** or **Explore writing** page. The Explore section gives you extra language and skills work, all aiming to help you become a better and more culturally aware communicator in English.

The **Look again** section takes another look at the target language for the unit, helping you to review and extend your learning.
Sometimes you will also find this recycling symbol with the goals, to show when a particular goal is not new but is recycling language that you have met before.

This symbol shows you when you can hear and practise the correct pronunciation of key language, using the audio CD.

The **e-Portfolio** DVD-ROM contains useful reference material for all the units, as well as self-assessment to help you test your own learning, and **Word cards** to help you test your vocabulary learning.

You can do more practice by yourself using the **Self-study Pack**, which includes a workbook and interactive DVD-ROM.

The DVD-ROM contains video and over 300 interactive activities.

1

1.1 goals
- talk about entertainment media
- talk about habits
- express preferences

Media around the world

Entertainment and you

LISTENING

1 Look at the TV channel logos below and talk with a partner.

1 What kind of programme do you think each channel shows?
2 What kind of TV or radio programmes do you enjoy? Think about:
- reality shows
- sport
- drama
- cookery shows
- nature programmes
- news

2 a ◆ **1.1** Listen to four people talking about TV and radio. Which channels does each person watch?

❶

AL DAWRI & AL KASS SPORT CHANNEL

Juan from Argentina

❷
FUJI TELEVISION NETWORK, INC.

Carmen from Spain

Aiko from Japan

❸

cinco SHOP

Yasir from Saudi Arabia

❹
MTV VIDEO MUSIC AWARDS LATINOAMERICA MEXICO '05

❺

BBC WORLD NEWS

b ◆ **1.1** Listen again. Who:

1 only watches TV on the Internet?
2 can't watch much TV these days?
3 doesn't like the adverts on TV?
4 enjoys radio more than TV?
5 loved a drama show as a teenager?
6 likes learning about things on TV?
7 watches cookery programmes?

3 Where you live, which is the best TV channel or radio station for:

- high-quality news?
- nature programmes?
- the most popular shows?
- good dramas?
- sports programmes?

VOCABULARY

Habits and preferences

4 Find the highlighted expressions in the script on p146 and answer the questions.

1 Which group of expressions is used to talk about:
   a habits?   b things you like?   c things you don't like?
2 Which expressions in box 3 do the speakers use to talk about:
   a current habits?   b past habits?
3 Which expressions can be followed by:
   a a noun?   b an -ing form?   c an infinitive?

1	2	3
I'm a big fan of ...	I'm not a big fan of ...	I hardly ever ...
I'm really into ...	I can't stand ...	I tend to ...
I prefer ... to ...	I'm not keen on ...	I'll ...
I'd rather ...	I find ... really irritating.	I used to ...

WRITING AND
SPEAKING

5 **a** What TV and radio do you like? Write five sentences with expressions from 4.

I'm a big fan of reality TV shows.
I tend to listen to the news on the radio.

b Compare with a partner.

1 Do you like the same types of TV and radio programmes?
2 Have your habits changed much in the last ten years?

Anything good on TV?

LISTENING

1 **a** Do you watch TV with other people? What happens if you don't want to watch the same programmes?

b ● **1.2** Listen to Paul and Rebecca talking about what's on TV.

1 What does Rebecca want to do?
2 What does Paul want to do?
3 What are their plans for later?

GRAMMAR

Talking about
the present

2 Which sentences A–C from the conversation are about:

1 a time up to now?
2 uncompleted activities happening now or around now?
3 things that are always true or happen all the time?

A Present simple
❓ Do you read books?   ➖ I don't like watching films more than once.
➕ I read magazines.

B Present progressive
❓ What are you doing?   ➖ I'm not reading anything at the moment.
➕ I'm trying to read.

C Present perfect simple
❓ Have you read it?   ➖ I haven't looked.
➕ We've seen it before.

3 **a** Complete the questions with the correct forms of the verbs in brackets.

1   *Do* you *prefer* TV, radio, books or the Internet? Why? (prefer)
2   _____ you _____ anything at the moment? What? (read)
3   _____ you _____ anything interesting recently? What? (read)
4   _____ you _____ a TV series at the moment? Which one? (follow)
5   _____ you _____ watching TV from other countries? Give examples. (like)
6   _____ you _____ any important news today? What? (hear)
7   _____ you _____ anything good on TV in the last week? What? (see)

Grammar reference
and practice, p134

b ● **1.3** Listen to check. ❷ Write three more questions about media habits for a partner.

PRONUNCIATION

Common pairs
of words 1

4 **a** ● **1.4** The highlighted words are some of the most common pairs of words in English. Listen to how you say them.

1 Do you watch TV in English?
2 Are you reading anything?
3 Have you heard the news recently?
4 Would you like me to record it?
5 Can you pass the remote?

b Practise saying the pairs of words on their own. Then practise asking the questions.

SPEAKING

5 **a** Ask and answer all the questions in 3a, and the questions you wrote in 3b.

b Tell the class something interesting you found out.

Fact or fiction?

READING

1 a Which of these do you use when you need to get information?

- the Internet
- reference books
- newspapers
- magazines
- advertisements
- encyclopedias

b Which do you tend to trust? Why?

2 Read the article. Match paragraphs 1–4 to subheadings a–d.

- a Can we believe what we read on the Internet?
- b Can we believe what we read on paper?
- c The difficulty of knowing what to believe.
- d A surprise online discovery.

Can you believe what you read?

1 When Mike Scott, a singer, read the page about himself on Wikipedia.com, he noticed several facts were wrong. So he started correcting them online. When he got to the end of the page, he looked up and saw that the information at the top of the page was changing back again. He couldn't believe his eyes. He wrote about it in his blog and minutes later, he got a message from a complete stranger. The person explained that he was a big fan of Mike Scott and maintained the Mike Scott Wikipedia page. He checked the page regularly and if any facts changed, he immediately changed them back.

2 Today, anyone can write a blog or an article online. Wikipedia, where anyone can post or change an entry, has become a popular way to do research. But is it a good place to get reliable facts? In recent years, many people, like Mike Scott, have found that their online biographies contain inaccurate information. Terry Millstone, a web-based journalist, says, 'Wikipedia seems like a really great idea but actually it's quite a dangerous website. People call this the great internet age, but there's never been a worse time to get accurate information.' Not everyone agrees with this view. Pete Morley, another journalist, says, 'People criticise Wikipedia because they're afraid of it. There's no other source of information which is so up-to-date and free.'

3 So, is it a better idea to place our trust in what we read in magazines, newspapers and books? There have been a number of scandals in the publishing world over the years, but one of the most extreme was the story of Stephen Glass. At only 25, he was a celebrated journalist working for the highly respected US political magazine, *The New Republic*. All that ended in May 1998 when it was discovered that one of Glass's biggest articles was a fake. Later, it was found that Glass had made up facts in 27 of the 41 articles he wrote for the magazine.

4 So, how do we know what to believe? Words have always had the power to influence people and, rightly or wrongly, we tend to trust the printed word. But with the rise of the Internet, that trust is at greater risk than ever.

3 Read the article again and answer the questions.

1 What did Mike Scott's fan do? Why?
2 What does Terry Millstone think about Wikipedia? Why?
3 What did Stephen Glass do?
4 Do you agree with Terry Millstone or Pete Morley?
5 What do you think the writer's opinion is? Why?

VOCABULARY

Talking about facts and information

4 Find words and expressions in the article with these meanings:

1 (2 *adj*) which can be trusted or believed = r_____
2 (2 *adj*) not completely correct or exact = i_____
3 (2 *adj*) correct, exact = a_____
4 (3 *noun*) reports about shocking things that people have done = s_____
5 (3 *noun*) something which seems real but isn't = a f_____
6 (3 *multi-word verb*) invented = m_____ _____
7 (4 *verb*) believe = t_____
8 (4 *noun*) belief = t_____

5 **a** Complete the questions with words and expressions from 4.

1 How often do you think information in advertisements or magazines is _____?
2 Would you buy a designer T-shirt or DVD which was _____?
3 Do you _____ what politicians say? Why? Why not?
4 Have there been any _____ about famous people in your country recently?
5 Do you think it's more important for newspapers to be entertaining or _____ and _____?
6 Have you ever _____ something _____ on your CV?

b Ask and answer the questions in groups.

It's a good way to ...

1 You can use place, way, time, idea with these adjectives to evaluate and recommend things. Which adjectives are they used with in the article?

But, is it a _____ place to get reliable facts? Wikipedia has become a _____ way to do research. There's never been a _____ time to get accurate information. Is it a _____ idea to place our trust in what we read in magazines, newspapers and books?	good bad popular different better worse great terrible

2 Look at quite and really in this sentence and answer the questions.

Wikipedia seems like a really great idea, but actually it's quite a dangerous website.

1 Which makes the meaning a lot stronger?
2 Which goes before a/an? Which goes after a/an?

3 **a** Complete these sentences with your own ideas to give recommendations.

1 ... is a good idea.   3 ... is an easy way to ...   5 ... is a popular place to ...
2 ... is a terrible idea.   4 ... is a safe place to ...   6 ... is a great way to ...

b Choose two or three sentences from 3a. Add quite or really.

Checking facts in more than one place is quite a good idea.

c Compare your ideas. Ask questions to find out more information.

4 **a** Think of recommendations for these things.

* websites   • computers   • eating out
* physical exercise   • finding information   • doing homework

Think about your own experiences and plan what you want to say.

b Talk together. What do you think about each other's ideas?

That new Korean restaurant is a really popular place.

Yeah, that's true. The best time to go is early evening, before the rush, and it's quite a good idea to book early.

Describe a book or a TV show

1.3 goals

◉ express preferences ♻
◉ evaluate ideas ♻
◉ describe a book or TV show

One Hundred Years of Solitude

Chef Ramzi

The West Wing

Born on a Blue Day

TASK LISTENING

1 **a** Look at the books and TV shows. What do you think they're about?

b ● **1.5** Listen to four people talking about them.

1   Were your ideas about the books and TV shows correct?
2   Did the people like what they read or watched? Why? Why not?

2 Would you like to read these books or see the TV shows? Why? Why not?

TASK VOCABULARY

Describing books and TV shows

3 **a** Can you remember what the people said? Complete sentences 1–10 with the information in the box. ● **1.6** Then listen to check. ℗

> book   amazing   interesting book   Gabriel García Márquez   his life   Martin Sheen
> boring   Márquez's own life   have all these problems   how to cook great meals

1   It's by someone called _____ .
2   It's quite a well-known _____ .
3   It's about this family who _____ .
4   People say it's _____ .
5   I found it _____ .
6   It's based on _____ .
7   It has _____ in it.
8   It looks at _____ .
9   It's a really _____ .
10   Basically, it shows you _____ .

It's by someone called Gabriel García Márquez.

b Look at the highlighted expressions. Which can you use to talk about:

1   a TV show?   2   a book?   3   both?

TASK

4 You're going to describe a book or TV show. Choose something you've read or seen. Then think about the language you need to:

• describe books or TV shows   *It's by someone called ...*
• express preferences   *I'm really into ...*
• evaluate things you've seen or read   *It's a really popular ...*

5 In groups, tell each other about the books or TV shows. Which would you most like to read or see?

6 Make a class list of recommended reading and viewing.

Across cultures Intercultural experiences

LISTENING

Federico from Buenos Aires, Argentina, lived in Egypt for a year.

1 Have you lived, worked or travelled outside your region or country? Talk together.

   1 Was it an easy or difficult experience? Why?
   2 Did you notice any differences from your culture? What?

2 **1.7** Listen to Federico talking about an experience he had in Egypt. How did he feel during the day? How about at the end of the day?

3 **1.7** Listen again and discuss these questions.

   1 Who did Federico go out for the day with?
   2 What language did they speak?
   3 What happened at lunchtime?
   4 What was the problem for Federico?
   5 Why was Manu upset?
   6 What do you think caused the problem between them?

4 **1.8** Listen to Federico talking about how he felt six months later. What cultural difference does he talk about?

VOCABULARY

Changes

5 Which sentences, A, B or C, are about:

   1 a present situation?
   2 a past situation?
   3 a process of change?

A   I found it quite difficult at first.
     I wasn't used to spending so much time in big groups.

B   After living in Egypt for six months or so, I began to understand what had happened.
     I slowly got used to being with a lot of people.

C   Now I'm OK with it.
     I'm used to it now.

---

6 a Think about changes in your life or the life of someone you know. Write five sentences with the highlighted expressions in 5. Think about:

   • moving abroad   • visiting another country   • moving to a different area
   • changing jobs   • changing schools   • learning a language

   I found it quite difficult when I first went into advertising.

b Compare your sentences with a partner. Are your experiences similar?

SPEAKING

7 a Think about these aspects of culture where you come from:

   • eating habits   • greetings   • personal space   • showing emotions
   • family life   • hospitality   • work–life balance   • sense of humour

Think about relationships between:

   • older and younger people   • men and women   • employers and employees

Which aspects of culture do you think:

   1 visitors can begin to understand quite quickly?
   2 take longer to get used to?
   3 you can only understand when you know the culture very well?

b Talk together. Do you have the same or different opinions?

1 EXPLORE Writing

Goal

© write a book review for a website

1 How do you make decisions about:

- where to go on holiday?
- which books to read?
- which TV shows to watch?

2 Look at the cover of *The Book Of The World*.

1 What do you think you'd find in the book?
2 What information do you think it gives about places?
3 Who do you think might buy it?

3 a Read two online reviews of the book and check your ideas.

b The site uses a five-star rating system. How many stars do you think each reviewer gave the book? Check your ideas on p118.

☆☆☆☆☆ **My favourite book,** 14 Jun 2010
By **L A Seadan 'LAS47'**
See all my reviews

This is an absolutely amazing book. If you are interested in seeing people around the world and their ordinary but colourful lives, then this book is definitely for you. Its organisation is especially clever: it organises countries from A to Z, rather than grouping countries by region, which means that you see a completely different part of the world every time you turn a page. It does something quite special – it exactly captures the mood of places I have been to, which is very unusual in my experience. It is written by travellers for travellers, not for someone doing a geography project.

It's really easy to read and still fascinates me. I love reading it, especially when I'm feeling bored of life or when it's raining outside. It's a wonderful source of inspiration as well. After reading it, my list of must-go-to places has tripled! This book deserves to be treasured by anyone interested in travelling the world, seeing its sights and meeting its people.

☆☆☆☆☆ **Coffee table book,** 14 Aug 2010
By **Aliya Bakaev**
See all my reviews

This is nothing more than a coffee table book. It contains some absolutely stunning photos and a quick guide to each country, [1]which is probably all you can expect from a book featuring every country in the world.

I browsed through it in a shop and was about to add it to my gift list. But when I went to the entry of my country of birth – Kazakhstan – I was disappointed to see that the main picture (taking over half the page) was taken in Tashkent, [2] which is in Uzbekistan. It's amazing that a travel book can get this kind of information completely wrong! It made me doubt all the other information in the book.

This book isn't especially helpful if you want to plan a trip, but it's a really nice book to get a snapshot of a country. Or you can just get some inspiration from the photos. They aren't your usual postcard shots, [3]which is refreshing to see.

4 Find the adjectives which go with these adverbs in the reviews.

absolutely *amazing* / _____
especially _____ / _____
completely _____ / _____
really _____ / _____

5 Look at the which clauses in the second review.

1 When is which used to:
   a add extra information?
   b say what the writer feels or thinks?
2 Find one more of each type of which clause in the first review.
3 Where do you put the comma (,) when you use which clauses like these?

6 a Write four sentences recommending one or two books. Try and use the language from 4 and 5.

It's an absolutely amazing book. The recipes are really easy to follow, which means you can cook lots of dishes straight away.

b Look at your sentences together. Would you like to read the books your partner recommended?

7 a Write a short book review for a website.

1 Choose a book to write about.
2 Think of positive and/or negative things to say about the book.

b Read some other students' reviews. Which book would you most like to read?

1 Look again ♻

Review

GRAMMAR Talking about the present

1 a Look at the game and complete the questions.

2 Have you seen any good films recently?

START

1 Go forward two spaces.	2 you / see / any good films recently?	3 you / study / anything at the moment?
6 you / change / anything in your life this year?	5 Go back one space.	4 what / you / usually do / on Friday nights?
7 Go to square 10.	8 What / do / at work at the moment?	9 Go back one space.
12 What have you …?	11 Start again.	10 you / learn / anything new at the moment?
13 What are you …?	14 What do you …?	**FINISH**

b Play the game in groups.

1 Take turns to toss a coin. For one side of the coin, move one space. For the other side, move two spaces.
2 When you land on a square, ask the question. Ask more questions to find out more.
3 If you land on the same square twice, ask a different player the question.

VOCABULARY Habits and preferences

2 a Make questions to find someone who:

1 used to play the same games as you as a child.
2 tends to go to bed at the same time as you.
3 can't stand the music you like.
4 hardly ever reads the same books as you.
5 prefers different websites from you.
6 is a big fan of a TV programme you love.

b Ask four or five people your questions. Who is similar to you? Who isn't?

Extension

SPELLING AND SOUNDS /f/

3 a 🔊 **1.9** Listen and <u>underline</u> the letters in these words which make a /f/ sound.

official different afford off stuff film often after yourself surf telephone pharmacy photograph laugh cough enough

b Find words in 3a to match spelling patterns 1–4 and think of another example for each pattern. /f/ is spelled:

1 f, particularly after l or r and before t.
2 ff after short vowels.
3 gh in these patterns: ough, augh
4 ph in some words.

c Spellcheck. In pairs, take turns to choose ten words and test your partner's spelling.

NOTICE and

4 a Look at the expressions with and. Which add emphasis? Which are verb + and + verb?

1 … so I can fast forward through all the ads and then watch the shows over and over. (🔊 **1.1** Juan)
2 I try and follow the news. (🔊 **1.1** Aiko)
3 It has hundreds of names and people and it just goes on and on. (🔊 **1.5** Carmen)
4 I don't know how you can read books again and again. (🔊 **1.2**)
5 Come and see the view from here. It's incredible.

b Complete sentences 1–5 with your own ideas. Then compare with a partner.

1 When I watched … I laughed and laughed.
2 I saw … and it went on and on.
3 There are lots and lots of … on TV these days.
4 … has got better and better.
5 Recently I went and saw … It was …

Self-assessment

Can you do these things in English? Circle a number on each line. 1 = I can't do this, 5 = I can do this well.

◎ talk about entertainment media	1	2	3	4	5
◎ talk about habits	1	2	3	4	5
◎ express preferences	1	2	3	4	5
◎ talk about information media	1	2	3	4	5
◎ evaluate ideas	1	2	3	4	5
◎ make recommendations	1	2	3	4	5
◎ describe a book or TV show	1	2	3	4	5
◎ write a book review for a website	1	2	3	4	5

• For Wordcards, reference and saving your work → e-Portfolio
• For more practice → Self-study Pack, Unit 1

Good communication

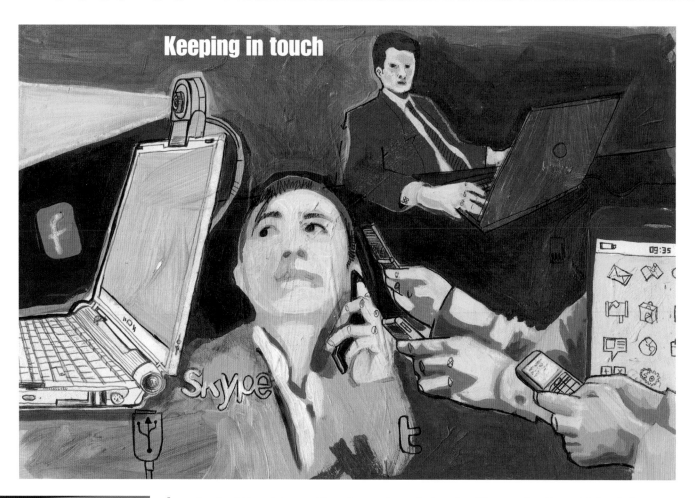

Keeping in touch

1 Look at the pictures. How do you keep in touch with your family and friends?

2 🔊 **1.10** Listen to two conversations. What method of communication is each about? What do the people think about it?

Paula from Argentina

Megan from Canada

Graham from Ireland

Deniz from Turkey

3 🔊 **1.10** Listen again. Which sentences are true and which are false?

Paula and Megan
1 They don't use Facebook very much.
2 They've made contact with old friends.
3 They often check old friends' profiles.
4 They have nothing to say to old friends.
5 They think you make good friends on it.

Graham and Deniz
6 Deniz always has her phone with her.
7 She turns it off at night.
8 She returns people's calls in the morning.
9 She doesn't mind getting work emails on holiday.
10 She finds it easy not to think about work.

4 Discuss the questions.

1 Do you agree with Paula and Megan about social networking?
2 Do you think Graham and Deniz have similar lifestyles? Give reasons.
3 Do you know anyone like Deniz?

5 **a** Look at some sentences from the conversations. Who says 1–6?

1 I'd say it must be impossible to relax, though.
2 I reckon you must get tired.
3 They say you need to take breaks from work.
4 Some people say you shouldn't take your work on holiday.
5 There's no point in being friends, really.
6 There's no harm in checking your emails from time to time.

b Look at the highlighted expressions in 5a.

1 Which expressions:
   a give the speaker's opinion?   b give other people's opinions?
2 Which expression:
   a introduces an expert's opinion?   b says it's OK to do something?
   c says there's no reason to do something?

6 **a** Look at this sentence from Graham and Deniz's conversation.
1.11 Listen and notice which words are stressed.

     •   •   •   •   •
I'd say it must be impossible to relax, though.

b You stress the most important words in a sentence (often nouns, main verbs, adjectives and adverbs). Look at sentences 2–6 in 5a. Mark the words you think are stressed.

c **1.12** Listen and read the script on p147 to check. Practise saying the sentences.

7 **a** Write one or two sentences giving your opinions about these statements. You can include other people's opinions too. Use the expressions in 5a.

> Using mobile phones on public transport is impolite.

> Texting is making our spelling worse.

> Women make better bosses than men.

> You should only have children if you're married.

b Talk about the sentences together. Do you have the same opinions?

It's good to talk

1 Use the adjectives to complete the opinions from Graham and Deniz's conversation.

amazing difficult tiring

1 It's _____ being on call all the time.   *it's* + adjective + *-ing* form
2 It's _____ to relax, sometimes.   *it's* + adjective + infinitive
3 It's _____ how much I miss the buzz of work.   *it's* + adjective + question word

In sentences like these, the *-ing* form and infinitive usually have the same meaning.

2 **a** Put the words in order to make sentences.

1 It's / face to face / to people / better / to talk *It's better to talk to people face to face.*
2 It's / seeing / easy / to stop / your old friends
3 It's / in contact / to keep / with your family / important
4 It's / you / much free time / stressful / when / don't have
5 It's / a lot of time / spending / boring / alone

b Talk together. Do you agree with the sentences in 2a? Why? Why not?

3 **a** Work alone. Tick (✓) the things you think are a waste of time.

At work: chatting to colleagues, surfing the Internet, having meetings ...
At home: tidying up every day, dressing up to go out, cooking complicated meals ...
Going out: waiting in queues, window shopping, walking everywhere ...

b Add another activity which you think is a waste of time to each list.

4 Discuss all the ideas. Try to agree on three things that are a waste of time.

Online friendships

2.2 goals
- talk about using the Internet
- speculate about the present and future

VOCABULARY

Using the Internet

1 Answer the questions in groups.

1 How much time do you spend online? Which sites do you use most?
2 Do you have a blog or web page? Do you ever read other people's pages?
3 Do you ever post a comment after you've watched a video or read a blog online?
4 How often do you look for information online? What search engine do you use?
5 Are you on a social networking site? Do you enjoy socialising online?

READING

2 a Read the title of the article. What do people use social networking sites for?
Can you think of any reasons why these sites could be bad for friendships?

b Read the article. Does it mention any of your ideas?

Could social networking sites mean the end of lasting friendships?

[1] A GENERATION THAT IS GROWING UP using social networking websites, such as Facebook and MySpace, is less likely to form lasting relationships and is more likely to act without thinking, an expert has warned.

[2] Many people who were born in 1990 or later have only known a world with the Internet, so they could grow up with an unrealistic view of the world and themselves, the annual meeting of the Royal College of Psychiatrists heard.

[3] Dr Himanshu Tyagi, a psychiatrist, said social networking sites have encouraged the idea that friendships and relationships can be formed and ended quickly and easily. He said, "It's a world where everything moves fast and changes all the time, where relationships are ended at the click of a mouse. Online, you can delete your profile and change who you are in a few seconds." He said that because everything happens so quickly on social networking sites, people may start to find the real world boring.

Dr Himanshu Tyagi

[4] He said teenagers who socialise online are more likely to make quick decisions without thinking about the consequences of their actions. They might not pay enough attention to their 'real world' selves, and might find it difficult to form relationships in the real world because they won't learn about body language, tone of voice and facial expressions online. He said that if you can't see someone's face or body language or hear the changes in their voice, this will influence your understanding of what's going on. He added that friendship means something very different to the 'internet generation'.

[5] But there are also benefits. When you're online, you often don't know the wealth, race or gender of the person you're communicating with. Dr Tyagi said, "No one is an outsider on the net. It may not be the best way to make lasting friendships, but it does make everyone equal."

3 Read the article again. In Dr Tyagi's opinion, why might young people:

1 have an unrealistic view of the world?
2 feel that relationships can be started and ended quickly and easily?
3 find the real world boring?
4 find it more difficult to form relationships in the real world?
5 be equal on the Internet?

4 Talk together about the questions.

1 Do you agree with Dr Tyagi? Why? Why not?
2 How did you meet your closest friends?
3 What's the first thing you notice about people? Is it different meeting people online?
4 Read the last paragraph again. What other benefits are there of using the Internet to socialise?

Speculating

1 a Look at sentences 1–7 from the article. Which modal verbs mean:

a I'm sure about this? (x2)   b This is a possibility? (x5)

> **modal + infinitive**
> 1 ⊕ If you can't see someone's face … this will influence your understanding of what's going on.
> 2 ⊖ They won't learn about body language, tone of voice and facial expressions online.
> 3 ⊕ People may start to find the real world boring.
> 4 ⊖ It may not be the best way to make lasting friendships.
> 5 ⊕ They might find it difficult to form relationships.
> 6 ⊖ They might not pay enough attention to their 'real world' selves.
> 7 ⊕ They could grow up with an unrealistic view of the world and themselves.

b 🔊 **1.13** Listen to check and practise saying the sentences. ℗

2 Which highlighted expression(s) A–G in the sentences below can you use:

1 to emphasise that you're sure?
2 to say you think there's a good chance of something? (x3)
3 to say you think there's only a small chance?
4 to compare the chances of different things happening? (x2)

I've changed internet provider. I ᴬmay well be connected by the end of the week. ᴮI'll definitely join a social networking site. ᶜI'll probably join Facebook.
She's ᴰlikely to be at work now. Why don't you try her mobile?
I'm ᴱunlikely to finish this today. I'll email it to you tomorrow.
You're ᶠmore likely to get online at the café later. It's ᴳless likely to be busy then.

3 How likely are these things in the future? Make sentences with these words about:

The world	You
1 online relationships / be / important	6 I / have an unexpected email in my inbox
2 newspapers and books / disappear	7 I / make a close friend online
3 everyone / do their shopping online	8 I / get my dream job
4 most people / speak / Mandarin	9 I / move to another country
5 people / stop / writing with pens	10 I / learn another language

Online relationships will probably be more important in the future.

4 Discuss the ideas in 3 together. Do you have the same ideas?

> I'd say newspapers and books are unlikely to disappear.

> I don't know. I think printed newspapers may well disappear in the next ten years.

Discuss an issue

TASK READING

1 Answer the questions together.

1 How many emails do you send a day? How many do you receive?
2 How often do you check your emails at work? What about at home?
3 Do you have an intranet system at work? Do you find it useful?

2 Read this extract from an article and discuss the questions.

1 Do you agree with Paul Johnson?
2 Can you think of any solutions to the problem?

EMAIL GUIDE

EMAIL AT WORK CAN SERIOUSLY DAMAGE YOUR HEALTH

Last year, the world sent five trillion business emails, which works out at 15 billion a day, as well as 40 billion personal messages every day. Yet the average office worker fails to respond to more than a quarter of their messages. We are drowning in a sea of email, and it's beginning to bother some people.

Paul Johnson has written the *Email Survival Guide*, a handbook to help you take control of your inbox. "People are addicted to email because it makes them feel wanted," he says, "but it's disruptive. People think it's an efficient way of communicating because it only takes 30 seconds to deal with it, but every time a message pings on to your screen, it takes your focus away from the work you're doing."

TASK LISTENING

3 a 🔊 **1.14** Listen to Eric and Graham discussing a management decision.

1 What has their firm decided to do? Why?
2 What do Eric and Graham say about the consequences of the firm's decision?

b Check in the script on p147.

Eric and Graham work for Vantage, a management consultancy firm.

TASK VOCABULARY

Speculating about consequences

4 a Look at sentences 1–7 from the conversation. Which are arguments for the intranet ban? Which are against it?

1 We'll have to walk around and talk to people.
2 It'll take longer to do everything.
3 You'll be able to make decisions immediately.
4 I just think it'll cause problems.
5 It might actually help us to get things done quicker.
6 It might be nice to have a chat sometimes.
7 We might need to give it a chance.

b 🔊 **1.15** Listen to check. 🅟

TASK

5 a Your firm is banning mobile phones and MP3 players in the office. Work in A/B groups. A, you're in favour of the ban. B, you're against it. Think of at least three reasons to support your argument.

b Think about the language you need to:
- give your opinions *I'd say ...   There's no harm in ...   It's important to ...*
- speculate about consequences *It might help us to ...   It'll cause ...*

> Banning mobile phones will cause problems.

> Like what?

> Well, people won't be able to text us ...

6 Work in A/B groups. Discuss the issue with your colleagues.

7 Discuss the ban with the whole class. What are the most convincing reasons:
- in favour of the ban?   • against the ban?

Keywords *so, such*

Sylvia

1 **1.16** Listen to Sylvia talking about something that has changed her life.

1 What is it?
2 Why does she like it?
3 What does she plan to do next?

2 a In which sentences, 1–4, does *so* or *such*:

a mean *really* or *very*?
b introduce the result of a situation?

1 He did it all **so** quickly **that** I didn't have time to make us a cup of tea.
2 It's **such** an easy and cheap thing to use **that** I'm going to get an internet phone as well.

3 And it's **so** cheap!
4 It's made **such a difference** to my life.

b Answer the questions. Listen again to check.

1 Which word, *so* or *such*, is followed by:
a an adjective or adverb?
b *a/an* + (adjective) + noun?
2 Which words have a strong stress in sentences 3 and 4? **1.16**

3 Decide together where *so* or *such* goes in these sentences.

1 A How are you doing? Busy? B I'm busy! Unit 2
2 It saves a lot of time. Unit 2
3 So many of us are wasting much time looking at it. Unit 2
4 I find a lot of channels really irritating because there are many ads. Unit 1
5 I didn't realise it was a long way.
6 It took a long time to get there that we missed the party.

4 Complete the sentences with your own ideas. Then compare them together.

1 I was so … recently that I …
2 I had such a … day yesterday that I …
3 I find it so difficult to … that I have to …
4 … is such a/an … person that …
5 I didn't know … was so …

> I was so stressed recently that I thought about quitting my job.

Expressions with *so* and *such*

5 a Replace the underlined words with the expressions in the box.

| so far   such as   or so   and so on |

1 After living in Egypt for six months approximately, I began to understand what had happened. Unit 1
2 A generation that is growing up using social networking websites, like Facebook and MySpace, is less likely to form lasting relationships. Unit 2
3 On this site, you can chat with friends, post and comment on photos, and things like that.
4 She's won all the competition events until now.

b In pairs, cover the box in 5a. Say the sentences and try to remember the expressions.

6 a You're going to tell a story about something that changed your life. Think about:

• a move   • an important test   • an achievement
• meeting someone   • seeing something

b Look at 1–5 and think about how you can use *so* and *such* in your story.

1 how you feel about the event now
It was such a great …
2 how you felt at the time *I was so worried …*
3 some things that happened
4 the result *I was so late that I …*
5 expressions with *so* or *such* you can use
There were ten of us or so.

7 Tell each other your stories. Ask questions to find out more.

2 EXPLORESpeaking

Goals
- ask for clarification
- clarify what you're saying

1 a 🔊 **1.17** Listen to three conversations Eric has on the same day. Who's he talking to in each conversation?

   1 a friend   2 a colleague   3 a stranger

b 🔊 **1.17** Listen again. What's each conversation about?

c Read conversations 1–3 to check.

2 a Which highlighted expressions do the speakers use to:

   1 ask for clarification?
   2 clarify what they're saying?

b Add these expressions to group 1 or 2 above.

> What I meant to say was ...
> What exactly do you mean?
> So you're saying ...?
> No, I was trying to say ...

c 🔊 **1.18** Listen to check. **Ⓟ**

3 Practise having the conversations together. Replace some of the expressions in the conversations with expressions from 2b.

4 Choose a question and make notes.

- Is it possible to get to know someone well online?
- Is the use of technology, like satellite navigation systems in cars, making people lazy?
- Is it a good idea for children to use the Internet for homework?

5 a Talk in A/B pairs.

   1 A, give your opinions about one of the questions in 4.
   2 B, listen and ask for clarification.
   3 A, clarify what you're saying.

❶

KEN ... and then everyone will be able to get on with their work and not lose concentration every time they get emails.

ERIC Do you mean people aren't working hard enough?

KEN No, what I'm trying to say is people want to work and they want to work hard but they can't because they're always getting emails from ...

❷

TICKET INSPECTOR Well, the thing is, sir, a train's broken down on the line, so there are no trains leaving from here.

ERIC Are you saying I can't use my ticket?

TICKET INSPECTOR No, I'm saying there are no trains going there from this station. You can use your ticket to get there by a different route.

❸

ERIC I don't know how to describe it really. We started exchanging emails and I just knew she was the one. I think I fell in love after the fourth or fifth email. And then when we met, we knew for sure it was love ...

DOM Yeah, OK. I can understand how you can get to know someone's personality a bit online, and by writing emails. What I don't get is, how can you fall in love when you've never seen the person, never heard their voice? I mean ...

ERIC Well ... how can I put it ... I just *did*. I have no idea how. I suppose it's ...

b Then change roles and talk about another topic.

c Change pairs and have more conversations.

> Do you mean dating websites should be banned?

> No, I'm saying you should be careful about who you agree to meet ...

Review

VOCABULARY *It's* + adjectives

1 **a** Make sentences about your family and friends.

1 It's nice when your friends ...
2 It's important to see ...
3 It's interesting having ...
4 It's boring ...
5 It's annoying ...
6 It's ...

b Talk about all the sentences together. Do you agree? Why? Why not?

GRAMMAR *will, could, may, might*

2 **a** What do you think your country will be like in 10, 20 or 50 years?

1 Who will govern your country?
2 How will most people travel?
3 What skills might people lose or gain?
4 How will people communicate?
5 What will entertainment be like?
6 What do you think your country might look like?

b Talk together and compare your ideas.

CAN YOU REMEMBER? Unit 1 – Talking about the present

3 **a** Complete Paul and Rebecca's conversation with the correct form of the verbs in brackets.

PAUL	What ¹_____ (you / watch)?
	What are you watching?
REBECCA	Er, it's a crime drama.
PAUL	Any good?
REBECCA	Yeah, but I can't concentrate because you ²_____ (talk).
PAUL	Sorry, it's just – there's a documentary about Darwin on in a minute. Did you see the review?
REBECCA	No, I ³_____ (not / read) the TV guide. Anyway, I ⁴_____ (watch) this. You could record it.
PAUL	Yeah, OK. ⁵_____ (you / see) the remote?
REBECCA	No, I ⁶_____ (not / know) where it is. Look, can you be quiet?
PAUL	I ⁷_____ (not / make) any noise, I ⁸_____ (just / look) for the remote.
REBECCA	Look, it's over there by the TV guide ...

b 🔊 1.19 Listen to the conversation and check your answers. 🅟

Extension

SPELLING AND SOUNDS /tʃ/

4 **a** 🔊 1.20 Listen and underline the letters in these words which make a /tʃ/ sound.

chair   chance   achieve   exchange   each
touch   kitchen   watch   catch   question
suggestion   tuna   Tuesday   cultural   future

b In pairs, answer the questions.

1 Where can ch occur (at the start, in the middle, at the end)?
2 Does tch occur after a short or a long vowel?
3 What patterns after t can make a /tʃ/ sound?

c Can you think of more words with these spelling patterns?

d 🔊 1.21 Spellcheck. Close your book. Listen and write ten words. Then check your spelling on p148.

NOTICE Adjective–noun collocations

5 **a** Complete the adjective–noun collocations from texts in the unit with these words.

facial	real (x2)	urgent
huge	quick	

1 People may start to find the _____ world boring. p16
2 Teenagers who socialise online are more likely to make _____ decisions without thinking. p16
3 They won't learn about body language, tone of voice and _____ expressions online. p16
4 It's not like a _____ friendship. 🔊 1.10
5 It's such a _____ waste of time. 🔊 1.10
6 What about _____ emails and stuff? 🔊 1.14

b Match up the adjectives and nouns. Then write five questions to ask a partner using the collocations.

meal	online	demanding	conversation
private	job	messages	quick delicious
personal	chat	relationship	

Self-assessment

Can you do these things in English? Circle a number on each line. 1 = I can't do this, 5 = I can do this well.

⊚ talk about methods of communication	1	2	3	4	5
⊚ express opinions	1	2	3	4	5
⊚ talk about using the Internet	1	2	3	4	5
⊚ speculate about the present and future	1	2	3	4	5
⊚ speculate about consequences	1	2	3	4	5
⊚ ask for clarification	1	2	3	4	5
⊚ clarify what you're saying	1	2	3	4	5

• For Wordcards, reference and saving your work → e-Portfolio
• For more practice → Self-study Pack, Unit 2

Success

Great ideas

READING

1 You're going to read about an inventor. Which of these facts do you think are about the inventor of:

* karaoke?   * the iPod?

a   He never became rich from his invention.
b   He's shy and doesn't usually do interviews.
c   He made people listen to music in a different way.
d   He used his invention to celebrate his 59th birthday.
e   He was a drummer in a band.
f   He has also designed computers.

2 Work in A/B pairs. A, read the article below and B, read the article on p119 to check your ideas.

Mr Song and Dance Man

1 Karaoke is a $10 billion-a-year industry, but the man who invented it has made almost no money out of it. Inoue Daisuke came up with the idea in 1971. He could have become one of the richest men in Japan, but he didn't patent his idea and doesn't seem worried about the lost opportunity. 'I took a car stereo, a coin box and a small amplifier to make the karaoke,' says the 65-year-old in his small office in Osaka. 'Who would consider patenting something like that?'
2 In the early 1970s, Inoue was a drummer in a bar band with six colleagues, playing in local clubs in Kobe. They played for middle-aged businessmen who wanted to sing traditional Japanese songs. Inoue says, 'Out of 108 club musicians in Kobe, I was the worst! And the clients in my club were the worst singers!'

3 One day, one of his clients asked Inoue to play for him on an overnight trip. Inoue, unable to leave his job, gave him a tape of the backing music instead. That night, the businessman gave an emotional performance and karaoke (meaning 'empty orchestra') was born.
4 Inspired by this success, Inoue made 11 boxes with tapes and amplifiers, and began renting them to bars in Kobe in 1971. His plan was to make a bit of money but he never thought the idea would be so popular. In fact, karaoke was soon picked up by larger companies and through the 1980s and 1990s, it swept across Asia, the US and Europe. Then in 1999, *Time Magazine* called Inoue one of the 20th century's most influential people, saying he had completely changed nightlife. 'Nobody was as surprised as me,' he says.

5 Inoue himself only used a karaoke machine for the first time to celebrate his 59th birthday. These days, he makes a living selling a cockroach repellent for the machines. 'Cockroaches get inside the machines, build nests and eat the wires,' he says. He's very excited about his next venture. 'My dream,' he says, 'is to train Japanese pet-owners to take better care of their pets.' Friends say he is the ideas man, while his wife, who works in the same Osaka office, helps bring the ideas to life.

3 **a** A, complete the summary of this article; B, complete the summary on p119.

1   Inoue Daisuke invented karaoke, but he didn't ...
2   He was a drummer in a band which ...
3   The idea for karaoke started when Inoue gave ...
4   Over the next twenty years karaoke became ... Inoue was surprised when ...
5   Now, Inoue ... In the future, he ...

b Tell each other about your articles. How are the two men similar or different?

VOCABULARY

Talking about a business idea

4 Look at the sentences from the articles. Match 1–3 with topics a–c.

a a description of the product
b the financial success of an idea
c the start of a project or invention

> 1 Inoue Daisuke came up with the idea in 1971.
> He didn't patent his idea.

> 2 You can use it to store thousands of songs.
> Critics said it looked fantastic and was easy to use.

> 3 The man ... has made almost no money out of it.
> He makes a living selling a cockroach repellent.

5 Complete the questions with verbs from the highlighted expressions in 4 in the correct form.

1 How did Inoue Daisuke _____ up with his idea?
2 Why didn't he _____ his invention?
3 Do you think Jonathan Ive _____ a lot of money out of the iPod?
4 What do you think is the easiest way to _____ a living?
5 Is it more important that a gadget is easy to use or _____ fantastic?

SPEAKING

6 Ask and answer the questions together.

Hopes, dreams and ambitions

VOCABULARY

Hopes, dreams and ambitions

1 What's Inoue Daisuke's dream for the future? What do you think of his idea?

2 ▶ 1.22 Listen to Aminata, Eduardo and Elisa talking about their hopes, dreams and ambitions. Match each speaker to one of the pictures A–C.

3 ▶ 1.22 Listen again. Complete sentences 1–8 with a–h. ℗

Aminata	1	One day, I'd like to	a	taking some lessons.
	2	At some point, I'd absolutely love to	b	be comfortable in the water.
	3	I'm thinking of	c	learn to swim.
Eduardo	4	I'm considering	d	be a guitar player.
	5	My dream is to	e	doing a degree in music.
Elisa	6	My aim is to	f	live in Tokyo for a year.
	7	My ambition is to	g	train at the JKA dojo.
	8	I've always wanted to	h	go there next year.

4 Choose five of the highlighted expressions from 3. Write sentences about your hopes, dreams and ambitions.

One day, I'd like to travel around the world.

PRONUNCIATION

Schwa /ə/

5 a ▶ 1.23 Listen to sentence 1 above. What kinds of word are usually stressed? What kinds of word often have a schwa?

One day, I'd like to learn to swim.

b Mark the stressed syllables and schwa sounds in sentences 2–8 above.

c ▶ 1.24 Listen and read the script on p148 to check. Practise saying the sentences.

SPEAKING

6 Talk to your partner about your hopes, dreams and ambitions. Do you think you can both achieve your ambitions?

7 Tell the class something interesting your partner wants to do in the future.

Your abilities

3.2 goals
- talk about abilities
- talk about achievements

READING

1 a What's an IQ test? Have you ever taken one?

b Read the article from an educational magazine. Which intelligence types might help with these activities?

- doing your accounts
- playing tennis
- writing a poem
- designing a building
- staying happy
- learning a song
- resolving an argument

What is intelligence?

➡ Not just a high IQ

The **theory of multiple intelligences** was proposed by Howard Gardner in 1983. He believed that the traditional intelligence test (known as an IQ test) didn't acknowledge the wide variety of abilities that people have. Here is a summary of the main types of intelligence that he identified:

1 Bodily-kinesthetic People who have bodily-kinesthetic intelligence learn best by doing something physically. They are good at building and making things. They may enjoy acting or performing and are generally good at physical activities such as sports or dance.

2 Interpersonal People who have a high interpersonal intelligence learn best by working with others and often enjoy discussion and debate. They are able to co-operate in order to work as part of a group. They communicate effectively and empathise easily with others.

3 Intrapersonal Those who are strong in this intelligence are typically introverts and prefer to work alone. They are capable of understanding their own emotions, goals and motivations and learn best when concentrating on a subject by themselves.

4 Verbal-linguistic People with high verbal-linguistic intelligence have a facility with words and languages. They are typically good at reading, writing, telling stories and memorising words along with dates. They tend to learn best by reading, taking notes, listening to lectures, and through discussion and debate.

5 Logical-mathematical This area has to do with logic, reasoning and numbers. People with this ability excel at scientific thinking and investigation, and have the ability to perform complex calculations. Traditional concepts of intelligence, or IQ, reflect ability in this area.

6 Musical This area has to do with rhythm, music and hearing. Those who have a high level of musical intelligence are able to sing and play musical instruments. They can also often compose music and may learn best by listening to lectures.

7 Visual-spatial People with strong visual-spatial intelligence are typically very good at visualising and mentally manipulating objects. They have a good visual memory and are often artistically inclined. They also generally have a good sense of direction and may have good hand–eye co-ordination.

> A lawyer probably needs interpersonal and verbal-linguistic intelligences.

2 Read the article again. Which intelligences do you think are important for these jobs? Why?

- lawyer
- politician
- poet
- engineer
- doctor
- singer
- DJ
- social worker

VOCABULARY

Abilities

3 Look at the highlighted expressions in 1–7 in the article. Which can be followed by:

a an infinitive?   b an -ing form?   c a noun?   d an -ing form or a noun?

4 a Which intelligences do you think you have? What about people you know well? Write five sentences. Explain your ideas and give examples.

I think I have musical intelligence because I'm able to learn tunes very quickly.

b Talk about your sentences together. What intelligences do most people have?

Your achievements

LISTENING

1 🔊 **1.25** Listen to interviews with Aminata, Margot and Charlie about their achievements. What are they most proud of?

2 Can you answer the questions about each person? 🔊 **1.25** Listen again to check.

Aminata	1	What did she want to learn? Why?	2	When did she start learning?
Margot	3	What's her book about?	4	What's she doing at the moment?
Charlie	5	What did he join?	6	What do they do together?

3 Do you think each of them found it easy to do these things? Why?

GRAMMAR

Present perfect and time expressions

4 Match the sentences from the listening with functions a or b.

1 I've **had** the bike for about a year now.
2 I've just **written** a cookery book.
3 I've **learned** to ride a bike recently.
4 I've always **wanted** to write.

a a situation or state which is still true
b a finished action which is important now

5 Match the highlighted words in 1–8 with categories a–e.

1 I've **always** wanted to write.
2 I've **just** written a cookery book.
3 I've **never** been able to go with them.
4 I've **already** written a novel actually.
5 I've learned to ride a bike **recently**.
6 It hasn't come out **yet**.
7 I've had the bike **for** about a year now.
8 I haven't written anything **since** the cookery book.

a the whole of your life until now *always* / _____
b part of your life until now _____ / _____
c something you expect to happen _____
d a short time ago _____ / _____
e something that happened sooner than expected _____

6 Notice the position of the highlighted time expressions. Then add them to the sentences in the quiz.

Find someone who:

recently
1 has won a competition ⋀. What was it? recently
2 has passed a test or an exam. just
3 has learned to drive. Why not? never
4 has done well in interviews. always
5 has achieved something today. What was it? already
6 has been married over ten years. for
7 hasn't taken a test or an exam they left school. since
8 hasn't done what they needed to do today. yet

Grammar reference and practice, p136

SPEAKING

7 a Ask questions to find who the statements in 1–8 are true for. Find out more about each situation.

b In pairs, tell each other what you found out.

Have you won a competition recently?

Actually, I've never won a competition.

Sell an idea

3.3 goals
- ◉ talk about a business idea
- ◉ talk about hopes, dreams and ambitions
- ◉ talk about achievements
- ◉ take part in an interview

TASK LISTENING

1 Read the advert. Why do people join *Connections*?

Connections

| My business idea | What's new? | Connect online | Contact us |

Do you have a great business idea? Do you want to make money out of it? *Connections* can help you. We specialise in bringing together entrepreneurs with suitable investors. We match you with the best investor for you and organise an interview with them. Interested? Then click on the link below to join our database ...
> Click here to join Connections.

2 a ● 1.26 Listen to the first part of Olga's interview with an investor she met through *Connections*. Label the picture with these words:

strap   handle   wheels   buggy   bag   top pocket   side pocket

How does the bag work?

Olga's 'easybag'

b ● 1.27 Listen to the rest of the interview.

1   What does Olga want from the interview?
2   How does she feel about the product?

Listen again or check in the script on p148.

3 a Discuss the questions.

1   Do you think the product will work? Why?
2   Do you think the investor will support Olga's idea? Why?

b ● 1.28 Listen to a phone call between the investor and Olga. Were you right?

Olga explaining her idea

TASK VOCABULARY

Facts and feelings

4 a Who says sentences 1–8, the interviewer or Olga?

1   Can you give us a bit more information about your background?
2   We'd like to ask you some questions about international sales.
3   I'm really excited about the product.
4   I'm very keen to hear your thoughts about the business plan.
5   It's good to see someone so passionate about their product!
6   We have some doubts about a few things in the business plan.
7   What I'm more concerned about is the marketing.
8   I feel very optimistic about its chances of success.

b Which highlighted expressions are: adjective + about?   noun + about?

TASK

5 You're going to have an interview with an investor at *Connections*.

1   A, look on p119. B, look on p128. Complete the section about you.
2   Think about the language you can use to describe your product, your experience and your hopes for the future.

I've worked in design since ...

My aim is to ...

I'm concerned about the distribution costs ...

6 Work in A/B pairs. A, you're the investor. Ask B questions and decide if you want to invest in his/her idea. B, you've got a great idea. Explain your idea and answer any questions.

7 Now change roles. Have another interview.

8 Talk in groups. Which idea do you think will be the most successful?

Across cultures Attitudes to success

LISTENING

Mariama from Britain

1 🔊 **1.29** Listen to Mariama and Remco talking about attitudes to success.

1 How does Mariama feel about talking about her achievements?
2 What two examples does Remco give to explain his attitude to success?

2 🔊 **1.29** Listen again. Are sentences 1–4 true or false?

Mariama

1 She says her American friends are happy to talk about what they've achieved.
2 She thinks British attitudes are similar to those of Americans she knows.

Remco

3 He says that he always plays sports to win.
4 He has a similar attitude at work.

Remco from the Netherlands

VOCABULARY

Attitudes to success

3 a Who says sentences 1–7 from the listening: Mariama, Remco or the interviewer?

1 Would you say you're a competitive person?
2 I'm not at all comfortable.
3 They're much more confident about coming forward.
4 You don't want to seem arrogant.
5 I want to win at all costs.
6 I don't try and bend the rules as much as I do in sports.
7 So you play by the rules at work?

b Look at the highlighted expressions in sentences 1–7 and answer the questions.

1 What's the difference between being confident and being arrogant?
2 What does it mean if you want to 'win at all costs'?
3 What's the difference between bending and playing by the rules?

SPEAKING

4 a Work alone. Read the quiz questions about attitudes to success and think about your answers.

All about winning?

1 Are you a competitive person?

2 Do you think it's ever OK to bend the rules to win something?

3 Do people you know think being competitive is a good thing?

4 Are you comfortable talking about your achievements?

5 Do you put non-professional achievements on your CV?

6 If an employer asked about your strengths in a job interview, what would you say?

7 Are people in your country generally happy to talk about their achievements?

b Now answer the quiz questions in groups.

1 Do you have the same or different attitudes to success?
2 Do you think people in different countries have the same or different attitudes to success?

3 EXPLORE Writing

1   **Talk together.**

 1   When do you take notes?
   • taking a phone message • in a lecture   • getting directions
   • in an interview   • listening to the radio • in a meeting
 2   Do you use any specific note-taking techniques?

2   **[1.30] Listen to part of a job interview. Answer the questions about Olga.**

 1   What kind of job is the interview for?
 2   What experience has Olga got?
 3   What product is she most proud of?

3 **a** **Look at note-taking tips a–f. Which do you follow when you take notes?**

 a   use section headings and subheadings   d   use abbreviations where possible, not full words
 b   list points under each subheading   e   revise your notes as soon as possible
 c   don't try to write every word   f   don't worry about correct spelling and grammar

 b **Look at the interviewer's unfinished notes about Olga. Match 1–4 with tips a–d above.**

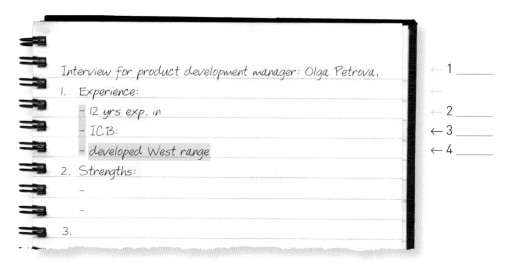

> Interview for product development manager: Olga Petrova, ← 1 _____
> 1. Experience: ←
>   – 12 yrs exp. in   ← 2 _____
>   – ICB: ← 3 _____
>   – developed West range   ← 4 _____
> 2. Strengths:
>   –
>   –
> 3.

4 **a** **In pairs, say what you think these abbreviations mean.**

1	yrs	3	8.00	5	pm	7	C21st	9	vs.	11	pw
2	75 g	4	no.	6	w/	8	etc.	10	approx.	12	PTO

 b **[1.31] Listen to check.**

5 **a** **[1.32] Now listen to the first part of the interview again. Complete the interviewer's notes about Olga.**

 b **[1.33] Listen to the next two questions the interviewer asks Olga. Make notes about her answers.**

 c **Compare your notes with a partner. Did you write down the same details? Then check your notes in script 1.30 on p149.**

6   **Work in A/B pairs. A, you're going to take notes in an interview for the post of student representative in a big international college. B, look at these five questions for the interview and think about your answers.**

 1   How long have you been at the college?
 2   What experience have you got of dealing with people?
 3   What are your strengths and weaknesses?
 4   How much time can you give to the job?
 5   What can you bring to the job?

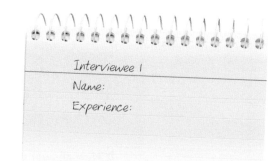

> Interviewee 1
> Name:
> Experience:

7   **Take turns to interview each other for the post and take notes about each other.**

8 **a** **Get into separate groups, As and Bs. Tell each other about the person you interviewed, using your notes to help you.**

 b **Decide who's best qualified in your group to get the post.**

3 Look again ♻

Review

GRAMMAR Present perfect and time expressions

1 a Complete the sentences with the best time expression. Which are true for you?

> *never*
> 1 I've /\ had a garden. I'd love to grow things.
> 2 I've lived in the same house /\ I was born.
> 3 I've /\ loved being alone. I'm not very sociable!
> 4 I've changed my job /\. I'm much happier now.
> 5 We've /\ started a family. We've got two small children.
> 6 I haven't achieved my ambition /\.
> 7 I've known my best friend /\ ten years.
> 8 We've /\ moved home. We haven't unpacked yet.

b In pairs, make sentences about:

- your interests • travel • friends and family

I've just …	I've … for …
I've always …	I've … since …
I've never …	I've … recently
I haven't … yet	I've already …

VOCABULARY Hopes, dreams and ambitions

2 a Put the words in order and make sentences about your hobbies, interests, hopes and dreams.

1 to / dream / My / is …
2 absolutely / to / love / I'd …
3 considering / point / At / I'm / some …
4 wanted / always / I've / to …
5 thinking / I'm / of …
6 like / One / to / I'd / day …

My dream is to have my own photography business.

b Talk in groups. Does anyone have the same hopes, dreams and ambitions as you?

CAN YOU REMEMBER? Unit 2 – *will, could, may, might;* **Expressing probability**

3 a Look at sentences a–f about Olga's plans for the evening. Put them in order from the most likely (1) to the least likely (6).

a I may go out for a meal tonight.
b I'm very unlikely to go to bed early.
c I'll definitely have a shower later.
d I might not watch television.
e I won't call my family.
f I may well see my friends.

b Write five sentences about your evening using the highlighted expressions in 3a.

c Talk together about your evenings. Who knows exactly what they're going to do? Who isn't sure?

Extension

SPELLING AND SOUNDS /s/

4 a 🔊 1.34 Listen and underline the letters in these words which make a /s/ sound.

celebrate city cycle address across essay story skin supermarket price chance advice answer ask describe close increase

b Find words in 4a to match spelling patterns 1–4. /s/ is spelled:

1 s in most words and always before a consonant.
2 c sometimes before e, i or y.
3 ss after a short vowel.
4 se or ce at the end of words, after long vowels and usually ce after n.

c Spellcheck. In pairs, take turns to choose ten words and test your partner's spelling.

NOTICE *One of the …*

5 a Complete the sentences from texts in the unit with these expressions.

richest   most successful   most important

1 He could have become one of the _____ men in Japan. **p22**
2 He may be one of the _____ industrial designers of our time. **p119**
3 ICB is one of the _____ firms internationally. 🔊 **1.30**

b Check your answers. What kind of adjective is one of the often followed by?

c Write a brief description of one of your favourite things.

My parents gave me a pearl necklace. It's one of the most valuable things I own.

d Listen to each other's descriptions. Ask questions to find out more information.

Self-assessment

Can you do these things in English? Circle a number on each line. 1 = I can't do this, 5 = I can do this well.

◎ talk about a business idea	1	2	3	4	5
◎ talk about hopes, dreams and ambitions	1	2	3	4	5
◎ talk about abilities	1	2	3	4	5
◎ talk about achievements	1	2	3	4	5
◎ take part in an interview	1	2	3	4	5
◎ take notes	1	2	3	4	5

- For Wordcards, reference and saving your work → e-Portfolio
- For more practice → Self-study Pack, Unit 3

What happened?

4.1 goals
- talk about accidents and injuries
- explain how something happened

Accident-prone

SPEAKING

1 **a** Do you take a lot of risks? Do the quiz and find out. Then check your score on p118.

Safety first

	Never	Sometimes	Usually	Always
1 I unplug everything when I'm away from home.	D	C	B	A
2 I get travel insurance when I go on holiday.	D	C	B	A
3 I read the instructions before I use something.	D	C	B	A
4 I break the speed limit when I'm driving.	A	B	C	D
5 I answer my phone when I'm driving.	A	B	C	D
6 I look both ways when I cross a road.	D	C	B	A
7 I listen to the safety instructions before a flight.	D	C	B	A

b Discuss the questions.

1 Do you agree with what the answers say about you?
2 Think about people you know who take risks. Do they have a lot of accidents?

READING

2 **a** You're going to read an article about why people are accident-prone. How do you think these things can make people have more accidents?

- upbringing • adolescence • watching TV • being left-handed

b Read the article to check.

Why so *clumsy?*

What makes one person have more accidents than another? Most people would say that it's to do with taking risks. Take fewer risks and you'll have fewer accidents. But is taking risks really a matter of choice?

Some experts believe that whether or not you take risks in life has a lot to do with your upbringing and, some believe, with your birth order. Parents are often stricter and more careful with their first child, and so first-born children tend to grow up taking fewer risks and being more cautious. Parents are often more relaxed with a second or third child, so these children tend to take more risks.

But why do children tend to be more accident-prone than adults? During childhood and adolescence, the body grows very quickly. There seem to be periods in these years when our brain and body are at different stages of development.

Our arms are longer than the brain thinks they are, so we knock things over; our legs are longer than the brain believes, so we trip over easily.

Another explanation has been offered by scientists in Spain who have found a possible link between the number of hours a child watches TV and how accident-prone they are. The research suggests that the more time a child spends watching TV, the less they are developing their physical co-ordination skills. If a child doesn't run around a lot, they don't begin to understand that the world is full of physical risk. Watching cartoons and action adventure films doesn't help either. It gives the child a false sense of how the world works and of how much danger it contains.

So, what about adults? Some studies have shown that left-handed people are more accident-prone than right-handed people. Why the difference? No one knows for sure. One theory is that we live in a right-handed world. Everything – from cars to door handles, from children's toys to engineering tools and equipment – is made by right-handed people for right-handed people. So left-handed children and adults are more likely to have accidents because the modern world is not designed for them.

3 **a** Can you remember what the article says about these things?

  1 Parents are usually stricter with …
  2 Adolescents are often clumsy because …
  3 Watching too much TV affects children's …
  4 Watching cartoons doesn't help children to understand …
  5 The world is designed for …

b Read the article again to check. Do you agree with these ideas? Why? Why not?

I dropped it!

LISTENING

1 🔊 **1.35** Listen to five conversations. Match them to pictures A–E.

VOCABULARY

Accidents and injuries

2 **a** Complete the highlighted expressions with the correct form of these verbs. 🔊 **1.35** Listen to check. **P**

| drop   cut   slip   bang   trip   fall   break (x2) |

  1 I _____ your camera. I think I've _____ it. I'm sorry.
  2 I _____ my head on the cupboard door! Ow!
  3 Oh, yeah, I _____ my wrist.
  4 I _____ on the ice and _____ over.
  5 And I've _____ my finger on the glass.
  6 I _____ over that stool.

b What other parts of the body do people break, cut or bang? What things do people drop or break in the home? What kind of things make people trip, or slip, over?

VOCABULARY

Saying how something happened

3 **a** Complete sentences 1–3 from the conversations.

1 I was on the way to	a washing up and I dropped it.
2 I was in the middle of	b take a photo and it just slipped out of my hand.
3 I was trying to	c work and I slipped on the ice and fell over.

b Which of these endings can follow 1–3?

  • change a light bulb • cooking dinner • the shops
  • the airport • open a bottle • having a shower

c Now imagine accidents in these situations. Write a sentence for each.

  I was on the way to the shops when I dropped my keys.

SPEAKING

4 **a** When was the last time you or someone you know did these things? Can you remember what happened?

  • dropped something • tripped over • cut yourself • broke something
  • fell over • banged your head • slipped

b Talk together. Who's the most accident-prone?

The power of nature

The Asian tsunami in 2004 killed over 200,000 people.

VOCABULARY
Natural events

1 a Which of these events can you see in pictures A–F?

> a flood   a hurricane   an eclipse   a tsunami *B*   the northern lights
> an earthquake   a forest fire   a volcanic eruption

b Have any of these events taken place in your country in the last 100 years?

LISTENING

2 🔊 **1.36** You're going to hear Fran and António talking about natural events. Which events in 1a do they talk about? What was the experience like for them?

3 🔊 **1.36** Listen again and discuss the questions.

1 What does Fran say about:
  • her street?   • the water?   • moving?   • her family?
2 What does António say about:
  • the beach?   • the time of day?   • the sky?   • his children?

GRAMMAR
Narrative verb forms

4 a Which verb A–C from Fran's story:

1 tells us about a finished action or event in the past?
2 explains the background to a past action or event?
3 tells us that an event happened earlier than another event?

> I was living^A in Sri Lanka when the tsunami hit^B.
> We found out there **had been**^C an earthquake.

| **Past simple** regular ending *-ed* |
| **Past progressive** *was / were + ing* |
| **Past perfect** *had* + past participle |

b Match A–C with the three past tenses on the right.

5 a Work in A/B pairs. A, circle the correct verb forms in Fran's story. B, do the same in António's story.

ASTRID ¹Did you have to / Were you having to move to a different town?

FRAN No, we ²stayed / were staying because the water then subsided very quickly, and then it was quite soon that we ³found out / had found out what had happened, that there ⁴was being / had been an earthquake and that it ⁵was causing / had caused a tsunami …

ASTRID Your family probably was very worried for you.

FRAN Well, my parents ⁶were actually visiting / actually visited me at the time.

ANTÓNIO Everyone just left their workplaces and they immediately ⁷headed / were heading down to the sea. … And as soon as the light ⁸started / was starting changing the birds ⁹went / had gone silent. … There were lots of people on the street who ¹⁰were selling / had sold special sunglasses and other things to watch the eclipse through and people ¹¹were walking / had walked around with little bits of card … I remember thinking that it was really odd that the whole town ¹²was going / had gone to the beach in the middle of a working day to see this strange event.

Grammar reference and practice, p137

b In pairs, look at both stories and check your ideas together. Then check in the script on p150.

Describing an experience

VOCABULARY

Adverbs for telling stories

1 a Look at the sentences from the stories below and discuss the questions.

1 Which group of adverbs, A or B, describes how or when something happened?
2 Which adverb means:
   • when you don't expect it, quickly?   • without waiting, at once?
3 Which group of adverbs, A or B, tells us how the speaker thinks or feels?
4 Which adverb introduces a statement which is:
   • a surprise?   • good news?   • a bad thing?   • clearly true?

A	1	They **immediately** headed down to the sea.
	2	**Suddenly**, my landlady came upstairs, shouting "Seawater, seawater!"
	3	The sky just changed colour very **slowly**.
	4	The water then subsided very **quickly**.
B	5	**Obviously**, I'd have liked my kids to see it too.
	6	But **unfortunately**, they were at school so they missed it.
	7	The water **amazingly** didn't come to the street I lived in.
	8	But **luckily** we were able to contact our family back at home.

b Look at 1–8 again. Which adverbs can go in a different position in the sentence?

PRONUNCIATION

Groups of words 1

2 a We speak in groups of words. This makes what we say easier to understand.
  1.37 Listen to these sentences from Fran's and António's stories.

1 Obviously, // I'd have liked my kids to see it too.
2 But unfortunately, // they were at school // so they missed it.
3 The water // amazingly // didn't come to the street I lived in.

b Practise saying the sentences.

SPEAKING

3 Work in A/B pairs. You're going to read about two natural events that happened in Mexico.

1 A, read Astrid's story on p121. B, read Nuria's story on p129.
2 Answer the questions and make notes.
3 Think about which adverbs from 1a you can use to make the story more dramatic.

4 Cover the stories and tell them to each other. You can use your notes to help you.

5 How do you think you'd feel in these situations?

Describe a dramatic experience

4.3 goals

◎ describe a dramatic experience
◎ explain how something happened
◎ say how you feel about an experience

Megan and her mum, Jane

TASK LISTENING

1 a You're going to listen to Jane's story about an accident. Look at the pictures. What do you think happened?

b 🔊 **1.38** Listen to check. Then answer the questions.

1 Where was Megan? What was she doing?
2 Where was Jane? What was she doing?
3 Why did it suddenly go quiet?
4 Why was Jane scared?
5 Why couldn't Megan move?

TASK VOCABULARY

Common verbs in stories

2 🔊 **1.38** Listen again. Complete the sentences from the story with these verbs in the correct form.

find out   realise   remember   know

1 I didn't _____ what they were doing.
2 So I went to _____ what was going on.
3 I immediately _____ what had happened.
4 I can't really _____ what happened next.

TASK

3 You're going to describe an experience: <u>either</u> an accident <u>or</u> a natural event you have experienced. First, think about how to:

- explain the background to the story   *I was living in ...*
- explain what you were doing   *I was on the way to ...*
- describe the events   *I went to ... I saw ...*
- say how you felt about the experience   *amazingly ... luckily ...*
- explain your understanding of the events   *Later, I realised ...   I didn't know ...*

4 Tell your stories in turn. Listen and ask questions to find out more.

5 Which story did you find the most interesting? Change groups and tell your new group that story.

Keyword *over*

Meanings of *over*

1 (1.39) Listen to Tomoko's story about redecorating her home. What improvements did she and her husband want to make?

2 Match the uses of *over* in sentences 1–6 from the story to meanings a–f.

1 My husband and I redecorated the living room **over** the summer.
2 It cost **over** 50,000 yen.
3 We have planes that fly **over** our house.
4 We decided to put a shelf **over** the door.
5 I went **over** the road to the local café.
6 I'm so glad it's **over**.

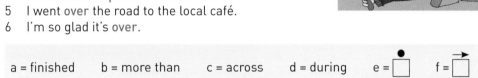

a = finished   b = more than   c = across   d = during   e = [ ]   f = [→]

3 a Work together to add *over* to sentences 1–6 below. Match each use with meanings a–f in 2.

Find someone who:
over
1 sometimes works / the weekend.   4 has flown a famous place in a plane.
2 can't wait for today to be.   5 goes a river on the way to work.
3 takes an hour to get to class.   6 has a picture their bed.

> Do you sometimes work over the weekend?
>> Yes, often actually.
> What kind of work do you do?

b Ask questions for 1–6. If the answer is yes, find out more about each situation.

Multi-word verbs with *over*

4 a Match 1–8 with a–h to make sentences.

1 I slipped on the ice
2 My son's so clumsy!
3 I tripped over
4 He came over to me
5 I went over the documents
6 Have you got over
7 Can we turn over?
8 They ran over an animal

a your bag on the floor.
b and there weren't any mistakes.
c There's something good on Channel 7.
d in the middle of the road.
e He's always knocking things over.
f and asked what the matter was.
g your cold yet?
h and fell over.

b Which of the multi-word verbs in 4a are about accidents? Which is about a car accident?

5 a Use the multi-word verbs in 4a to complete these questions.

1 Have you ever _____ _____ a drink in someone else's house? What did you do?
2 Do you usually _____ _____ your emails before you send them?
3 How often do friends and family _____ _____ to your home?
4 What's the best way to _____ _____ the end of a relationship?
5 What kinds of TV programme make you _____ _____ immediately?

b Ask and answer questions 1–5 together.

4 EXPLORE Speaking

1 Discuss the questions.

1 Do you socialise a lot with people from your work or studies?
2 What are the advantages and disadvantages of socialising with colleagues?

Goal
⊚ refer to an earlier topic or conversation

2 a 🔊 1.40 Listen to a conversation between two friends, António and Don. Who's Pam? How's she feeling about the next day?

b 🔊 1.41 Now listen to Pam. Did her meeting go well?

3 a Complete the expressions from conversations 1 and 2 with these verbs in the correct form.

> say (x3)   mention (x2)   talk (x2)

1 Yeah, she _____ that. I think she's pretty nervous actually.
2 You never _____ her before.
3 I've forgotten what we were _____ about.
4 Weren't you _____ about the diagrams?
5 What were you _____?
6 I was just _____ that Pam's quite nervous.
7 As I was _____, we really need to ...

b Check in conversations 1 and 2.

4 Complete Don and Pam's conversation with expressions from 3a. Then practise it.

DON So, how did it go, Pam?
PAM Oh, it was awful. I really messed it up.
DON Really? António said you were good. Oh, and he asked if we'd like to go round to his for dinner on Friday, so we need to reply.
PAM Dinner, hm, yes. Anyway, what ¹_____?
DON Erm, that António invited us to dinner.
PAM No, not about dinner.
DON Er, sorry, I've ²_____ .
PAM You were just ³_____ that António thought I was good.
DON Oh yes. He ⁴_____ that you were a bit nervous, but he thought you'd be great at the job!
PAM Oh, that's a relief!
DON Anyway, as I ⁵_____, we need to tell António if we can go to dinner on Friday.

5 a You're going to talk about some of these topics:

- your plans for the weekend
- your next holiday
- a news story
- how you feel about your job
- something else

Plan what you want to say about two of the topics.

b Work in groups of three, A, B and C.

A, start talking about one of the topics in 5a.
B, interrupt A and ask C about one of the other topics.
C, answer B's question, and then ask A to continue.

c Now change roles and do 5b again.

António and Don

Pam in a meeting with António and her new colleagues

❶

DON Erm, have you got somebody called Pam starting at your office tomorrow?
ANTÓNIO Yes, actually. She's the new head of HR.
DON Yeah, that's right. Well, she's my new girlfriend!
ANTÓNIO What? You never mentioned her before.
DON Well, you know, we haven't been seeing each other very long.
ANTÓNIO So, what's she like?
DON Well, I think she's amazing, of course. I hope you'll like her.
ANTÓNIO I'm sure I will. We're having a meeting tomorrow so she can get to know everyone.
DON Yeah, she mentioned that. I think she's pretty nervous actually.
ANTÓNIO Wow! Look at that rain!
DON Yeah, and I didn't bring my waterproofs. I'm going to get soaked!
ANTÓNIO Sorry. I've forgotten what we were talking about. What were you saying?
DON Oh, I was just saying that Pam's quite nervous about tomorrow.
ANTÓNIO Oh, yeah, Pam. Well, erm, it will be really interesting to meet her.

❷

PAM Hello, everyone. My name's Pam and I'm the new head of HR. I hope I get the chance to meet you all properly later on. António mentioned a little get together in the café downstairs after work, so I hope you can come to that. Erm, so, I just wanted to talk a little bit about what I've been asked to do here and why. Now if you have a look at these diagrams, … Ah, I can't seem to make this work … OK, forget the slides, I can manage without them. As I was saying, we really need to … erm … sorry, I've forgotten what I was talking about.
ANTÓNIO Er, weren't you talking about the diagrams?
PAM Er, yes. Thanks, António. Sorry. Yes, I was going to show you some diagrams to help illustrate an idea for reorganising the department. I don't know if this will make any sense without the slides …

4 Look again ♻

Review

VOCABULARY Adverbs for telling stories

1 a Complete these adverbs with *a, e, i, o, u*.

> _ bv _ _ _ sly   l_ ck_ ly   _ m_ z_ ngly
> s_ dd_ nly   _ nf_ rt_ n_ t_ ly

b Add the adverbs to sentences 1–5.

1 _____, I've never eaten noodles.
2 I'm into music but _____, I can't sing or play an instrument.
3 _____ I love my sister, but we don't get on very well.
4 _____, when I was younger, my parents taught me to manage money.
5 Sometimes, I _____ feel scared for no reason.

c Change the underlined parts of the sentences to make them true for you.

GRAMMAR Narrative verb forms

2 a Work in pairs. Complete the story with the verbs in the box in the correct form.

> have   hear   drive   ring   get   not see

When my wife ¹_____ to say she ²_____ the baby, I immediately ³_____ in the car and ⁴_____ quickly towards the hospital. I was nearly there when I ⁵_____ a loud siren. I ⁶_____ the police car behind me. ...

b Add one or two more sentences to finish the story. Then compare your ideas with another pair.

CAN YOU REMEMBER? Unit 3 – Facts and feelings

3 a Complete sentences 1–6 to make them true for you.

1 I'm excited about ...
2 I've always been passionate about ...
3 I'm having doubts about ...
4 I need some information about ...
5 I'm optimistic about ...
6 I've got a few questions about ...

b Compare your sentences with a partner. Ask questions to find out more.

> I'm feeling quite optimistic about my new job.
>
> That's good. What is it?
>
> I'm going to be working on a conservation project.

Extension

SPELLING AND SOUNDS /k/

4 a ● 1.42 Listen to some words with the /k/ sound from Fran's story. Complete the spelling of these words with c, k or ck.

1	__ould	5	lu__y	9	a__tually
2	loo__ed	6	s__ary	10	lu__ily
3	li__e	7	be__ause	11	__onta__t
4	__anals	8	qui__ly	12	ba__

b Read these spelling patterns for /k/. Check your answers.

1 We use c before a, o or u. (can, come, cup)
2 We use c before most consonants. (clean, act)
3 We use k before e, i or y. (likely, sky)
4 We use k or ke after a long vowel. (break, broke)
5 We use ck after a short vowel. (sick)

c ● 1.43 Spellcheck. Listen and write ten words. Then check your spelling on p150.

NOTICE Time expressions: past and present

5 a Read the sentences. Which are about:

- now?   • the past?

1 My parents were actually visiting me at the time.
2 We didn't know at that time that there was going to be an earthquake.
3 I was going to tell him about the new job, but at that moment my wife rang me.
4 I'm studying for some exams at the moment.
5 In those days, people didn't watch TV. They listened to the radio.
6 These days, the Internet is a big part of most people's daily lives.

b Write two or three sentences about:

- things you're doing now   • your childhood

c Talk about your sentences together.

Self-assessment

Can you do these things in English? Circle a number on each line. 1 = I can't do this, 5 = I can do this well.

⊚ talk about accidents and injuries	1	2	3	4	5
⊚ explain how something happened	1	2	3	4	5
⊚ talk about natural events	1	2	3	4	5
⊚ describe a dramatic experience	1	2	3	4	5
⊚ say how you feel about an experience	1	2	3	4	5
⊚ refer to an earlier topic or conversation	1	2	3	4	5

• For Wordcards, reference and saving your work → e-Portfolio
• For more practice → Self-study Pack, Unit 4

A change of plan

A helping hand

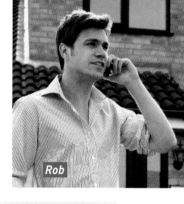

Rob

1 a Talk together. Have you ever done any of these things?

- locked yourself out
- lost your car keys
- got on the wrong bus or train
- broken down

b What did you or would you do in these situations?

2 **1.44** Listen to three phone calls between friends, Jon, Rob and Amy. Answer the questions about each call.

A	Jon and Rob	1	Who's visiting Rob this weekend?	2	Why can't Rob pick her up?
B	Jon and Amy	3	Why can't Jon pick her up?	4	What does Amy offer to do?
C	Jon and Rob	5	What's Rob going to do?	6	What happens to Rob's phone?

3 a Tick (✓) the things that are true for Rob. Correct the sentences which are wrong. **1.44** Then listen to the conversations again to check.

1 The battery on his mobile is running out.
2 He can't get into his house.
3 He's lost his car keys.
4 His car's in the garage.
5 He can't get a taxi.
6 He'd arranged to go on a bike ride.
7 There are no windows open.
8 He's late for work.

b How do you think Rob's going to get back into his house?

c **1.45** Listen to Rob's conversation with Amy and his mum, Maria. Were you right?

4 Complete sentences 1–3 with a–c.

1 I'm supposed to be going on that bike ride today,
2 I'm supposed to be picking my mum up from the train station,
3 Rob's meant to be picking his mum up from the train station,

a but he's locked himself out of the house.
b but my car keys and wallet are in the house.
c but I'm too tired.

5 Complete sentences 1–4 with your own ideas. Then write two more.

1 I'm supposed to ... but I've got a cold.
2 I'm meant to ... but it's raining.
3 ... but I've lost my wallet.
4 ... but the bus is late.

I'm supposed to be going out with an old friend tonight, but I've got a cold.

Sorting out arrangements

1 Look at the sentences from the conversations. Which future form do the speakers use:

a to describe a plan they've already made (before speaking)?
b to express a decision (at the moment of speaking)?
c to describe something they're sure will happen (because it's been arranged)?

1	I'll call Amy now, then I'll call you back. OK?	*will* + infinitive
2	She's staying this weekend.	present progressive
3	I'm going to find a ladder.	*be going to* + infinitive

Grammar reference and practice, p138

2 **a** Read the conversation between Rob and his mum and (circle) the best forms.

MARIA	How can I help, darling?
ROB	Just sit down and relax, and ¹ (I'll make) / I'm making a cup of tea.
MARIA	Oh, good. Do you have any plans today?
ROB	Well, I have to buy some food, so ² I'll go / I'm going to go shopping at some point today.
MARIA	Right. ³ I'll come / I'm coming with you if that's OK. I need a few things at the shops.
ROB	OK. Do you want to do anything later?
MARIA	Well, actually, I'm quite tired after the journey. I think ⁴ I'll go / I'm going to bed early tonight.
ROB	Good idea. By the way, I've got a surprise for your birthday, Mum.
MARIA	Oh, really? How exciting! What ⁵ will we / are we going to do?
ROB	Well, ⁶ we'll go / we're going out to dinner, then ⁷ we'll go / we're going to the theatre.
MARIA	That sounds lovely. What ⁸ will we / are we going to see?
ROB	Er, I've forgotten the name. When I've made the tea, ⁹ I'll look / I'm looking for the theatre programme.

b Compare your ideas and explain your choices. 🔊 **1.46** Then listen to check. ❷

PRONUNCIATION

Common pairs of words 2

3 **a** 🔊 **1.47** Close your books and listen to six sentences. Write the sentences you hear.

b Check your ideas in the script on p151.

c 🔊 **1.47** Each sentence has pairs of words that often go together. Listen again. Practise saying the pairs of words on their own. Then practise saying the sentences.

going to   want to   have to   at the   to the   for the

SPEAKING

4 **a** Work in A/B/C groups. You're three friends. Choose one of these ideas together.

A wants to pick up his/her brother from the airport but the car won't start.
A has to go to work but there's no public transport this morning. A can't drive.
A has promised to take his mum to the theatre but he's got an emergency at work.

b Work alone. Read the different roles below and think about what you want to say.

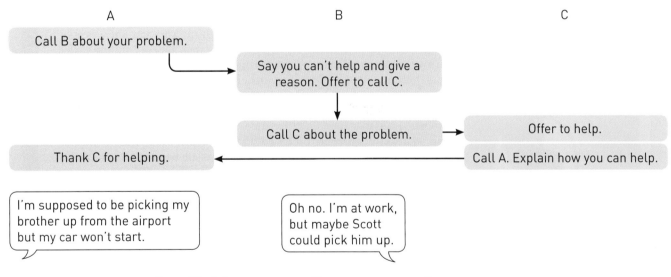

A
Call B about your problem.

B
Say you can't help and give a reason. Offer to call C.

Call C about the problem.

C
Offer to help.

Call A. Explain how you can help.

Thank C for helping.

I'm supposed to be picking my brother up from the airport but my car won't start.

Oh no. I'm at work, but maybe Scott could pick him up.

5 **a** Work in your groups. Have your conversation.

b Change roles. Choose a different problem and have another conversation.

Fate?

5.2 goals
◎ talk about something that went wrong
◎ talk about changes of plan

LISTENING

1 a ◆**1.48** Listen to Pierre and Munizha talking about fate. Circle the correct words in the summary.

Pierre thinks things ¹happen / don't happen for a reason, but that people ²can / can't control how they respond to events in their lives.

Munizha ³believes / doesn't believe that things happen by chance, but says that people ⁴like / don't like believing in fate because it can make certain things seem special (like falling in love).

b Do you think things happen for a reason? Talk together.

READING

2 Work in A/B pairs. Both read the introduction to the True Story competition. Then, A, read the story below and find answers to these questions. B, read the story on p123 and answer the questions there.

1 How did Hans meet Chin Mae?
2 Why didn't they get married?
3 How did he try to contact her later?
4 What happened on January 7th?
5 What happened to Hans's letter?
6 How did the story end?

File Edit View Favorites Tools Help

Address www.newwriting.com/competitions/june/truestory ⌄ → Go Links »

New writing.com

July issue > Readers' stories from around the world > **June competition**

True Story competition

Here are the two winners of our True Story competition, judged by you, the reader. You had to tell us the story of how you met your partner in no more than five hundred words. Here are the two stories from our winners, **Hans Klinsman from Germany and Maggie Renbourne from Ireland.**

I first met Chin Mae when she came to Bonn thirty years ago. She was only supposed to be in Germany for two weeks, but then she met me and we fell in love. We were going to get married, but then she had to go back to Korea for family reasons. I couldn't go with her and I'm not a good letter-writer, so in the end, we lost touch. I couldn't forget her, though. Some years later, I realised there was no way that I was going to be happy with any other woman. I had to try and find Chin Mae. So I wrote a letter and sent it to her last address – her parents' home. I didn't get a reply, which was no surprise really. I thought there was no chance that she'd still be single. She probably had a husband and children. So I tried to get on with my life.

It was three months ago – January 7th, 7.00 in the morning – when I was woken by the phone ringing. I'd been dreaming, and in my dream the phone was ringing and it was Chin Mae, trying to contact me. I'd had that dream many times over the years. When I eventually picked the phone up, I heard Chin Mae's voice. Of course I thought I was still dreaming, but this time it really was her. She said she never got my letter; her parents forgot to give it to her. Just recently, she was helping her mother move home and she found it. It had fallen behind a bookcase and it had been there for over twenty years! As soon as she read it, she knew she had to try to find me. I'd moved home, but luckily, I'd kept the same telephone number.

I immediately flew to Seoul and Chin Mae met me at the airport. It was a wonderful moment. She hadn't changed a bit. I'm so glad my letter ended up where it was supposed to be. I'm fifty this year, and I've just married the woman I've always loved.

3 a Cover the story and think about how to tell it. Use the questions in 2 to help you.

b In pairs, tell each other your stories. What do you think of the stories?

VOCABULARY

*no chance,
no way*

4 Look at sentences 1–5 from the stories. Match the highlighted expressions to the meanings a–d.

1 There was no chance that she'd still be single.
2 There was no way we could have the party.
3 It's no coincidence that I met him on that day.
4 I didn't get a reply, which was no surprise really.
5 It was no use ruining everyone's evening.

a I expected it.
b it wasn't possible. (x2)
c it wasn't by chance.
d it was pointless.

5 **a** Work in pairs. Choose two topics and write sentences with the highlighted expressions in 4.

 • sports events • politics • news stories • social events

There's no chance that Marsel İlhan will win the match tomorrow.

 b Change partners and compare your ideas.

What went wrong?

GRAMMAR

Future in
the past

1 **a** Look at three sentences from Maggie's story.

1 Do they refer to present or past plans?
2 Which two forms suggest an event <u>didn't</u> happen?

> It was supposed to be this great party.
> We were going to have this big dinner.
> All my friends were coming.

 b Find an example of each form to suggest an event didn't happen in Hans's story.

2 **a** It's Maggie's husband's fortieth birthday. Look at the pictures. What were her plans for the evening?

"It was my husband's birthday, his fortieth, so I wanted to do something special for him. But I'd been away on a business trip and hadn't had time to plan anything, so I decided to surprise him when he got home from work. Well, my plan was this: while he was at work I was going to ... "

Grammar reference
and practice, p138

 b 🔊 **1.49** Listen to the story to check. What went wrong with Maggie's plans?

3 What do you think happened after Maggie's husband arrived home? Write the end of the story. 🔊 **1.50** Then listen to the ending. Were you right?

SPEAKING

4 **a** Think about plans you've had which changed. Use these or your own ideas.

 • meeting friends • going on holiday • going on a business trip
 • commuting/travelling • planning an event

1 What were you planning to do?
2 What went wrong?
3 What did you do about it?
4 What happened in the end?

> I was supposed to
> go to Brazil with my
> friends in August,
> but ...

 b Tell each other your stories. Ask questions to find out more.

Attend a reunion

5.3 goals
- ◎ discuss plans and arrangements
- ◎ talk about changes of plan
- ◎ catch up with old friends' news

Dear Carolina,

We are organising a ten-year reunion party on 11th November for all former National University of Singapore students who graduated ten years ago. Would you like to come?

TASK LISTENING

1 Read the beginning of the email and talk about the questions.

1 Would you like to go to a reunion party like this? Why? Why not?
2 Is there someone you haven't seen for a long time that you'd like to see again? What do you think he/she is like now? How do think you've changed?

2 ●❙ **1.51** Listen to Carolina and Iqbal talking at the NUS reunion. Do they seem satisfied with their lives?

TASK VOCABULARY

Catching up

3 a ●❙ **1.51** Listen again. Who says these things, Carolina or Iqbal? ℗

1 You're looking well.
2 You haven't changed a bit.
3 When we were at university, you were going to be a doctor.
4 I'm not a doctor, no. That didn't work out.
5 The last time I saw you, you were going to study finance.
6 Did you ever travel around Europe?
7 I remember you always wanted to do that.

b Write a word to help you remember each expression. Then try to remember the highlighted expressions in 1–7 in groups.

1 looking   2 changed   3 ...

TASK

4 a You're going to meet some old friends at a university or college reunion. You're A, B or C. Read your role card and complete 1–3 with your own ideas. A, look on p119; B, look on p121; C, look on p125.

b Think about how to:
- catch up with old friends
- talk about changes of plan
- talk about your plans

> You're looking well.

> You were going to ...

> Next year, I'm going to ...

5 Talk in groups of three.

6 Talk in new groups. Tell each other about the old friends you met.

Across cultures Saying no

1 a 🔘 **1.52** Listen to Mark and Victor talking about misunderstandings. Are they talking about work or friends?

b 🔘 **1.52** Listen again and answer the questions.

Mark
1 Where was Mark working?
2 Where did he have to go? Why?
3 What did he think had happened?
4 What actually happened?

Victor
1 Where is Victor from? Where does he live?
2 Who is Sarah?
3 How did Victor upset Sarah?
4 What has he learned from the experience?

2 What do you think was the reason for the misunderstanding in each case?

sorry I couldn't make it :)

3 a Look at these extracts from emails and conversations. Which is saying no to:

1 a job application? 3 a business deal? 5 a suggestion?
2 a request for help? (x2) 4 an invitation?

Ⓐ We found the discussions very interesting. However, we feel that, on this occasion, we will not be able to work together.

Ⓑ *I'm afraid I can't* **come** *to your wedding. It's my brother's birthday.*

Ⓒ That's a great idea, but I'm not sure it will work in this case.

Ⓓ Sorry, I'd love to **help**, but I'm too busy.

Ⓔ Actually, I don't think I'm the best person to ask. Why don't you try Sara?

Ⓕ Unfortunately, we are not able to offer you anything at this time, but we will keep your details on file for future reference.

b Do you say no in similar ways in your language? Give examples.

Lim, would you mind lending me 10 dollars? I can pay you back tomorrow.

Erm, actually, I haven't got much money on me. Sorry. Maybe Siew can lend you some.

4 a Work alone. Look at the highlighted expressions for saying no in 3a. Which ones could you use in these situations?

1 A friend asks you to lend her some money, but she owes you money already.
2 A colleague who you don't like much asks you to a party.
3 An acquaintance contacts you to ask you for work. You don't have anything suitable.
4 Someone asks you to help them with a computer problem. You're busy.
5 A new employee suggests a crazy idea in a big meeting.
6 A stranger asks to borrow some money for a taxi in an emergency.

b Take turns to start conversations for situations 1–6. Use expressions from 3a to say no.

c What would you really say and do in these situations? Why?

5 a Think about a situation when:

1 you've found it difficult to say no to a request.
2 you've said yes to something when you didn't mean 'yes'.

b Talk together about the situations. Would you do the same thing as your classmates?

1 Read the emails between Kyoko, Maya and Melissa.

1 What does Maya promise to do? Does she do it?
2 Where is Kyoko going to stay?
3 What does Kyoko offer to do?
4 Who's Melissa? What does she recommend?

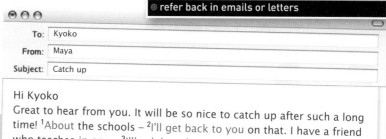

To: Kyoko
From: Maya
Subject: Catch up

Hi Kyoko
Great to hear from you. It will be so nice to catch up after such a long time! [1]About the schools – [2]I'll get back to you on that. I have a friend who teaches in one – [3]I'll ask her about it. By the way, we have a spare room if you need somewhere to stay.
Maya x

Thanks, Maya. That's great that I can stay with you – thanks a lot. The info about the schools would be really helpful. Speak soon.
Kyoko

Hi Maya
Haven't heard from you for a while. [4]You were going to send me something about schools in the area. Have you heard anything? [5]Did you manage to talk to your friend? Don't worry if not. Is there anything you'd like me to bring from Tokyo?
Kx

Hi Kyoko
Sorry I haven't been in touch. My son's been ill so things have been a bit difficult. I spoke to my friend, Melissa, some time ago, and asked her to contact you directly. [6]I'll remind her to get in touch. [7]About bringing something from Tokyo, do you think you could get me some green tea?
Maya

Kyoko, from Tokyo, is going to Dublin to study English. She's just emailed her old college friend, Maya, who lives in Dublin.

File Edit View Insert Format Tools Message Help

Dear Kyoko
Maya asked me to contact you about schools in this area. Here is some information, [8]as promised.
I teach at Addison's Language Centre. It's small and friendly, with excellent teachers.
[9]As far as Business English is concerned, the best place is probably Westbrook's (information attached). Look forward to meeting you in April!
Best wishes,
Melissa

2 Match highlighted expressions 1–9 in the emails with categories a–d.

Referring back in an email or letter:
a to a topic (x3) *About ...,*
b to a promise (x3)
Making offers and promises to:
c write back with more information (x1)
d ask somebody to do something (x2)

3 a Write three requests for a partner.

b Read your partner's requests. Respond using language from 2.

Could we do our homework together?
Sure, if I'm free. I'll get back to you on that.

c Read the responses. What do you think of them? Talk together.

4 a Work in pairs. Imagine:

1 an old friend from another country is going to visit you to do a language course.
2 you're going to visit a friend in another country to do a language course.

What could you offer to do to help? Is there anything your friend could do for you?

b Work with a new partner, in A/B pairs. Use the expressions in 2.

1 A, write an email to your friend explaining your plans.
2 B, read your friend's email. Reply and offer to help in some way.
3 A, remind your friend what he/she promised to do and offer to do something in return.
4 B, reply. Explain what happened and say what you have or haven't done.

5 Read another pair's emails. What did each person offer to do? Did they do it?

5 Look again ♻

Review

VOCABULARY *be supposed to, be meant to*

1 a Make sentences with be supposed to and be meant to and these words.

1 go to work now / but car won't start
2 do homework at the moment / but too tired
3 see friend later on / but not feeling well
4 have a meeting now / but boss late
5 get a bus home / but have to work late

I'm supposed to be going to work now, but my car won't start.

b Work together to think of other reasons for not doing these things.

I'm supposed to be going to work now, but I'd rather watch the tennis.

GRAMMAR Future in the past

2 a Put the words in order to make sentences about past plans. Which two suggest something didn't happen?

1 a big / have / going to / I was / birthday party / twenty-one / I was / when
2 supposed to / I was / summer / on holiday / last / be going
3 in Italy / my / were coming / about / friends / two years ago / to visit me

b Think of two or three things you planned to do, which didn't happen, for example:

• a party   • a celebration   • a trip or holiday
• a day out   • a move   • a change of job

c Tell each other what happened. Who was the most disappointed?

CAN YOU REMEMBER? Unit 4 – Accidents and injuries

3 a Which words and expressions in B can you use with the verbs in A?

A	B
drop slip	over your head
cut bang trip	your finger something
fall break	on something

b Which accidents and injuries in 3a are most likely when you're doing these things?

running for the bus   cycling
driving   swimming
cooking   doing the washing up
going down stairs

c Compare your ideas in groups. Do you agree? Give examples.

Extension

SPELLING AND SOUNDS /r/

4 a 🔊 **1.53** Listen and underline the letters which make a /r/ sound.

wrong   wrote   wrap   promises   garage
ride   right   research   worry   borrow
arriving   correct

b Find words in 4a to match spelling patterns 1–4. /r/ is spelled:

1 r in most words.
2 wr at the beginning of some common words.
3 rr after a short vowel or schwa /ə/.
4 rr before -ow or -y. (There are some exceptions, e.g. very, battery.)

c Spellcheck. In pairs, take turns to choose ten words and test your partner's spelling.

NOTICE *this* in stories

5 a You can use this instead of a/an when you tell stories informally. Look at two sentences from Maggie's story on p123. Then add this to sentences 1–4.

It was supposed to be this great big party …
We were going to have this big dinner …

1 There was incredible bolt of lightning.
2 My friends and I were preparing everything when suddenly we heard huge crash.
3 I was walking down the road when I saw man robbing a bank.
4 I've just bought great new computer game.

b Think about something surprising that happened to you recently. Think about how you can use this when you tell the story.

c Tell each other your stories.

Self-assessment

Can you do these things in English? Circle a number on each line. 1 = I can't do this, 5 = I can do this well.

◎ discuss plans and arrangements	1	2	3	4	5
◎ make offers and promises	1	2	3	4	5
◎ talk about something that went wrong	1	2	3	4	5
◎ talk about changes of plan	1	2	3	4	5
◎ catch up with old friends' news	1	2	3	4	5
◎ make offers and promises in emails or letters	1	2	3	4	5
◎ refer back in emails or letters	1	2	3	4	5

• For Wordcards, reference and saving your work → e-Portfolio
• For more practice → Self-study Pack, Unit 5

6

Let me explain

Saving money

VOCABULARY

Linking expressions

1 Read the introduction to a newspaper article. Why did Kath Kelly decide to live on a pound a day?

HOW I LIVED ON £1 A DAY

At 47, Kath Kelly made a sudden decision to change her life. Out one evening with friends, Kath – who was sharing a house and working as a part-time language teacher – complained that she could not afford a wedding present for her brother Danny. So she announced that she would survive on £1 a day for the 12 months up to his wedding.

She came up with lots of great ways to save money.

2 a How many ways of saving money can you think of? Make a list.

b Look at Kath's advice for saving money.

    1   Match the tips to pictures A–F.
    2   Were any of your ideas the same as Kath's?

KATH'S MONEY-SAVING TIPS

1 Go to a library **if** you want to use the Internet or read the papers.

2 Do your shopping at the end of the day **when** small food shops reduce their prices.

3 Keep your teabag **after** making a cup of tea. Use it at least twice, but leave it in the cup longer each time.

4 Visit people and leave notes if they're out **instead of** making phone calls.

5 Pick fruit from bushes and trees **whenever** you walk anywhere.

6 Never ignore a market researcher **in case** they have free samples to hand out.

c Which ideas do you think are practical? Why? Do you do any of these things?

3 a Look at the highlighted linking expressions in 2b. Which can be followed by:

    a   subject + verb?   b   *-ing* or a noun?   c   either a or b?

b Complete the advice for saving money with linking expressions and your own ideas. Then write three more tips for saving money.

    1   Cycle or hitchhike ...   4   Re-use plastic bags ...
    2   Use leftover food in the fridge ...   5   Grow your own fruit and vegetables ...
    3   Use email to contact friends ...   6   Enter magazine competitions ...

    Cycle or hitchhike whenever you need to travel.

4 Tell the class your top five tips. Then choose the best five as a class.

Living cheaply

1 **Read the rest of the article about Kath Kelly.**

1 How did she save money?
2 Did she buy the wedding present?
3 How did the experience change her?

Kath Kelly

She continued to see her friends, but gave up going to cafés and pubs to see them. "Instead of meeting for lunch in a café, as we used to, we'd take sandwiches and home-made soup and eat in the park." Kath made the soup every morning from chicken carcasses given away by her local butcher and whatever cheap vegetables she could find. She found out that small food shops often sell whatever is left over at the end of the day very cheaply because they cannot keep it overnight. She picked fruit from bushes and trees and looked out for free buffets. "I was the queen of the buffet. Every time there was a public event and a crowd was needed, I was there. I dragged my mates out to free events, too. I couldn't buy drinks for them or anything like that so I'd take them to art openings and book launches." She got rid of her mobile phone and cycled to friends' houses if she wanted to speak to them, leaving a note if they were out, and she used the library for free internet access.

"I was the queen of the buffet."

She also picked up coins dropped in the street and managed to collect £117 – a third of her annual budget. She said: "I kept it for emergencies, but in the end I didn't need it so at the end of the year I gave it to charity." Kath says one of her best tips is to hand out small gifts whenever you can – what you receive in return will usually be of a greater value.

She even managed a free trip to France to visit her brother by hitchhiking through the Channel Tunnel. During the 365 days of her experiment she successfully kept to her budget, going over only once, when she had to visit a dentist. By the end of the year, Kath was able to use some of the £10,000 salary she had saved up to buy a special wedding present for her brother Danny and his bride Sarah.

She had also formed a relationship with 38-year-old Bruce Taylor, manager of the farm where she worked as a holiday volunteer. Kath left her shared house so she and Taylor could live together, and has written a book about her year of living cheaply called *How I Lived On Just A Pound A Day*. The experience has changed her outlook on life dramatically. She said: "Before, I enjoyed spending money on treats, like chocolate and weekends away, but now I don't see the need for expensive things. I don't spend much at all, though it is probably more than £1 a day."

2 **Read again. Why did Kath:**

1 ask her butcher for chicken carcasses?
2 take her friends to free public events?
3 give £117 to charity?
4 hitchhike?
5 spend more than her budget once?
6 move house?

3 **Do you think Kath enjoyed her year of living cheaply? Why? Why not?**

Multi-word verbs: managing money

4 **What can you remember about Kath? Match 1–6 with a–f. Then read the article again to check.**

1	Kath Kelly survived on	a	her mobile phone.
2	She looked out for	b	her budget once.
3	She gave up	c	£1 a day for twelve months.
4	She saved up	d	her budget.
5	She kept to	e	bargains.
6	She only went over	f	enough money for a wedding gift.

5 **Complete the questions with the multi-word verbs from 8.**

1 Have you ever _____ money to buy a gift for someone special?
2 Do you find it difficult to _____ a budget?
3 Do you ever _____ bargains? Where?
4 Have you ever _____ something you enjoyed in order to save money?
5 Do you think you could _____ a similar budget to Kath's? Why? Why not?

6 **Ask and answer the questions together. Do you think you're good with money?**

What do I do next?

READING

1 Read two true stories about following instructions. What did each person do wrong?

1 A motorist in Germany caused thousands of euros worth of damage after following his satellite navigation system too carefully. When the 53-year-old from Freiburg was instructed to "Turn right now", he immediately drove his 4x4 off the road, went through a building site, up a stairway and crashed into a small toilet block.

2 An elderly Swedish woman ended up travelling along a baggage chute at Stockholm airport after misunderstanding instructions on check-in signs. The woman was supposed to be boarding an international flight, but instead of going to the departure lounge, she followed her suitcase onto a luggage belt.

2 a What would you do if you didn't understand the instructions for:

- using a new camera?   • ordering online?   • assembling flat-pack furniture?

b Have you ever had a problem with instructions? What happened?

LISTENING

3 a (2.1) Listen to Vishal's phone call to a computer helpline.

1   What's the problem?   2   Do they manage to solve the problem?

b Put this summary of the phone call in the correct order.

The technician:
a   tests the signal and says it's OK.
b   explains how Vishal can check his internet connection.
c   tells Vishal to test his equipment using a different socket.
d   gives Vishal some advice about his router.
e   suggests turning the computer off and on again.

c (2.1) Listen again to check.

VOCABULARY
Using equipment

4 a Complete 1–8 from the conversation with these verbs in the correct form.

> open   press   unplug   check   click on   turn ... off
> switch ... off   plug ... in   shut ... down

1   Have you tried **switching** everything _off_ and on again?
2   If you're phoning about a technical problem, please _____ two.
3   Have you _____ it _____ and on again?
4   You'll need to _____ your internet connection.
5   _____ Control Panel and _____ Network Connections.
6   I've checked and I've _____ everything _____.
7   You'll have to _____ everything _____.
8   _____ your router and computer.

b (2.2) Listen to check. ℗

c Find:

1   three pairs of verbs that are opposites   2   two verbs that have the same meaning

d Have you had a computer problem recently? Can you remember how you fixed it?

PRONUNCIATION
Linking
consonants and
vowels

5 **a** When a word ending in a consonant sound is followed by a word beginning with a vowel sound, the two sounds usually link. Look at the example in 1, and mark the sounds that link in 2–5.

1 turn‿it‿on 2 switch it off 3 plug it in

4 shut it down 5 click on it

b 🔊 **2.3** Listen to check. Practise saying 1–5.

SPEAKING

6 **a** 🔊 **2.4** Listen to instructions for using a piece of equipment. What do you think it is?

b Think about a piece of equipment you often use. Write instructions for how to use it. Don't say what the equipment is.

c Listen to each other's instructions. Can you guess what they are for?

Have you thought about … ?

GRAMMAR
Verb + *-ing*

1 **a** Some verbs can be followed by *-ing*. Complete sentences 1–6 from the conversation with a–f.

1 My router **keeps**
2 Have you **tried**
3 Try and **avoid**
4 You should **think about**
5 Have you **considered**
6 I can't **face**

a leaving your router on all the time.
b getting a new one?
c switching everything off and on again?
d going wrong.
e moving everything again.
f turning it off at night.

b In which sentences 1–6 is the speaker:

a complaining? b giving advice and suggestions?

2 **a** Complete Vishal's conversation with Nicky using the expressions in the box. Put the verbs in the correct form.

> try talking   avoid going   can't face going   consider telling   keep asking

VISHAL I ¹_____ to work tomorrow.
NICKY Really? Can you work at home?
VISHAL No, I'm having computer problems.
NICKY Oh, no. Anyway, I thought you liked your job. What's the problem?
VISHAL My boss ²_____ me to do her work! She asked me every day last week.
NICKY Have you ³_____ to her about it?
VISHAL No, I find her really difficult to talk to. And she always comes and sits with me at lunch, when I want to relax.
NICKY Well, can you ⁴_____ to lunch at the same time as her?
VISHAL No, not really. The whole team eats together most days.
NICKY Hm. Have you ⁵_____ someone else about the problem?
VISHAL Yeah, maybe I should.

Grammar reference and practice, p139

b 🔊 **2.5** Listen to check. ❓ What would you do in Vishal's situation?

SPEAKING

3 Think of two or three things in your life you aren't happy about. It could be:

- some equipment that doesn't work
- an arrangement you don't want to keep
- something you have to do at work
- someone who's annoying you at the moment

4 Talk together about your problems. Make suggestions and give each other advice. Try to use the verb + *-ing* expressions from 1a.

> My computer keeps crashing.

> Have you thought about getting a new one?

Give expert advice

6.3 goals
- ⊚ give advice
- ⊚ talk about how you manage money
- ⊚ give reasons for advice

TASK LISTENING

1 Can you think of two things that help a marriage or relationship to be successful and two things that can cause problems?

2 a •2.6 Listen to Jörg, on a radio programme, giving advice about how couples should manage their money. Put Jörg's advice in the order he gives it.

a Couples should have a joint account.
b You should have your own account.
c Couples should have a budget.
d Couples should be open about money.

b •2.6 Listen again. What reasons does he give for his advice? Do you think it's good advice?

TASK VOCABULARY

Giving reasons

3 a Complete sentences 1–7 with the reasons Jörg gives for his advice.
•2.6 Then listen again to check.

1 It's important to manage money in the right way because ...
2 Since it's such ... you need to make sure you're always open about your finances.
3 It's easy to find out how to budget as there's a lot of advice ...

4 Many marriages break down because of ...
5 Couples who argue a lot – well, it's often due to ...

6 It's extremely time-consuming to ... so it's a good idea to pay bills from one joint account.
7 It's important to have your own money, so that you can ...

b Look at the highlighted expressions for giving reasons.

1 Which are followed by nouns? Which are followed by subject + verb?
2 In which sentence, 6 or 7, can you use so or so that?

> It's important to have a savings account so that you can feel secure.

4 a Complete these statements with different highlighted expressions from 3a and your own advice about managing money.

It's important to ...   It's a bad idea to ...
It's difficult to ...   It's easy to ...

b Talk about your sentences together. Do you agree with each other?

TASK

5 a You're going to explain how to do something you know about, for example:

- investing money
- doing a sport
- writing a blog
- being a good driver
- taking care of a pet
- raising children

b First, think about the language you need to:

- give advice • give reasons for advice

6 a Talk in groups. Give reasons for your advice. Ask and answer questions.

b Talk in new groups. Tell them what you learned.

Keyword *mean*

I mean

1 a **2.7** Listen to a conversation between two old friends. How do they know each other? Why is Felipe in Italy?

b You can use I mean to add or correct information, or give yourself time to think. Look at script 2.7 on p152 and <u>underline</u> the four examples of I mean.

Felipe and Sabrina in Arezzo, Italy

Patterns with *mean*

2 a Match sentences 1–3 from the conversation with functions a–c.

1 I **meant to** call you last week … but I've been so busy.
2 This photo **means a lot** to me.
3 My conference starts at 9.00, so that **means leaving** here on Sunday night.

a an intention
b a consequence
c something important in your life

b Complete the questions. Then discuss them.

1 Imagine you accept a job on the other side of the world. What would it mean _____ in your life?
2 Do you own something that means _____ you? Why is it important?
3 Is there anything you meant _____ last week but didn't? Why didn't you do it?

Softeners with *mean*

3 a **2.8** Sabrina and Felipe are discussing a plan to eat out. What's the problem with:

a Felipe's passport? b Burger World?

b Complete the highlighted expressions 1–4 with a–d.

1 I've been **meaning to** ask you,
2 I **don't mean to** sound rude,
3 I **don't mean to** worry you,
4 I **didn't mean to** upset you.

a but … it would be nice to go somewhere more Italian.
b It was just funny seeing that beard again.
c but your passport's falling apart.
d could you give me Marco's phone number?

> If I moved to Japan, it would mean learning a new language and leaving my family …

c You can use these expressions to soften what you are going to say. Which function a–c from 2a do they all have?

d Complete these sentences with a highlighted expression from 3b.

1 … but I can smell gas. I think it's coming from the kitchen.
2 … are you driving to Emily's party on Saturday?
3 … but I really don't like your dress. It just doesn't suit you.
4 I'm sorry I shouted. …

4 a Work alone. Imagine an old friend from a different country is visiting you. Think of:

• two or three things you could do • somewhere to eat out • a hotel for your friend

b Work in pairs. A, your friend is visiting. B, you're visiting your friend.

A, suggest things you can do together.
B, you don't like some of your friend's suggestions. Say what you want to do. Use expressions from 3b to soften your objections and make requests.
A, respond and make new suggestions. Use I mean to give yourself time to think and to correct or add ideas.

1 Can you think of examples of these different kinds of games? Which have you played?

- card games
- board games
- outdoor games
- puzzles

2 Look at the photos of a Chinese game called Mahjong. Match A–D in the photos with the rules explaining the game in 1–4.

1 Each player takes turns to pick up a tile.
2 The aim is to collect tiles of the same kind.
3 You throw away the tiles you don't want in the middle.
4 At the end of the game you count your score. You get more points for particular tiles, like ones and nines.

3 a ●● 2.9 Listen to Liu Ying and Jen playing Mahjong.

1 Do they both know how to play?
2 How do you win the game?

b Read the conversation to check.

4 a Look at the highlighted expressions 1–7 in the conversation. Which ones:

1 say you don't understand? (x2)
2 say you partly understand? (x1)
3 explain something? (x4)

b ●● 2.10 Listen to check. ℗

5 a Complete the rest of the conversation using the highlighted expressions.

JEN But how do you get a high score?
LIU YING Well, there are various tiles that are worth more points, like the winds and dragons.
JEN Sorry, ¹_____ . Winds and dragons? How do I know what they are?
LIU YING You can tell from the picture on the tile. Look, this is the East Wind and this is the Red Dragon.
JEN OK, ²_____ . But what are these tiles then?
LIU YING Oh, this one's a season, and that's a flower. ³_____ collect them as that helps you win points.
JEN Oh right. ⁴_____ that card game, you know, whist.
LIU YING Exactly. So, shall we carry on or do you want me to go over it again?

b Replace 1–4 in the conversation in 5a with the expressions in the box below.

> I don't know what you mean.
> You're supposed to ...
> I think I've got that.
> It's similar to ...

6 a Think about a game or sport you know well. If possible, bring the game into class to help you describe it. Then prepare to explain the rules.

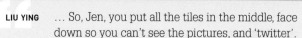

LIU YING ... So, Jen, you put all the tiles in the middle, face down so you can't see the pictures, and 'twitter'.
JEN ¹Sorry, I'm lost. What does 'twitter' mean? Isn't it some sort of website?
LIU YING Well, yes, but in Mahjong it just ²means you mix all the tiles up – like shuffling cards – and 'twitter' is the sound the tiles make when you move them around. It sounds like the birds in the trees.
JEN Ah, nice!
LIU YING Yes. Anyway, everyone has thirteen tiles, and that's what you play the game with. I suppose the tiles are like cards, really.
JEN Like cards?
LIU YING Yes, so you could say ³it's like a card game with tiles. Anyway, ⁴the idea is to collect sets of three or four tiles of the same kind – and then you display them in front of you and you win points.
JEN Hm. I'm sorry, ⁵I don't get it. What's the objective of the game? How do you win?
LIU YING Oh sorry. ⁶I meant to say the aim is to get rid of all the tiles in your hand first. So the game ends when one player has got rid of all of their tiles, and the winner is the person with the highest score. OK?
JEN OK. So, you collect sets of tiles. ⁷I get that bit. But how do you get a high score?

b Talk together and take turns to explain the rules of your game. Use the language in 4 and 5 to ask questions and to explain, until you're sure everyone understands the rules.

7 What do you think of the games? Which ones would you like to play?

6 Look again ♻

Review

1 a Match 1–5 with a–e to make sentences.

1 <u>I try and avoid travelling</u> by public transport,
2 <u>I've tried making</u> Chinese food a few times.
3 <u>I can't face going</u> for a run
4 <u>I've thought about moving</u> abroad,
5 <u>I've considered working</u> for myself,

a but I don't know if I would earn enough.
b when it's cold or wet.
c It's delicious and very easy to cook.
d but I don't want to leave my family and friends.
e in case I catch flu from someone.

b Complete the <u>underlined</u> sentence beginnings with your own ideas.

I try and avoid travelling overnight, as I can never sleep.

c Talk together. Do you have the same ideas?

VOCABULARY Multi-word verbs: managing money

2 a Read Laura's email and complete sentences 1–4.

```
○○○                                            ○
... I'm really proud of my son. He wanted to travel around Chile
so he put 5,000 pesos in the bank every week for six months.
He stopped going to the fitness centre to save more. He had
240,000 by the end of it. It wasn't a lot so he decided on a
budget. I think it was 1,500 pesos a day. He managed this OK,
he said, though there were one or two days when he spent a
bit more. He said he had a great time. He didn't buy me any
presents on his travels. He said he didn't have enough money!
```

1 He saved up ...   3 He kept to ...
2 He gave up ...   4 He only went over ...

b Do you know anyone who has saved money for something special? Use the multi-word verbs to talk about them.

CAN YOU REMEMBER? Unit 5 – Future in the past

3 a Work alone.

1 Write a diary for this week with five or six arrangements in it.
2 Imagine two or three arrangements have been cancelled. Cross them out.

b Work in pairs. Today is Wednesday. Tell each other about your week so far. Then arrange to meet on Thursday or Friday this week.

> On Tuesday, I was supposed to go to the cinema with Howard, but he was ill.

Extension

SPELLING AND SOUNDS /ɔː/

4 a ⏺ 2.11 Listen and underline the letters in these words which make an /ɔː/ sound.

orchestra   morning   door   ordinary
award   resource   wardrobe   score   forty
law   four   drawing   warm   before   poor

b Look at the words in 4a again and complete rules 1–4 with: our or aw ar ore oor
/ɔː/ is usually spelled:

1 _____ at the beginning of words.
2 _____ after w.
3 _____, _____ or _____ in the middle of words.
4 _____, _____, _____ or _____ at the end of words.

c Can you think of more words with the patterns in 4b?

d ⏺ 2.12 Spellcheck. Listen and write ten words. Then check your spelling on p153.

NOTICE Collocations

5 a Complete the collocations with the words in the box. Then check your ideas in the article on p47.

access   friends   dramatically   ~~present~~
phone   together   fruit   events

N + N	Adj + N	Vb + N	Vb + Adv
wedding *present*	mobile _____	pick _____	change _____
internet _____	free _____	see _____	live _____

b Write five questions with the collocations.

c Ask and answer your questions.

> Have you ever bought somebody a wedding present?

Self-assessment

Can you do these things in English? (Circle) a number on each line. 1 = I can't do this, 5 = I can do this well.

◉ give advice	1 2 3 4 5
◉ talk about how you manage money	1 2 3 4 5
◉ give detailed instructions	1 2 3 4 5
◉ give reasons for advice	1 2 3 4 5
◉ say you don't understand	1 2 3 4 5
◉ ask for help	1 2 3 4 5
◉ explain something	1 2 3 4 5

• For Wordcards, reference and saving your work → e-Portfolio
• For more practice → Self-study Pack, Unit 6

7 Personal qualities

A high achiever

1 Read the 5-minute interview with Carlos Acosta. What kind of person do you think he is?

ArtsComment

The 5-minute interview: Carlos Acosta

The Cuban ballet dancer Carlos Acosta has danced for many ballet companies including the Royal Ballet in London and the National Ballet of Cuba, where he was principal. In recent years, he has danced all over the world as an International Guest Artist. He has won numerous international prizes and is considered by many to be the best male dancer in the world.

" **A phrase I use too often is ...**
'You know' or 'You know what I mean'. You know what I mean?
I wish people would take more notice of ...
The importance of art in society. We need to have more support from the government. Not just in the UK – everywhere.
The most surprising thing that happened to me was ...
When my father went to jail. That was very surprising.
I'm good at ...
Learning things quickly, especially movement. And I can remember things for a long time.
I'm very bad at ...
Art. I can't paint or draw. I just don't have any talent.

The ideal night out is ...
Time spent with normal people, just having a good time and learning.
You know me as a dancer but in another life I'd have been ...
A musician or a sportsman. I wanted to be a footballer when I was a child.
The best age to be is ...
Now. I'm mature but I still have youth – it's a good balance.
In weak moments I ...
Just have to have faith in myself and trust the people around me.
In a nutshell, my philosophy is this:
Do whatever makes you happy, however you want it.
Because life is special. "

2 a Read the interview again. Find four facts about Carlos's life and two of his opinions.

b Close your books. Talk together. What can you remember about Carlos Acosta?

3 Complete the sentences from the interview so they're true for you.

A phrase I use too often is 'I don't believe it!'.

> I'm good at maths.
>
> > Really? What's 23 multiplied by 15?

4 a Listen to each other's sentences. Ask questions to find out more details.

b Tell the class the most surprising thing you found out about your partner.

It's the kind of job that ...

1 a Read these opinions about success. Do you agree? Why? Why not?

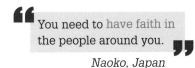

" You need to have faith in
the people around you. "

Naoko, Japan

" You have to have discipline to keep
going, mentally as well as physically. "

Anne, Ghana

" You can't be successful if
you don't have any talent. "

Lucilla, Brazil

" You have to have initiative. You can't
wait for someone to tell you what to do! "

Craig, Scotland

" It's good to have an open mind about things.
You never know what's going to happen next. "

Asim, Egypt

" You need to have confidence.
People listen to confident people. "

Juan, Spain

b What personal qualities do you need:

1   in the army?
2   when you work alone?
3   in an emergency?

4   when you fail at something?
5   if you want to be famous?
6   to be a dancer?

c Talk together. Do you have the same or different ideas?

Anne is Ghanaian

2 🔊 **2.13** Listen to Anne talking about being a dancer. Put these topics in the order she talks about them:

- competition • body shape
- motivation • disappointment

3 🔊 **2.13** Listen again. Which of these things does she say are important?

You need to ...
1   ... really want to be a dancer.
2   ... be pushed by your parents.
3   ... have discipline.
4   ... be skinny.
5   ... have confidence in yourself.
6   ... be able to take rejection.
7   ... have some luck.

4 Talk together. Do you agree with the statements?

1   Parents should push their children to be successful.
2   Success is about being in the right place at the right time.

5 Look at the sentences from Anne's interview. In which other jobs are these qualities important? Make a list.

1	You need to be You have to be	someone the kind of person the sort of person	who that	never gives up. can take rejection well. keeps going.
2	It's That's	something the kind of job the sort of thing	that	needs a lot of discipline. requires a lot of confidence. people don't really understand.

> Acting is the kind of job that looks easier than it really is.

6 Work alone. Write three or four sentences about your job, and the sort of person it would suit. Use expressions from 1 and 5.

Nursing is the kind of job that requires a lot of patience. You also need to have discipline ...

7 a Tell each other about the jobs. Try and find someone who would be suitable for each job.

b Tell the class who you chose and why.

A great character

**READING**

1 Why do you think people keep pets?
What are the advantages and disadvantages of having pets?

2 a You're going to read an article about the personalities of people and their pets. Before you read, do you think these statements are true or false?

1 Married couples become more alike after being together for a long time.
2 Animals don't have personalities like humans do.
3 Pets become more like their owners over time.

b Read the article. What does it say about 1–3?

NEWSONLINE

Can pets and their owners 'become more alike over time'?

Pets and their owners are just like married couples and they get more alike over time, a psychologist claimed yesterday. Prof Richard Wiseman asked almost 2,500 people to complete online questionnaires about their characters and those of their pets. He found that many dog lovers, cat owners and even reptile keepers said they shared many of the same traits – such as happiness, intelligence, independence and a sense of humour – as their pets.

But he also discovered that the longer an animal had been with its owner, the more likely it was to have picked up their characteristics. Prof Wiseman said: "For years owners have insisted their pets have a unique personality. This work suggests they might be right, but it also reveals that people's pets are a reflection of themselves." He went on to say: "It's like with married couples. They grow to look like each other and to have similar personalities. It's possible we are seeing a similar effect."

3 Do you know anyone who has a pet? Do you think they and their pet are similar? Give examples.

LISTENING

4 Which photo A–E shows: a dog   a hamster   a parrot   a goldfish   a lizard

5 a ◖2.14◗ Listen to five people talking about pets. Match the people 1–5 with the pets in photos A–E.

Ⓐ  Ⓑ  Ⓒ  Ⓓ  Ⓔ

b ◖2.14◗ Listen again. Are any of the people similar to their pets? In what way?

c Check in the script on p153.

Personality

6 **a** These adjectives and nouns often go together.
Which adjective is used with each noun 1–3 in the listening?
Check in the script on pp153–4.

1	a	difficult great miserable	character	**2**	a/an	interesting strange calm	person	**3**	a bright nice charming	guy/woman

b Choose expressions from 6a to complete these sentences.

1 My boss is a _____ . She's not easy to get on with.
2 It was fascinating talking to your sister. She's a very _____ .
3 My new assistant is a _____ . He learns things really quickly.
4 That teacher is such a _____ . She never smiles at anyone.
5 The new managing director is a _____ . I just don't understand him.
6 My brother finds it easy to get whatever he wants. He's such a _____ .

7 **a** Think of people you've met in the last five years. Think about how to describe them using the expressions in 6a.

b Talk together. Ask questions to find out more.

> My new neighbour's a very interesting person.
>
> Interesting? In what way?

Similarity and difference

Comparing

1 **a** Complete the sentences from the listening with the words in the grey boxes.
Then check in the script on p153.

Comparatives	A _____	B _____
1 He's _much_ friendlier than a lot of the ones you see.	much	a little
2 I am _____ more fussy.	a lot	a bit
3 Watching him is _____ better than watching television.	lots	slightly
4 I am _____ more intelligent than him.	far	marginally

as ... as ...	C _____	D _____
5 We certainly are _____ as tolerant as we used to be.	almost	just
6 I enjoy my food _____ as much as he enjoys his.	nearly not quite	

Grammar reference and practice, p139

b Match meanings 1–3 with A–D in the highlighted expressions above.

1 a small difference (x2)   2 a big difference   3 the same

Contrastive stress

2 **a** You can stress a word to compare or contrast it with something else.
2.15 Listen and notice which words have contrastive stress in this sentence:

Watching him is far better than watching television.

b Which words can you stress to make a contrast in these sentences?

1 Tim's generally a calm person, so she tends to be calm now too.
2 I enjoy my food just as much as he enjoys his.
3 If their owner gets stressed, then they get stressed too.

c **2.16** Listen and look at the script on p153 to check. Practise saying the sentences.

3 Choose a friend or family member and use the highlighted expressions in 1a to write five or six sentences about:

1 the ways you're similar and different.
2 how you've both changed over the years.

4 **a** Discuss your sentences. Ask questions to find out more.

b Talk together. Who would you most like to meet?

> My brother's a really nice guy, but he's not nearly as bright as me!
>
> Do you get on with him?

Talk about people who have influenced you

TASK LISTENING

1 Discuss the questions.

1 Can you remember the name of your first:
   • teacher? • friend? • colleague? • boss?
2 What kind of person were they? What do you remember about them?
3 Which kinds of people tend to be role models for young people in your country?

2 a 🔊 **2.17** Listen to Tara talking about two people who have influenced her. Who are they?

b 🔊 **2.17** Listen again. How did each person influence Tara? Make notes. Then read the script on pp153–4 to check.

TASK VOCABULARY

Describing someone's influence

3 a Can you remember who Tara is talking about in each sentence?

1 Her confidence made a huge impression on me.
2 She really got me interested in the subject.
3 She really helped me to be myself, I suppose.
4 She made me much more confident.
5 She encouraged me to go on to university.
6 She really had faith in me.
7 She inspired me to do better.

b Which highlighted expressions above are followed by:

   • a verb? • a noun? • a comparative adjective?

Tara from Iran

TASK

4 a You're going to talk about two or three people who have influenced you. They can be:

   • a teacher
   • a boyfriend/girlfriend
   • a friend
   • a family member
   • a colleague
   • someone famous

Influences in your life

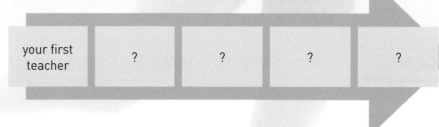

| your first teacher | ? | ? | ? | ? |

b Think about how to talk about:

1 their personality   *He was a great character.   She was the sort of person that ...*
2 how they changed you   *He made me much more ...   He got me interested in ...*

5 a Talk about your people in groups. Ask questions to find out more.

> My mum encouraged me to learn a musical instrument.

> Really? Is she a musician then?

b Who has had the biggest influence on each of your lives?

Across cultures Roles in life

1 a 🔊 **2.18** Listen to Hayes from the USA and Alex from Greece talking about their different roles in life. Listen and write H or A next to the roles they say are important to them.

- friend
- wife
- teacher
- father
- colleague
- son
- daughter
- businesswoman

b 🔊 **2.18** Listen again and answer the questions.

1 How does Hayes introduce herself to people? Why?
2 How does her dad feel about being retired?
3 In Greece, what does Alex say children are expected to do?
4 Why does Alex's brother live with his parents?

c Do you think you have more in common with Hayes or Alex?

2 Discuss the questions about where you live.

Work roles

1 Do people introduce themselves by saying their job title, like Hayes?
2 At what age do most people retire? Do people generally see retirement as a positive or negative thing? Why?
3 How much holiday do people usually take a year?

Family roles

4 Do people usually give priority to their family or their work?
5 Do very old people usually live in a care home or with their children?
6 If someone loses their job, do they rely on their family or the state for support?

3 Which highlighted expressions are used to talk about roles? Which are used to talk about opinions?

1 I see myself as a father first.
2 Maybe work isn't regarded as so important over there.
3 I also think of myself as a colleague to people at work.
4 It's difficult to say what I define myself as first.
5 I'd describe myself as a hard-working person.
6 Retirement is perceived as a bit lazy really.
7 Work is seen as a big thing here.

4 a What roles do you have in your life? What do you see yourself as first? Why?

b Compare your ideas in groups.

5 How are these people seen where you live? What about other places you know?

- working mothers
- househusbands
- unemployed people
- retired people
- divorced people
- people without children

1 Discuss the questions.

1 Do you travel for work and stay in hotels?
2 What are the most important features of a hotel for you?

2 Katherine and Mauro are organising their company's annual conference in Buenos Aires. Read Mauro's email and complete Katherine's list of the pros and cons of each venue.

Possible venues	Pros	Cons
The Excelsior	more facilities	
The Hotel Arts	good food	

Goals

- ◎ compare and contrast two alternatives
- ◎ organise ideas 1

Katherine   Mauro

4 Complete an email from Katherine to another colleague, Belinda, with the highlighted expressions from the first email.

○○○

Delete Reply Reply All Forward Print

Hi Katherine
I've visited the two hotels we're considering for the conference. They're lovely and would both be fine. However, there are some differences that are probably worth thinking about.

The Excelsior is much bigger (24 floors!) so it's got more facilities for guests. Although we'll probably be working too hard to use the swimming pools and tennis courts, some people might appreciate the shopping arcade. On top of that, there are plenty of places to eat, including a buffet Italian restaurant as well as a more formal dining room and a café with Wi-Fi access.

The Hotel Arts is very different in size and style. It's much smaller but has a large conference room (seating 160) which would be fine for us. The business centre isn't quite as well equipped, though I think it would be sufficient for our needs. There are fewer places to eat but the food sounds good. It's a beautiful place in an art deco building, quite stunning in fact.

As for price, the Excelsior offers some pretty good discounts, but the Arts is slightly cheaper. On balance, I have to say I'd go for the Arts. The Excelsior is so enormous that it might feel rather impersonal, whereas the Arts feels a bit more special.

Anyway, let me know what you think, and please pass on your ideas to Belinda for her final decision.
Best wishes
Mauro

FROM: Katherine
TO: Belinda
SUBJECT: Annual conference

Dear Belinda,

Mauro and I would like to go ahead and book the Hotel Arts, Buenos Aires for the conference this year. ¹_____, we feel it's the best venue. It has really lovely conference rooms ²_____ internet facilities in every room.

³_____ it wasn't the cheapest place, it's perfect for our needs and is close to the airport. We felt that the Excelsior was just too big really, ⁴_____ the Arts is actually quite cosy. ⁵_____, you have the last word on this, so have a look at the websites and let me know if you disagree.

Best wishes
Katherine

---

3 Which highlighted linking expressions in the email:

a add information? (x2) Underline the information which is added.
b contrast two ideas? (x4) Underline the ideas which are contrasted.
c conclude an argument? (x1)

5 a Work in groups. Imagine you work for a large international company in Dubai and you have to organise a business trip over a weekend.

1 What does your company do? What's the aim of the weekend?
2 Look at the facilities in two different venues on p124. Which would be best for your weekend? Why?

b Write an email to another colleague comparing and contrasting the hotels and saying which you think would be best.

6 Read other people's emails. Which is the most popular venue? Why?

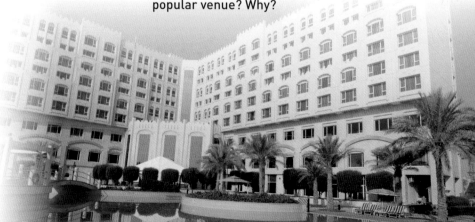

Review

VOCABULARY Personality

1 a Add vowels to make personality adjectives.

1 m__s__r__bl__	5 br__ght
2 ch__rm__ng	6 d__ff__c__lt
3 c__lm	7 __nt__r__st__ng
4 gr____t	8 str__ng__

b 🔊 **2.19** Listen to five descriptions of people. Write down the names of people you think fit these descriptions.

c Talk in pairs. Tell each other about the people you listed.

GRAMMAR Comparing

2 a Which words or expressions used in comparative sentences mean:

1 a big difference? 2 a small difference?
3 exactly the same?

Comparatives	as ... as ...
much a little far slightly a bit a lot marginally	not quite not nearly just almost

b Choose two famous people. Write sentences to compare them. They can be:

- two sportspeople
- two singers
- two actors
- two politicians

c Read your sentences to each other. Do you know the people? Do you agree?

> Ajda Pekkan is a lot more talented than Sertab Erener.

CAN YOU REMEMBER? Unit 6 – Multi-word verbs

3 a Complete these sentences with the correct particle: in to over off down up

1 I never go _____ my budget.
2 I haven't saved _____ enough money to go on holiday this year.
3 I find it difficult to keep _____ a daily budget.
4 I always shut _____ my computer at night.
5 I never leave things plugged _____ when I'm away.
6 I don't like walking into a room at night if the lights are switched _____.

b Change the sentences so they're true for you. Talk together. Who's the most careful person?

SPELLING AND SOUNDS /iː/

4 a 🔊 **2.20** Listen to the words and underline the letters which make an /iː/ sound.

creature meet reason easy complete believe each between knee these teacher colleague employee seen agree field receive

b Find words in 4a to match spelling patterns 1–4. /iː/ is spelled:

1 e + consonant + e in many words.
2 ea at the beginning and in the middle of words.
3 ee in the middle of some words and at the end of words with a stressed syllable.
4 ie in the middle of some words. But ei after c.

c Spellcheck. In pairs, take turns to choose ten words and test your partner's spelling.

NOTICE Comparing with *like*, *alike*

5 a Complete these sentences with like or alike.

1 Pets and their owners are just _____ married couples.
2 They get more _____ over time.
3 It's _____ with married couples.
4 They grow to look _____ each other.

b Check your ideas in the text on p56.

c Match the highlighted expressions with the meanings a–d.

a have a similar appearance
b similar to
c similar (in personality or appearance: *adjective*)
d exactly the same as

d Talk about these questions together.

1 Who do you look like in your family?
2 Do you know anyone who's just like you?
3 Do you know a couple who are very alike in personality? Have they become more alike over time?

Self-assessment

Can you do these things in English? Circle a number on each line. 1 = I can't do this, 5 = I can do this well.

◎ describe qualities you need for different activities	1	2	3	4	5
◎ describe personality	1	2	3	4	5
◎ make comparisons	1	2	3	4	5
◎ say how a person has influenced you	1	2	3	4	5
◎ compare and contrast two alternatives	1	2	3	4	5
◎ organise ideas 1	1	2	3	4	5

- For Wordcards, reference and saving your work → e-Portfolio
- For more practice → Self-study Pack, Unit 7

Lost and found

Clutter, rubbish, stuff

READING

1 a Read the introduction to an article on a lifestyle website. Which word on line 1 means:

- things you throw away? • lots of things in a small space? • things in general?

Is clutter a problem in your home?

b Read the rest of the article and the comments. What could be the benefits of decluttering?

---

www.declutteryourlife.com

 **Declutter your life!**

Clutter. Rubbish. Stuff. Call it what you like, we've all got so much of it we're drowning in it. It gradually takes over our houses and our lives. All this stuff has become a huge source of stress today, affecting everything from our lifestyle choices to our personal development.

Decluttering – clearing out all that clutter and living a cleaner, simpler life – is becoming increasingly popular.

Don Aslett is a cleaning specialist. He believes that we're addicted to stuff. "By the time we become adults, we believe that things make us happy," he says. "If one little thing gives us pleasure, then surely more things will increase our pleasure. And we think things can change us, make us better. For instance, 'the kids won't do their homework – I'm sure it'll help if we buy a computer' or 'I'm unpopular – a new shampoo should help.' " He believes that we buy things to solve all the problems in our lives, and so we keep getting more stuff. And of course, we're wrong.

Michelle Passoff

Michelle Passoff makes her living from other people's clutter – she's a 'clutter consultant' and author of *Lighten Up! Free Yourself From Clutter*. "A long time ago, I noticed that when something big happened in my life, I would go on a cleaning binge: I'd tidy up the front room; I'd put the kids' toys away in their cupboards; I'd clean up the kitchen." She found that cleaning helped her feel less stressed about the big problems in her life. "But then one day I had a thought: suppose I did it the other way around. If I had a big clear-out, would big things happen in my life?" She found that they did. She found that, without so many possessions, she could concentrate on the important things in her life, like relationships with friends and colleagues.

Do you hoard things and never throw them away? Go on, declutter your life. Click <u>HERE</u> to find out more.

How do you feel about clutter?

Comments

In my neighbourhood, there's one day a month when you can put old furniture and stuff you don't want out on the street. I think it's good to give away stuff you don't need any more. **Ana, Spain**

I don't agree with these people. My wife and I enjoy buying new things and we're perfectly normal. We have two happy and healthy kids. When you're happy, the things around you have happy memories, so you want to keep them. **Manuel, Brazil**

Every year, when the weather starts to improve, we give the house a good clean and get rid of a lot of our old stuff. It's not much fun but it does feel good when you've done it. So maybe they have a point, but the idea of a 'clutter consultant' is ridiculous. **Roger, UK**

---

2 Read the article and comments again. Who believes these things?

1 It's nice to have possessions that remind you of good times.
2 Cleaning can reduce stress.
3 No one needs a clutter consultant.
4 People are wrong to think buying new things will make their lives better.
5 It's a good idea to let other people have the things you don't need.

3 What do you think about each of the opinions in 2? Talk together.

VOCABULARY

Multi-word verbs: tidying and cleaning

4 Complete these sentences with the words in the box. Then read the article to check.

> away (x3)   up (x2)   of

1 Do you hoard things and never throw them _____?
2 I'd tidy _____ the front room.
3 I'd clean _____ the kitchen.
4 I'd put the kids' toys _____ in their cupboards.
5 Every year, we … get rid _____ a lot of our old stuff.
6 It's good to give _____ stuff you don't need any more.

SPEAKING

5 Discuss the questions.

1 Do you find it easy to throw things away?
2 Do you always tidy up before visitors come round?
3 How often do you get rid of old stuff and replace it? Do you usually sell it, give it away or throw it away?

Freecycle

VOCABULARY

Describing products

1 Read the information on the website.

1 Do you think Freecycle is a good idea? Is there anything like this where you live?
2 Are there any offers you'd be interested in?

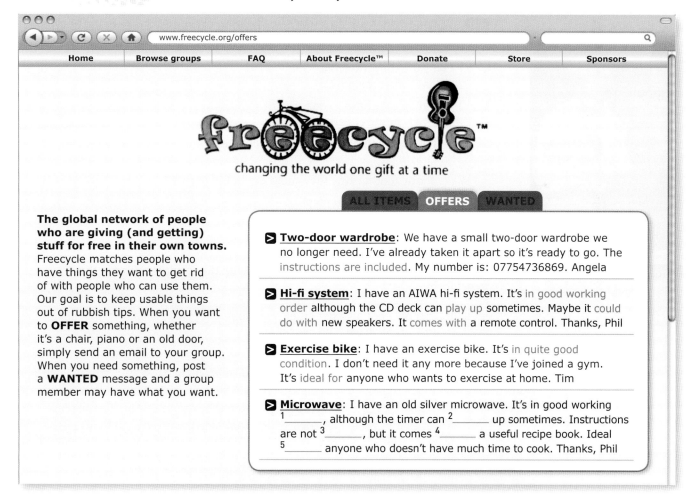

2 a Look at the highlighted expressions. Which are good points? Which are bad?

b Cover the first three offers. Complete the final offer with words from the highlighted expressions.

WRITING AND SPEAKING

3 Think of something you have in your home that you no longer need. Write a short description of it for Freecycle.

4 Read each other's descriptions. Talk together and choose something you need.

A nightmare journey

8.2 goals
- talk about unexpected travel situations
- discuss options and decide what to do
- make deductions

LISTENING

1 What can go wrong when you're travelling? Talk together.

2 **2.21** Alice and Javier are on a journey. Listen to conversations A–F and answer the questions. Did any of the problems you mentioned happen?

Javier   Alice

A	1	Why are they travelling?
	2	What's the problem?
B	3	What do they have to do?
C	4	What's the problem?
	5	What do you think is going to happen next?
D	6	What's the problem?
	7	Is there another way they could get to the party?
E	8	What does Javier suggest?
	9	What does Alice think they should do?
F	10	Do they get to the party on time?

VOCABULARY
Travel situations

3 Complete Alice's description of her journey with these expressions in the correct form.

> get a lift   get on   get off   get stuck   get lost
> give us a lift   break down   be cancelled

"

We had a nightmare journey. We ¹_____ the wrong train and had to ²_____ in some little town somewhere. We couldn't get a connecting train here, so we had to go all the way back but all the trains ³_____; there was a replacement bus service. And then the bus ⁴_____, so we got off and waited for ages. Then we decided to try and hitchhike here and we ⁵_____ straight away but our problems didn't end there. There was lots of traffic and we ⁶_____ in a traffic jam for ages, so we tried to go a different way but then we ⁷_____. Anyway, Donna, the woman who ⁸_____, was really nice and drove us all the way here. But now we've missed your party!

"

SPEAKING

4 a Think about a travel problem you've had. It could be:

- a train or bus you were on was cancelled
- you got on the wrong train or bus
- you got lost
- you got off at the wrong stop
- your train, bus or car broke down
- you got stuck in a traffic jam

b Tell each other what happened.

Lost

GRAMMAR

Modals of deduction and speculation

1 a Look at the sentences from the conversations. Which highlighted modal verbs can you use to say:

1 you're sure something is true?   2 something is possible? (x2)
3 you're sure something is not true?

> The train must go from here.

> There might be a local bus that goes past.

> Oh, no. This can't be our train!

> There could be one further along.

b Find one more example of each modal verb in the scripts on p154.

2 a During their car journey, Alice, Javier and Donna got lost. Complete their conversation with appropriate modal verbs from 1a.

> ALICE   This ¹_____ be the right road. None of the signs say Beauville on them.
> DONNA   You're right. Sorry, guys. I think we're lost.
> JAVIER Well, maybe we should head towards the nearest town. I'm sure there ²_____ be a shop with a map there.
> DONNA   Maybe. But we're not near any towns at the moment.
> ALICE   Oh, look, there's a garage coming up. It ³_____ sell maps.
> DONNA   I'll stop so you can go in and ask.
> …
> JAVIER No, no maps. And he's never heard of Beauville!
> ALICE   What! Let's call Andy. She lived round here. She ⁴_____ know the area pretty well.
> JAVIER OK, you can use my phone. I haven't got her number though.
> ALICE   Oh no! Er, I think it's 0151 …
> JAVIER No, it ⁵_____ be that. It's the wrong area code.
> ALICE   Oh, no. What are we going to do?

Grammar reference and practice, p140

b ◄ 2.22 Listen to check. ℗

PRONUNCIATION

Emphatic stress

3 a You can use emphatic stress with must, can't, could and might to express more certainty or less certainty. ◄ 2.23 Listen to the sentences from 1a again. In which group (1 or 2) does the emphatic stress make the sentence:

a   more certain?   b   less certain?

1   The train must go from here.
    This can't be our train.

2   There might be a local bus that goes past.
    There could be one further along.

b Practise saying the sentences together.

SPEAKING

4 a Read the situation. Discuss the four choices and decide what to do. Then turn to the appropriate page and continue.

> That man might be able to help.

> No, he's going too fast.

> Well, there must be someone in the house.

> **A** You're on holiday with friends in an area that you don't know. You've gone out walking in the countryside and have got lost. You need to find your way back to the holiday house that you're staying in. You can see a river to your right, a house in front of you and fields to your left. There's a man on a bicycle coming towards you along the path. Discuss what to do.
> **S** (p132) ask the man for help   **F** (p121) go towards the fields
> **K** (p118) go towards the house   **C** (p125) go towards the river

b Who got home in the fewest stages? Who took the longest to get home?

Target activity

Find something at lost property

TASK LISTENING

1 Discuss the questions.

1 Which of your possessions would you least like to lose? Why?
2 Have you ever phoned or been to a lost property office? Why?

2 ▶ **2.24** Listen to three people phoning a lost property office.

1 Look at pictures A–F. Match one item with each conversation.
2 Does the office have the items?

TASK VOCABULARY

Describing objects

3 a Match sentences 1–7 from the conversations with the pictures they refer to.

1 It's a small, brown, leather wallet.
2 It's a black and grey sports bag with a shoulder strap.
3 It's got some cash inside.
4 It has pink stripes on the outside.
5 It also has a little silver stripe on the bottom.
6 There's a heart design on the front.
7 It's got pockets on the side.

b Work together to answer the questions.

1 In which order do you say adjectives describing colour, material and size?
2 What other adjectives do you know describing colour, material and size?
3 What's the opposite of the highlighted expressions in 5 and 6?

4 a Think of one of your possessions. Write three or four sentences to describe it. Don't say what it is.

b Listen to each other's sentences. Can you guess what the things are?

TASK

5 Work in A/B pairs. A, you work in a lost property office. B, you've lost something, so you phone A to see if the office has it. A, look on p120; B, look on p126. Think about the language you need to:

describe objects   ... in good condition   ... on the outside   ... on the top
make deductions   *That sounds like it could be my bag.*   *These must be your glasses.*

6 a B, call A. Does the office have the thing you lost?

b Change roles. A, look on p120; B, look on p126. Then have another conversation.

c Have two more conversations like this. A, look on p127; B, look on p133.

d Did you find the things you lost?

Keyword *have*

Uses of *have*

1 **a** 🔊 **2.25** Listen to a conversation between Mani and Salil.

1 What has Mani lost? 2 Where does she think she left it?

b In which sentences 1–4 does have or had:

a describe an action?
b describe an obligation?
c make the present perfect?
d make the past perfect?

1 I've left it somewhere probably.
2 I'd just been to the dry cleaners.
3 I had to go into town for a meeting.
4 I had some food at the café.

c Read Mani's email to Salil.

1 What happened to her coat?
2 Add have in the correct form in eight more places in the email.

> ⦿⦿⦿
>
> Guess what! I *'ve* found my coat. It took most of the day to find it. I couldn't get through to lost property on the phone so I to go there, but nobody handed it in. I thought it might be at the office so I to go all the way into town to check, but it wasn't there either. I some lunch with Lorna, and I then saw an old man wearing my coat! I asked him about it and he said he found it at the bus stop outside the office. I said he could keep it, as I just bought a new one. You found your phone yet? Anyway, I to go now. See you later.
> Mx

Causative *have*

2 **a** Look at the extract from the conversation in 1a and answer the questions.

SALIL Didn't you take it to have it cleaned or something?
MANI Yeah, I had it dry cleaned.

1 Did Mani clean her coat or did someone else do it?
2 Complete the pattern: have + noun + _____

> You can use get instead of have in this pattern. It has the same meaning. *I got it dry cleaned.*

b Look at the verb–noun collocations. Prepare questions to ask a partner with causative have.

- fix your car
- clean your windows
- cut your hair
- manicure your nails
- do your accounts
- clean your home

Do you have your windows cleaned or do you do it yourself?

c Ask and answer your questions. Who is the most self-sufficient?

Common expressions with *have* + noun

3 **a** Match 1–7 with a–g.

1 Were you talking to someone?
2 Hello, Kuba, you wanted to talk?
3 Have you seen my new phone?
4 Can you fix my computer for me?
5 When's the meeting?
6 Is Don free on Friday?
7 Do you want to go on the business trip?

a Yes, can I have a word with you in private?
b I don't know. I haven't had a chance to ask him yet.
c I'm not sure, but I have a feeling it's on Tuesday.
d I'll have a go, but I'm not very good with PCs.
e Well, I had a chat with this old lady at the bus stop.
f Not really, no, but I don't have a choice.
g No, can I have a look?

b Prepare questions to find someone who:

1 had a look at the weather forecast this morning. What did it say?
2 always has a word with their boss when they have a problem.
3 has a go at fixing things in the home.
4 hasn't had a chance to do their homework.
5 has something boring to do at the weekend, but doesn't have a choice.
6 has a feeling that something exciting will happen today.

c Ask and answer the questions. Try and find out more information.

> Did you have a look at the weather forecast this morning?
>
> Yes.
>
> What did it say?
>
> It's going to be hot.

Goals
- describe objects you don't know the name of
- use vague language to describe things

1 Look at the pictures. How would you describe each object? Talk together.

2 **2.26** Listen to three conversations. Which object A–C do the people talk about in each?

1 Which is a gift?
2 Which is for someone's home?
3 Which has been left at a friend's house?

3 a **2.26** Listen again. In what ways are the three objects similar to or different from:

1 a piano?
2 a chest of drawers?
3 a string bag?

b Check your ideas in conversations 1–3.

4 Which group of expressions is used to:

a compare?
b describe something vaguely?
c categorise?

1	It's a sort of chest of drawers. It's a kind of instrument.
2	It looks like a chest of drawers. It's sort of like a string bag. I suppose it's a bit basket-like.
3	I'd like to buy the big thing we saw yesterday. I'd have to get a smallish one … … sort of reddish, brownish colours.

5 a Work alone.

1 Think of an interesting object. It could be:
   • a holiday souvenir
   • a gift you received
   • a possession
   • an ornament
2 Think about how to describe it with the language in 4.

b In groups, listen to the descriptions. You could try to guess what the object is or try to draw it.

1

SARA	What furniture are we going to put in this room?
RALPH	Well, I'd like to go back to that antiques shop and buy the big thing we saw yesterday.
SARA	What big thing?
RALPH	You know, it looks like a chest of drawers, but it's taller.
SARA	A wardrobe?
RALPH	No … it's got a special name, but I can't remember the word. It's a sort of chest of drawers.
SARA	Oh. Is it a 'tall something'?
RALPH	Tallboy. That's it!

2

TIM	Hi Grace, did you have fun last night?
GRACE	Yeah, it was great. Tim, I think I left my bag at your house. Could you check for me?
TIM	Yeah, I've got a load of stuff here, so you'll have to describe it to me. What's it like?
GRACE	Well, it's a *bilum* …
TIM	What's a … *bilum*?
GRACE	Well, it's difficult to describe … it's sort of like a string bag, from Papua New Guinea.
TIM	String?
GRACE	Well, not exactly. It's a bit like rope, maybe, but much more delicate than rope. I suppose it's a bit basket-like. And it's all different earthy colours, sort of reddish, brownish colours.
TIM	OK, well, if I find it I'll let you know …

3

EMILY	Do you think an *mbira* is a good thing to bring back from Mozambique for Paul?
MIKE	A what? What is it?
EMILY	Oh, it's a kind of instrument, a bit like a piano, but not nearly as big, of course. You can hold it in your hands. In fact, I think you can call it a thumb piano.
MIKE	Oh really? What does it look like?
EMILY	There are lots of different kinds, but I'd have to get a smallish one to fit in my case. It's made of wood and the keys are made of metal.
MIKE	Yeah, I think Paul will like that.

8 Look again ♻

Review

GRAMMAR Modals of deduction and speculation

1 **a** Read situations 1–5 and make sentences with might, could, can't and must to explain them.

  1 A man is running down the street, shouting, "Get out of the way!"
  2 You arrive at work at 9 am, but there's no one there.
  3 You are woken up at 4 am by a knock on the door.
  4 A close friend stops returning your emails and texts.
  5 Your computer suddenly switches itself off.

> He must be late for something.
>> Or he could be a policeman.

  b Work in pairs. Write two more situations and give them to another pair to explain.

VOCABULARY Travel situations

2 **a** Match the words to make travel expressions.

get give	stuck down on/off a lift
break be	somebody a lift cancelled lost

  b Complete sentences 1–4 with expressions in the right form.

  1 You're on the way to a wedding. You / in a traffic jam and haven't moved for half an hour.
  2 You're driving to a meeting when you see that a car has /. A woman and a child are standing near the car.
  3 Your evening flight home /. There isn't another flight until the morning.
  4 You / the last bus home. Some people on the bus are having a fight.

  c What would you do in these situations?

CAN YOU REMEMBER? Unit 7 – Matching people to jobs and activites

3 **a** Complete the sentences about karate using the words in the box.

someone   something   person   thing

  1 You need to be _____ who has a good physical memory.
  2 You have to be the kind of _____ who has a lot of discipline.
  3 It's not _____ that needs a lot of strength.
  4 It's the sort of _____ that requires regular practice.

  b Write similar sentences about these activities.
  • yoga • sky diving • chess • boxing

  c Talk about the activities together. Do you agree?

Extension

SPELLING AND SOUNDS /ɑː/

4 **a** ⏺2.27 Listen and underline the letters which make an /ɑː/ sound.

  argument dance dark article bar calm
  alarm half castle star example halve
  arm large far

  b Find words in 4a to match spelling patterns 1–3. /ɑː/ is spelled:

  1 ar in most words.
  2 al before f, m, v in some words.
  3 a in the middle of some words. This is pronounced /æ/ by some speakers.

  c ⏺2.28 Spellcheck. Listen and write ten words. Then check your spelling on p155.

NOTICE Using synonyms

5 Writers often use a range of words to describe the same thing (synonyms) in articles.

  1 Think of three more words which have a similar meaning to clutter:
     rubbish s_____ t_____ p_____
  2 Write five sentences to show how we use the different words.
  3 How many words and expressions can you remember which have a similar meaning to declutter?

  Check in the article on p62.

Self-assessment

Can you do these things in English? Circle a number on each line. 1 = I can't do this, 5 = I can do this well.

◉ talk about attitudes to possessions	1	2	3	4	5
◉ describe objects	1	2	3	4	5
◉ talk about unexpected travel situations	1	2	3	4	5
◉ discuss options and decide what to do	1	2	3	4	5
◉ make deductions	1	2	3	4	5
◉ describe objects you don't know the name of	1	2	3	4	5
◉ use vague language to describe things	1	2	3	4	5

• For Wordcards, reference and saving your work → e-Portfolio
• For more practice → Self-study Pack, Unit 8

Make up your mind

Power cut

Kurt's home

Phillip's home

READING

1 **a** Look at the pictures. What do you think has happened?

b Read both stories. Were you right?

SUBSCRIBE TO THE FEED ... ◼ POSTS ◼ COMMENTS

I remember we were at home and my son was being born. We had decided to have a home birth. It was in the middle of the night and the midwife, who was a friend of ours, was there. Anyway, we were in the middle of everything and suddenly the room went dark. The heating went off too. There we were in the dark and the cold. There are a lot of power cuts in Sweden because of the weather, so I got the torch and lit candles all around the room and got another lamp and we just kind of managed. Just after our son was born – his name's Kurt, too – the lights came back on. It was really nice, as if he was being welcomed into the world or something.

Kurt, from Karlstad, Sweden

→ latest blog ...

I remember there was a big storm in England in 1987. It happened in the middle of the night and it caused chaos in many parts of the country. Part of our roof was blown off and there was a power cut. Some pipes upstairs burst and there was water shooting out everywhere. The thing is, I was just a kid and I slept through the whole thing. I woke up and my home looked completely different. There was a huge hole in the roof. And when I went into the garden I saw that a tree had blown down in the garden. It was a complete mess.

Phillip, from Nottingham, England

2 **a** Cover the stories. What can you remember about these things in the stories?

Kurt's story:	1 his son	2 the heating	3 candles	4 the lights
Phillip's story:	1 a storm	2 the roof	3 water	4 outside the house

b Read again to check. How do you think Kurt and Phillip felt afterwards?

VOCABULARY

Problems in
the home

3 **a** Match problems 1–8 with pictures A–H.

1   The tap's leaking.
2   The pipe's burst.
3   The handle's come off.
4   The window's stuck.

5   The batteries are flat.
6   The washing machine's not working.
7   The bathroom's flooded.
8   There's a power cut.

A

B

C

D

E

F

G

H

b In which sentences in 3a does 's mean: • has? • is? • has or is?

c Which problems do you think are the most serious? Which are the least serious?

d Cover the two stories and look at the pictures on p70. Which expressions in 3a can you use to describe what happened?

e Complete these sentences with expressions from 3a and your own ideas.

1 We don't have any clean plates because ... *the dishwasher's not working.*
2 We had to use candles all evening because ...
3 We'll have to call a plumber because ...
4 Don't go in the kitchen because ...
5 We can't get out of the front room because ...
6 You won't be able to open that window because ...
7 That torch won't work because ...
8 There's no hot water because ...

SPEAKING

4 Discuss these questions.

1 Which problems in 3a would you be able to solve yourself?
2 In which situations would you get help? Who would you call?
   • a plumber • an electrician • an engineer • a friend • someone else
3 Have you ever had problems like these at home? What happened?

What shall we do?

LISTENING

1 a ●2.29 Listen to Lidia and Ben. What problems do they have?

b ●2.29 Listen again. What ideas do they have for:

a lunch?
b stopping the flood?
c Ben's shirt?

VOCABULARY

Discussing problems and solutions

2 Which highlighted expressions from the conversation do you use to:

a say you'll try something?
b say what you need to do?
c ask for suggestions?

1	What are we going to do about lunch? What shall we do?
2	I'll give it a try. I'll have a go.
3	We'll have to call someone. We're going to have to call a plumber.

SPEAKING

3 a Work alone. Imagine you're in situations a–c with a partner. Think about what you could do.

a You're both working at home in the evening and there's a power cut. You don't have any candles, and the batteries in your torch are flat.
b Your five-year-old son is locked in the bathroom and the door handle's come off. He's starting to panic.
c You've got ten people coming for dinner and your cooker's not working.

b In pairs, choose a situation and discuss what to do. Use the highlighted expressions in 2.

c Choose a new situation and discuss what to do.

4 Talk in groups. Did you do the same things?

Decision-making

9.2 goals
- talk about decision-making
- discuss solutions ♻
- discuss the consequences of decisions

READING

1 a How do you make decisions about:

- your work?
- buying things?
- your home?
- money?

Which decisions do you find easy to make? Which are more difficult?

b Talk together. How similar are you?

2 Read the introduction to an article about thinking strategies. What does the technique help people to do?

Six Thinking Hats™

Do you find it difficult to make decisions? The Six Thinking Hats™ technique, developed by creative thinking expert Dr Edward de Bono, helps people to make better decisions by changing how they think. The six hats represent six different ways of thinking. Dr de Bono believes that most of us only use one or two of these hats when making decisions, solving problems or coming up with ideas. This technique allows you to practise the six different approaches by trying on each of the six hats.

3 Read the rest of the article. Which hat represents someone who:

a thinks positively?   c thinks creatively?   e manages situations?
b focuses on challenges?   d thinks emotionally?   f focuses on the facts?

 Put on the red hat and trust your intuition when you look at situations – listen to your heart, not your head. You don't have to explain your views or justify them.

Look at the facts you have and see what you can learn from them. Use the white hat to identify what information is needed and think about how to get it.

 The black hat helps you to recognise all the reasons why a plan might not work. Use it to check for potential problems which could affect your plans now or in the future.

Try to be optimistic and look for all the benefits of a decision. The yellow hat will help you to keep going when everything looks gloomy and difficult.

When new ideas are needed, try on the green hat. Brainstorm ideas and don't criticise what anyone says. The green hat will help you to come up with new plans and develop creative solutions to problems.

 Wear the blue hat if you're holding a meeting. When new ideas are needed, suggest people try on the green hat. When you need to evaluate an idea, use the yellow and black hats, and so on.

4 Discuss the questions.

1 What do you think of the Six Thinking Hats strategy?
2 Which hat do you think most represents the way you think and make decisions?

VOCABULARY
Decision-making

5 In pairs, discuss which verbs you think go with 1–9. Then check your ideas in the introduction and article.

1 _make_ decisions	4 l_____ to your heart	7 b_____ ideas
2 s_____ problems	5 l_____ at the facts	8 d_____ solutions
3 t_____ your intuition	6 c_____ up with a new plan	9 h_____ a meeting

SPEAKING

6 a Think about a decision you have to make. It could be from one of the topics in 1a.

1 In turn, explain the situation to a group.
2 Each think about the situation from the point of view of all six hats.
3 Start with the blue hat and plan your discussion.

b Talk together. Did the discussion help you with your decision?

Problems and solutions

LISTENING

1 **2.30** Listen to Simon, Lidia and Yelena talking about their new business. What kind of business is it? What are they discussing?

2 a **2.30** Listen again. Who:

1 is running the meeting?
2 suggests opening a terrace?
3 is not happy about doing more hours?
4 comes up with new ideas?
5 has prepared something?
6 is a bit negative about all the ideas?

b Which Thinking Hats do you think each person is using? Why?

Simon, Lidia and Yelena

GRAMMAR

Real and unreal conditionals

3 a Look at these extracts from the conversation. In which sentences a–e does the speaker feel a situation:

1 is realistic and possible?   2 is unrealistic or impossible?

a	**Simon**	If we open a terrace, we'll be able to serve a lot more people.
b	**Lidia**	But it's too expensive. And if we did that, it would take a lot longer to serve people outside.
c	**Lidia**	Hm, that's a problem for me. I mean, if I didn't have three children, I'd do it, no problem.
d	**Yelena**	Well, I suppose this is impossible, but if we employed another person, we wouldn't have to do so many hours.
e	**Lidia**	That's not a bad idea. But if we employ another person, we'll take home less money.

b Complete the patterns for real and unreal conditionals.

| 1 | Real conditional | if + _____ , _____ + infinitive |
| 2 | Unreal conditional | if + _____ , _____ + infinitive |

Grammar reference and practice, p140

c We can use real and unreal conditionals to make suggestions and discuss consequences. Look at sentences d and e in the grammar box. Which is a suggestion? Which introduces a negative consequence?

PRONUNCIATION

Groups of words 2

4 a **2.31** When you speak, you use groups of words. This makes you easier to understand. Listen to the first sentence in 3a.

a   If we open a terrace // we'll be able to serve a lot more people.

b Look at sentences b–e in 3a and write // between groups of words. **2.32** Then listen and read the script on p155 to check. Practise saying all the sentences.

SPEAKING

5 a You're going to discuss different ideas.

1 Add a suggestion for your life and for your country, then complete the notes.
2 Think about which conditionals to use. Which ideas are realistic and possible for you? Which are unrealistic or impossible?

	Suggestions	**Positive consequences**	**Negative consequences**
Your life:	have your own business move abroad	*choose your own hours*	
Your country:	reduce the driving age to 15 host the Olympic Games		

b Discuss the suggestions together. Do you agree about the consequences?

Reach a compromise

9.3 goals
- describe problems in the home
- discuss solutions
- discuss the consequences of decisions
- negotiate

TASK LISTENING

compromise (n):
/ˈkɒmprəmaɪz/ when
you agree to something
which is not exactly what
you want: *We reached a
compromise in the end.
I've agreed to work on
Monday evening if I can
take Saturday off.*

1   Look at the dictionary entry and think of situations where you have to compromise. Talk together.

2   Imagine you live with friends. What disagreements can you imagine about:

- cleaning?
- noise?
- cooking?
- eating?
- washing up?
- the shower?
- shopping?

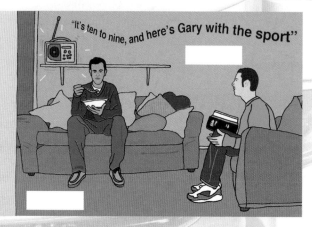

"It's ten to nine, and here's Gary with the sport"

3   a   ◆ 2.33 Listen to Brad, Nasser and Luis and write their names in the picture. Brad speaks first.

b   Discuss the questions. ◆ 2.33 Then listen again to check.

1   Which three problems from 2 do they discuss?
2   What compromises do they reach?
3   What do you think Brad, Nasser and Luis would be like to live with?

TASK VOCABULARY

Negotiating

4   a   What are the flatmates talking about in sentences 1–6?

A	1	How about if we take turns to do it?
	2	We could do that, I suppose. Or we could just do our own stuff.
B	3	Let's say you can listen to it in the kitchen if the door's shut.
	4	But if I agree to do that, could you please do something for me?
C	5	That way, you can take as long as you like.
	6	But that would mean making a rota.

b   ◆ 2.33 Listen again to check.

c   Which two highlighted expressions, A–C, can we use to:

1   explain consequences?   2   suggest a solution?   3   give a condition?

5   Which highlighted expressions could you use in these sentences?

1   Let's buy our own food. _____ we can get just what we need.
2   A I haven't got time to cook today.
    B _____ I do it today? You can cook tomorrow instead.
3   I could do the week's shopping now. _____ get stuff for tonight.
4   A Please don't go to the film tonight. I want to see it but I've got too much to do.
    B OK, _____ don't go tonight, can we please make sure we go tomorrow?
5   A Let's get the train on Friday evening.
    B But _____ leaving straight after work. I can't face doing that.

TASK

How about if we all eat together?

But that would mean being here every night.

6   a   Work in A/B/C groups. You're flatmates, and you need to discuss some problems. A, look on p121; B, look on p124; C, look on p131.

b   Talk in your groups. What solutions did you find? What compromises did you have to make?

EXPLORE

Across cultures Dealing with conflict

SPEAKING

1 What would you do in these situations?

- A colleague criticises your work to your boss.
- Your flatmate paints the flat a colour you hate.
- A close friend stops calling you.
- A relative really annoys you when you're out shopping together.

LISTENING

Çigdem is from Turkey. She lives in England with her husband and two children and is a health professional.

2 **a** ⏺ **2.34** Listen to an interview with Çigdem. Match each section 1–4 to topics a–d.

a parents and children	c work issues
b dealing with tension	d talking openly

b In pairs, choose a or b to complete each sentence. ⏺ **2.34** Then listen to check.

1	If a client is unhappy, Çigdem:		
	a talks about the problem with them.	b	avoids the problem.
2	If her husband's family have a problem:		
	a they try to solve it.	b	they ignore it.
3	Çigdem's mother:		
	a doesn't get involved in her life.	b	tells her what to do.
4	Çigdem says that people in Turkey:		
	a tend to say what they think.	b	don't argue in public.

c What differences does Çigdem mention between how people deal with conflict in England and Turkey?

VOCABULARY

Dealing with conflict

3 **a** Who is Çigdem talking about in 1–7?

1 They often don't try to resolve the conflict.
2 I would still always show him respect.
3 People have a lot more arguments and disagreements.
4 I wouldn't shout or swear at him, but I would argue my case.
5 If someone's done something which causes tension, nobody says anything.
6 We still have quite angry rows.
7 I'll discuss it with them and usually we'll reach a compromise.

conflict?

resolve conflict

b Test each other in A/B pairs. A, say the nouns; B, try to remember the verbs. Then change roles.

SPEAKING

4 Discuss your ideas in groups.

1 What do you do when you're angry with:
   - a colleague? • a relative? • a friend? • a child?
2 How do you think conflict should be resolved at work or at home? Give an example from your experience.
3 How do you feel about getting angry in public? Is it acceptable in your country?
4 Is it the same or different in other cultures you know of?

75

1 In your country, do most people you know:

* own their home?
* rent their home?

What do you think are the pros and cons of buying or renting your home?

2 Read the postings and the two comments.

1 What's Tomas's problem?
2 In the comments, who sympathises with Tomas? Who doesn't? What reasons do they give?

3 Who do you agree with? Why?

Goals

◎ write a web posting explaining an argument
◎ organise ideas 2

Tomas

File   Edit   View   Favorites   Tools   Help

Address   www.yourrights.com   ✓ → Go   Links »

Rights > rented property > comments

I've lived in my flat for twenty years. I rent it from someone who lives abroad and he's always charged a very low rent. The thing is, I've been here so long, I can't imagine living anywhere else. Anyway, I found out yesterday that my landlord is going to double my rent from the beginning of next month. That means I can't afford to live here any more. <u>As well as always paying my rent on time, I've also</u> looked after this property as if it was my own. It doesn't seem fair that I've got no rights at all. *Tomas*

To post a comment click here

Comments ▼

Sorry, but I think what the landlord's doing is fine. You've <u>not only</u> had a very low rent <u>but</u> you've <u>also</u> stayed in one home for twenty years. The point is <u>not that you always paid your rent on time, but that</u> it was never your property in the first place. The fact that you've lived there for such a long time doesn't make it yours. To my mind, that's a good thing – it's <u>neither your property nor</u> your problem. I can see why you're upset, but I don't think you appreciate how lucky you've been. *Ian*

What's happened is just plain wrong. You've <u>not only</u> lived there for twenty years, <u>but also</u> been a good tenant. It's clear that the landlord <u>either wants to sell the property or</u> move into it himself, so he's decided to charge you a rent you can't afford. <u>Of course</u> it's his property in law, <u>but at the same time</u> he should be grateful to you for looking after his flat all this time. To be fair, it's <u>both his and</u> yours, and the law should recognise that somehow. *Amie*

---

4 a Cover the texts. Can you remember how to complete expressions 1–7?

Linking ideas	Contrasting two ideas
1 as well as … _____	5 not that … _____
2 not only … _____	6 either … _____
3 neither … _____	7 of course … _____
4 both … _____	

b Complete the sentences with your own ideas. Then compare with a partner.

1 Of course it's important to fix things in your home, …
2 Their home is neither big …
3 He's not only allergic to pets …
4 The house belongs to both her brother …

5 The flat needs redecorating. You either have to paint it yourselves …
6 She's really cross with him. It's not that he broke the window, …
7 As well as being a lovely flat, …

5 Read another posting on the site on p118. Write a comment in response.

1 Brainstorm ideas in groups.
2 Organise your own ideas into sentences. Use the expressions in 4a.

6 a Read each other's comments. Choose one to write a reply to.

b Read the reply to your comment. Does the writer agree or disagree with your opinion?

Review

GRAMMAR Real and unreal conditionals

1 a Put the words in order to begin conditional sentences.

1 enough money / had / If / I
2 a good film / If / there's / tonight / on
3 nearby / there was / If / a good pool
4 really needed to / If / a language / learn / I
5 time / later / If / some / I / have
6 I wanted / any car / have / If / I / could

b Complete the sentences with your own ideas.

1 If I had enough money, I'd give up my job.

VOCABULARY Problems in the home

2 a Use the expressions in the box in the correct form to replace the underlined expressions.

> burst   come off   flat   not work
> be stuck   flood   a power cut

1 A What's happened?
   B The lights have gone out. *There's a power cut.*
2 The batteries in my torch are dead.
3 Oh no! The bathroom floor is covered in water.
4 The dishwasher's broken.
5 The water's coming from here. The pipe has a hole in it.
6 I can't open the door. The handle's broken.
7 Open a different window. That one doesn't open.

b What could you do in situations 1–7? Take turns to start conversations.

CAN YOU REMEMBER? Unit 8 – Modals of deduction and speculation

3 a Complete the conversations with must, might, could or can't.

1 A Shall I throw these old books away?
   B No, they _____ be mine.
2 A Do you think this is our coach?
   B It _____ be ours. It's exactly 5.54.
3 A I'm afraid there's no connecting train.
   B What do you mean? That _____ be true.
4 A I've lost my keys again!
   B They _____ be here somewhere. When did you last use them?

b Work alone. Write sentences using the underlined expressions in 2–4.

Do you think there will be a train strike this week?

c Work in pairs. Listen to your partner's sentences and respond using must, might, could or can't.

> Do you think there will be a train strike this week?
>> I hope not. They must be able to agree by now!

Extension

SPELLING AND SOUNDS /ɜː/

4 a 🔊 **2.35** Listen and underline the letters which make an /ɜː/ sound.

world   burst   birth   working   emergency
dirty   learn   alternative   earn   first   urgent

b Find words in 4a to match the spelling patterns in 1 and 2. /ɜː/ is usually spelled:

1 er, or, ear, ur or ir in the middle of words.
2 ear or ur at the beginning of words.

c Spellcheck. Complete the spelling of these words. Then check in a dictionary.

1 f__niture   4 __th   7 conf__m
2 th__teen   5 p__pose   8 det__mined
3 h__d   6 reh__se   9 __ban

NOTICE on, off

5 a Can you remember how to complete 1–6 from texts in this unit with on or off?

1 The heating went _____ too. **p70**
2 Just after our son was born, the lights came back _____ . **p70**
3 Part of our roof was blown _____ . **p70**
4 The handle's come _____ . **p70**
5 Would you mind not having the radio _____ all the time? 🔊 **2.33**
6 When new ideas are needed, suggest people try _____ the green hat. **p72**

b Check 1–4 on p70; 5 in 🔊 **2.33** ; and 6 on p72.

c Choose verbs from 1–6 above to complete these sentences.

1 Could I _____ on that shirt?
2 Blow the candles out. The power's _____ on.
3 I don't know how much this card costs. The price label's _____ off.
4 The lights _____ off five times in the storm.
5 I can't stand _____ the TV on all the time.

Self-assessment

Can you do these things in English? Circle a number on each line. 1 = I can't do this, 5 = I can do this well.

◎ describe problems in the home	1	2	3	4	5
◎ discuss solutions	1	2	3	4	5
◎ talk about decision-making	1	2	3	4	5
◎ discuss the consequences of decisions	1	2	3	4	5
◎ negotiate	1	2	3	4	5
◎ write a web posting explaining an argument	1	2	3	4	5
◎ organise ideas 2	1	2	3	4	5

• For Wordcards, reference and saving your work → e-Portfolio
• For more practice → Self-study Pack, Unit 9

10 Impressions

10.1 goals
◉ talk about memory
◉ talk about what you remember

Witness

LISTENING

1 How good do you think your memory is? Think about:

• names • places • faces • phone numbers • conversations • song lyrics

2 **a** If you saw a crime, would you be a good witness? Look at this CCTV image for 30 seconds. ⏺ **2.36** Then close your books, listen to the questions and take notes.

17/02/2011 14:31

b Compare your notes with a partner. Then look at the picture to check. What did you remember? What things didn't you notice?

3 **a** ⏺ **2.37** Listen to one of the witnesses, Hiromi, telling her friend what she saw. Do you think she has a good memory of what happened?

b ⏺ **2.37** Listen again and look at the CCTV image. What four things does Hiromi get wrong?

4 Have you or has anyone you know ever witnessed a crime? What happened?

VOCABULARY

Remembering
an event

5 **a** Complete the sentences from Hiromi's account. Look at the script on p156 to check.

1 I can't remember what	a No, no ... I've only just moved there.
2 But I can remember that	b it's all a bit worrying, really.
3 I've forgotten	c a lot of what happened.
4 I noticed someone	d he was wearing a rugby shirt.
5 That reminds me.	e crossing the street.
6 Looking back on it,	f he looked like.
7 Did you recognise him?	g He had a baseball cap on.

b Discuss the questions. Try to use the highlighted expressions in 5a.

1 In what order did people arrive in class today?
2 What date does your course start and finish?
3 What did you do in the first class of your course?
4 Did you know anyone in the class before the course started?

False memories

1 You're going to read about witnesses in court cases. Discuss the questions.

    1 What do these people in the courtroom do?
- the judge • the jury • a lawyer • a witness

    2 What do you think are the most difficult things they have to do?

2 Read this article from a journal for law students. According to the article, what is the problem with using witnesses in court?

The problem with witnesses

The honesty of witnesses is the basis for the judicial process in many countries around the world. But research has shown that you can't always rely on these witnesses to give an accurate account of events.

Several studies have shown that people frequently not only forget the details of things that happened but also remember things that didn't happen at all. In one study, people were shown a picture of a car accident. Later, some were asked what they saw when the cars 'hit' each other, while others were asked what they saw when the cars 'smashed' into each other. People who were questioned using the word 'smashed' were more likely to recall seeing broken glass in the original picture. The introduction of false information changes people's memories. It can make us believe something that didn't happen or exist.

The problem is made worse by the effect of telling a story on our memory. When we tell a story, we always have a particular audience, so we change certain details. When we tell a friend about our day, for example, we want to make it interesting so we might exaggerate some things and leave out boring details. And every time we tell the story, our memory of it changes. In court, once witnesses have given an account of an event, they tend to remember what they said in their account rather than the actual event. Even more worryingly, once a witness has identified a person as guilty, he is likely to identify that same person later on, even when the person identified is not actually guilty.

3 Read the article again. Find three reasons why you can't always rely on witnesses.

4 Discuss the questions.

    1 What's your opinion about using witnesses in court?
    2 What do you think would help to solve the problems discussed in the article?

5 **a** Verbs are followed by different patterns. Complete the sentences with the correct word from the article or the script, then check your ideas above and on p156.

    1 They tend to remember _____ they said in their account.
    2 I can remember _____ he was wearing a rugby shirt.
    3 Then I remembered _____ pick up the phone.
    4 I remember _____ how he got in there.

b In which sentence 1–4 is remember followed by:

    a *-ing*?   c a question word?
    b *to* infinitive?   d *that*?

6 **a** When you learn a verb, it's important to know which patterns follow it. Look at the dictionary entry for forget. Which patterns from 5b does it have?

b Which patterns can follow these verbs? Check your ideas on p130.

    remind   know   understand   find out

forget /fə'get/
▶ *verb* to be unable to remember a fact, something that happened or how to do something: *I've forgotten his name.*
1 ▷ [+ *that*] *I forgot that the meeting was today.* **2** ▷ [+ question word] *I've forgotten how this machine works.* ▷ **3** [+ *ing*] *I'll never forget seeing the Himalayas for the first time twenty years ago.*
4 ▷ [+ *to* infinitive] to not remember to do something: *Sorry, I forgot to post your letter.*

Grammar reference and practice, p141

7 **a** Complete these questions with your own ideas.

    1 Can you remember what ...?   4 When did you first understand ...?
    2 Have you ever forgotten ...?   5 Do you know ...?
    3 Can you remember seeing ...?   6 Would you like to find out ...?

b Ask and answer the questions in 7a.

It's scratched

10.2 goals

◉ talk about complaining
◉ complain about goods or services
◉ ask for a refund or replacement and explain why

LISTENING

1 **a** Talk together. What kind of behaviour annoys you? What would you do if:

1 someone went to the front of a queue without waiting in line?
2 someone broke the rules on public transport?
3 you got poor service in a restaurant, a café or a shop?

b What do most people do where you live?

2 ◖◗**2.38** Listen to Tariq talking about complaining in the UK and France. What difference does he mention?

VOCABULARY

Problems with things you've bought

3 **a** Match problems 1–8 with A–H in the pictures.

1 It's the wrong size. 5 It's dented.
2 It's faded. 6 It's torn.
3 It's chipped. 7 It's cracked.
4 It doesn't work. 8 It's scratched.

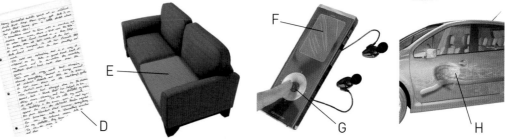

An old photo can be faded.

So can a T-shirt.

b Cover 3a. In pairs, take turns to point at a picture and say what's wrong.

c What other things can be the wrong size, faded, etc.? Think of two more examples for each highlighted expression.

4 Have you ever had a problem with something you've bought? What did you do?

Making a complaint

LISTENING

1 Read the email Mariah wrote to Anybooks.com. What complaints did she make?

File Edit View Insert Format Tools Message Help

To: help@anybooks.com
Cc:
Subject: Damaged book – Ref: 18635PK

Dear Sir/Madam,
I am writing to complain about the poor service I've received from Anybooks.com. I ordered a book from your website recently. When it arrived, several pages were missing and one page was torn. I wrote to you on 12th June asking for a replacement, but have received no reply. Could you please confirm that you received my earlier email, and that you will send me a new copy of the book? My account number is 18635PK.
Yours faithfully,
Mariah Dewey

2 **a** Mariah doesn't get a reply to her email so she phones the customer service department. What do you think will happen?

b ◖◗**2.39** Listen to the phone call. Were you right?

3 ◖◗**2.39** Listen again and answer the questions.

1 How does Mariah feel? Why?
2 What two things does the customer services person do?

PRONUNCIATION

Intonation in questions

4 **a** ⏵**2.40** Listen to the questions from the phone conversation. Which questions, A or B, end with a falling ↘ intonation? Which end with a rising ↗ intonation?

   A I'll have to put you on hold. Is that OK?
       Is that 35PK?
   B What's your order number, please?
       And when will I get the new book?

b Complete the rules with: yes/no questions *wh* questions

   _____ usually end with a rising ↗ intonation. They're often used to check something.
   _____ usually end with a falling ↘ intonation. They're often used to ask for information.

c Practise asking the questions in 4a.

5 **a** You work in customer services. A customer phones you to complain about a service or product they've ordered online. Write questions to ask for or check the following information:

   • name • email • order number: 26490FR • order date: 16th July

b Ask and answer the questions together. Try to use the correct intonation.

GRAMMAR

Present perfect simple and progressive

6 The present perfect simple and progressive link the past and present. Read the sentences and discuss the questions below.

> **A** **The present perfect simple:** have/has + past participle
> I've written two emails but I haven't received a reply.
> I've just ordered you a replacement copy.
>
> **B** **The present perfect progressive:** have/has + been + -ing
> I've been waiting to speak to someone for ten minutes.
> I've been trying to contact you for two weeks now.

   1 In which sentences, **A** or **B**, does the speaker want to emphasise:
      • how long something takes?
      • the result of a finished activity?
   2 Which form can you use to talk about the number of times something happened?

7 **a** Complete this extract from a complaint to a music website. Which verbs are present perfect simple? Which are present perfect progressive?

> ... I ordered an MP3 player from your site on February 12 this year. Unfortunately, when it arrived, I found that it didn't work. Since that time, I ¹_____ (write) three emails asking for a refund, but so far I ²_____ (not have) a reply. For the last two days, I ³_____ (phone) the number given on your website but I ⁴_____ (not get) through. I'm not at all happy with the service your company ⁵_____ (provide) on this occasion. In fact, this is not the first time I ⁶_____ (have) problems with Musico.com. I ⁷_____ (buy) CDs and DVDs from your site for many years, and on more than one occasion they ⁸_____ (arrive) with the cases cracked. I ⁹_____ (not complain) before because ...

Grammar reference and practice, p141

b Discuss your choices with a partner. Do you agree?

SPEAKING

8 **a** Work in A/B pairs.

   A, you want to complain about something you've bought from a website.
   Look on p127 and complete the information on the first role card.
   B, you work on the helpline. Look on p131 and complete the information.

b A, phone B and have a conversation.

c Now change roles and look at the next role card. Have another phone conversation.

d Listen to another pair's conversation and answer the questions.

   1 What problem did the customer have?
   2 Has the customer services person solved the problem?

Resolve a dispute

TASK LISTENING

1 **a** Make a list of possible problems between neighbours.

loud noise, parking ...

b Talk together.

1 What would you do if you had a problem with a neighbour?
2 Would you find it easy to discuss the problem?
3 What do you think you'd say?

2 🔊 **2.41** Listen to two neighbours, Ian and James, talking. What's the problem?

TASK VOCABULARY

Softeners

3 **a** Match 1–6 with a–f. 🔊 **2.41** Then listen again to check.

1	I've been meaning to talk to you,	a	have a bit of peace and quiet.
2	It's just that	b	kicked the ball quite close to our windows.
3	It's a bit	c	his ball ruins our plants and flowers.
4	Well, to be honest, we'd like to	d	you could have a word with him about it.
5	Well, to be fair, he has	e	annoying.
6	I'd be grateful if	f	actually.

b The highlighted expressions help to soften the complaint. Look at the script on p157 and find two more softeners with the same meanings as 1 and 6.

c In pairs, add the highlighted softening expressions to these complaints.

1 A Is everything OK? How's your food?
  B Well, / the soup is a bit cold.
2 A Could you lend me some money?
  B OK, but / you haven't paid me back from last week.
3 Your music is very loud. If you could turn it down, /
4 You never do the washing up. It's / irritating.
5 / You borrowed some books from me a few months ago, and I need them.

Well, to be honest, the soup is a bit cold.

TASK

> I've been meaning to talk to you, actually, about your ...

4 **a** Work in A/B pairs.

A, you're going to speak to your neighbour about a problem. Look on p129 and think about what language you need to use.
B, look on p130 and prepare to talk to your neighbour about a problem.

b Now change roles. Look at the next role card and have another conversation.

5 Talk in groups. Did you resolve the disputes with your neighbour?

Keyword *of*

Adjectives with *of*

1 **2.42** Listen to a conversation between Hiromi and her new neighbour, Gill. Did they make a good impression on each other?

2 **a** Some adjectives go with *of you*. Match 1–3 with responses a–c from the conversation.

1 I've made you some cakes.
2 Would Toshi like to come round and play?
3 We've just moved here from Japan.

a Really? That's so **brave of you**!
b Oh, that was very **kind of you**. They look delicious.
c How **thoughtful of you**. I'm sure he'd love that.

b Which **highlighted** expressions are used:

1 to give a compliment? 2 to say thanks?

Can you think of more expressions like these?

That's nice of you.

That's clever of you.

c **2.43** Listen to what five people say. Respond with a compliment or thanks.

3 **a** Complete each sentence with an appropriate adjective.

fond   capable   sick   proud   afraid

1 I'm _____ of spiders. I always think they're going to bite me.
2 Real Madrid are _____ of winning the league. They've got a great team.
3 I'm very _____ of Agata. She's such a nice person.
4 I'm very _____ of what we've achieved. We all worked hard on this project.
5 I'm _____ of my job at the moment. I've been doing the same thing for ten years.

b Think of sentences about you with the expressions in 3a. Then talk together.

I'm afraid of the dark.

Really? It doesn't bother me.

Verbs with *of*

4 Read this extract from an article about first impressions.
What four things does it say you can do to give a good first impression?

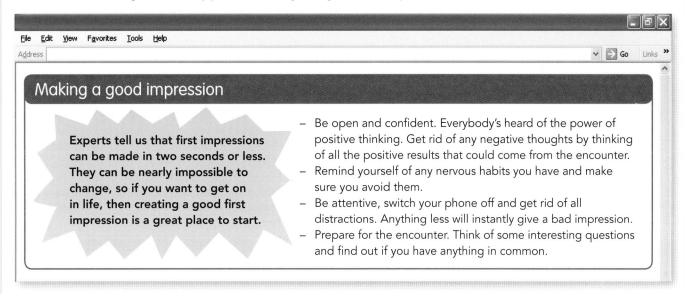

Making a good impression

Experts tell us that first impressions can be made in two seconds or less. They can be nearly impossible to change, so if you want to get on in life, then creating a good first impression is a great place to start.

– Be open and confident. Everybody's heard of the power of positive thinking. Get rid of any negative thoughts by thinking of all the positive results that could come from the encounter.
– Remind yourself of any nervous habits you have and make sure you avoid them.
– Be attentive, switch your phone off and get rid of all distractions. Anything less will instantly give a bad impression.
– Prepare for the encounter. Think of some interesting questions and find out if you have anything in common.

5 **a** Some verbs go with *of*. Cover the article. Can you remember how these sentences continue?

Everybody's **heard of** the power ...
Get rid of any negative ...

Remind yourself of any nervous ...
Think of some interesting ...

b Read the article again to check.

6 How many more ways can you think of to make a good first impression?

1 When was the last time you had a long weekend? What did you do?

2 🔊 **2.44** Listen to two conversations between Mariah and Pat and answer the questions.

Conversation 1 (Monday):
When do they decide to take a day off? Why?
Conversation 2 (Friday evening):
How much time do they get together in the end?

3 a 🔊 **2.44** Listen again. Are the following statements true or false?

1 Mariah isn't worried about writing her essay.
2 She thinks she can finish it before Thursday.
3 Pat thinks it's better to take Thursday off.
4 Mariah says driving was a bad idea.
5 Pat didn't enjoy his day off.
6 Mariah is looking forward to the rest of the weekend.

b Read conversations 1 and 2 to check your ideas.

4 Look at the highlighted comments 1–7 in the conversations.

1 What is each comment about?
 1 Mariah's essay
2 Which express:
 • positive feelings? • negative feelings?

5 a Add expressions from the box to which was and complete the conversation below.

| great excellent important nice tricky |
| understandable unfortunate typical a shame |

A How was your weekend?
B Nice. Some good friends who I don't see much came to stay, ¹_____
A Oh right. What did you do?
B Well, on Saturday Erin wasn't very well, ²_____ , but on Sunday I cooked a nice meal and later we went for a long walk, ³_____ . What about you?
A Well, I had to go in to work on Saturday, ⁴_____ because I was supposed to be going out with an old friend.
B Oh no. Why did you have to work?
A Well, somebody new was starting and they got in a mess, ⁵_____ , but nobody else was around, so I went in to help.

b Compare with a partner. Did you choose the same expressions?

c Write four more lines to finish the conversation. Use two expressions with which.

d Listen to another pair's conversation. Which ending do you prefer?

6 Take turns to start a conversation with the underlined questions in conversations 1 and 2. Make comments about how you feel.

Goal

⊚ add comments to say how you feel

❶

PAT Shall we do something nice this week? We could take a day off work.
MARIAH Well, I've got that essay to write, ¹which I think is going to be a bit tricky.
PAT Why, when do you have to finish it?
MARIAH It's got to be in on Friday, but I'd like to finish it by Wednesday evening at the latest.
PAT Yeah?
MARIAH ²Which is probably impossible.
PAT Why?
MARIAH Well, I've still got a lot to do – I'm waiting for a book I've ordered to arrive.
PAT Look, why don't we both take the day off on Thursday?
MARIAH Yeah, maybe, or Friday. Take a long weekend.
PAT ³Which would be better, I suppose.
MARIAH Yeah, let's do that. I'll take my essay into university in the morning, and then we can both relax.
PAT Yeah, yeah. It'll be good to spend some time together.

❷

PAT So, how was your day? I thought you'd be back earlier. Did you get your essay in on time?
MARIAH Yeah, just. I decided to drive to the university, ⁴which was unfortunate.
PAT Why? Was the traffic bad?
MARIAH Yeah, it was awful. It took hours to get in. I was so stressed …
PAT ⁵Which isn't good in the car.
MARIAH No, I had to listen to the radio to calm myself down.
PAT So much for the long weekend together.
MARIAH Yes, sorry. Did you have a nice day?
PAT Yes, I didn't do much, ⁶which actually was very relaxing. I even fell asleep after lunch.
MARIAH Well, we've still got the rest of the weekend free, ⁷which is great.
PAT Er, yeah, did I tell you my parents rang? They've invited us for lunch on Sunday, so I said yes.
MARIAH Yes, of course. That'll be nice. Ah well, we've still got tomorrow.

Review

GRAMMAR Present perfect simple and progressive

1 **a** Complete Rita and Hasan's conversation. Use the present perfect simple or progressive.

HASAN Hi.

RITA You're late again! You **_'ve missed_** (miss) dinner. You **_'ve been working_** (work) late all week and you ¹_____ (miss) dinner every day too. It's not good for you.

H I know. But I ²_____ (had) lunch with clients three times, so it's not so bad. I'm sorry about the late nights. You know I ³_____ (have) interviews all week.

R Yes, but what if you don't get another job? This ⁴_____ (go on) for too long now. You need to talk to Tim about your hours.

H I have. I ⁵_____ (have) three meetings with him this week.

R Oh good. You didn't tell me about that.

H No, I haven't had time. I ⁶_____ (do) other things.

b ● **2.45** Listen to check. ℗ What advice would you give Rita and Hasan?

c Think about the questions.

1 What have you achieved this week?
2 What haven't you managed to do? Why not?

d Talk about your week together. What advice can you give your partner?

VOCABULARY Problems with things you've bought

2 **a** Complete these sentences with an appropriate word.

1 It's the wrong s_____ .
2 The colour's f_____ .
3 The cup's ch_____ .
4 The phone doesn't w_____ .
5 The car's d_____ .
6 Some pages are t_____ .
7 The window's cr_____ .
8 The TV screen's s_____ .

b Describe problems you've had with:

- clothes
- cars
- furniture
- books
- shoes
- electronic goods

CAN YOU REMEMBER? Unit 9 – Decision-making

3 **a** Match the verb–noun collocations.

hold   solve   brainstorm   look at
trust   make   come up with

a decision   a problem   a meeting   the facts
a new plan   ideas   your intuition

b Which of these things have you done at home, work or college in the last week? Write two or three sentences.

We held a meeting to brainstorm ideas for the website.

c Talk together about what you've done.

Extension

SPELLING AND SOUNDS /uː/

4 **a** ● **2.46** Listen and <u>underline</u> the letters in these words which make an /uː/ sound.

balloon   afternoon   June   route   threw   choose
moon   include   rule   super   group   flew

b Find words in 4a to match spelling patterns 1–4. /uː/ is spelled:

1 oo in the middle of most words.
2 ou in the middle of some words.
3 ew at the end of most words.
4 u after j, l, r and s in some words.

c Can you think of more words with these patterns?

d ● **2.47** Spellcheck. Listen and write ten words. Then check your spelling on p157.

NOTICE Noun phrases with *of*

5 **a** Read two sentences from texts in this unit.

- In the UK, if someone goes to the front of a queue … nobody complains. ● **2.38**
- In one study, people were shown a picture of a car accident. p79

b Complete questions 1–6 with these nouns.

impression   picture   couple   copy   part   front

1 What's the most boring _____ of your job? What's the most interesting?
2 Do you form an instant _____ of people?
3 Do you have a _____ of *Cambridge Learner's Dictionary*?
4 Do you have a _____ of anyone in your wallet? Who?
5 Would you ever go straight to the _____ of a queue? In what situation?
6 Can you tell me a _____ of things about your childhood?

c Ask and answer all the questions.

Self-assessment

Can you do these things in English? Circle a number on each line. 1 = I can't do this, 5 = I can do this well.

◎ talk about memory	1	2	3	4	5
◎ talk about what you remember	1	2	3	4	5
◎ talk about complaining	1	2	3	4	5
◎ complain about goods or services	1	2	3	4	5
◎ ask for a refund or replacement and explain why	1	2	3	4	5
◎ make a complaint politely	1	2	3	4	5
◎ add comments to say how you feel	1	2	3	4	5

- For Wordcards, reference and saving your work → e-Portfolio
- For more practice → Self-study Pack, Unit 10

11 Truth and lies

Gossip

1 a Discuss the questions.

1 How many people have you talked to today?
2 Did you talk about any of these topics?

- friends
- the weather
- work
- politics
- your plans today
- a problem
- something that frightened or shocked you

b ◉ **3.1** Listen to conversations A–G and match them with the topics above.

HAVE YOU HEARD ABOUT ...?

Pass it on

Psssst!

oooh!

2 a ◉ **3.1** Listen again. In which conversation do people:

> When I'm driving to work with my friend, we often gossip about people we know.

1	complain	3	argue	about something
2	boast	4	gossip	or someone?

5	whisper	
6	scream	something?
7	shout	

b How often do you do these things? Do you remember the last time?

3 a Do you think these sentences are true or false?

1 Gossiping can be good for you.
2 More than half of what people talk about is gossip.
3 Women gossip a lot more than men.
4 People gossip more now that they have mobile phones.
5 Most gossip involves being critical of others.

b Now read a factfile about gossip. Check your ideas from 3a.

The truth about gossip

- Primarily, gossip allows people to develop and maintain a sense of community, which can relieve stress.

- Two-thirds of all human conversation is about social topics: who is doing what with whom; how to deal with difficult social situations; the behaviour, relationships and problems of family, friends, partners, colleagues and neighbours.

- Men gossip for just as long and about the same subjects as women, but tend to talk more about themselves.

- Men are more likely to gossip with work colleagues, partners and female friends, while women gossip more with same-sex friends and family.

- Mobile phones have increased the amount of time people gossip in general.

- Thirty-three percent of men gossip on their mobiles every day or almost every day, compared with twenty-six percent of women.

- Only about five percent of gossip-time is devoted to criticism and negative evaluation of others.

4 Discuss the questions.

1 How much do you gossip? Who with?
2 Do you gossip on your mobile phone? How often?
3 What kinds of things do you gossip about?
4 Do you think gossiping is a good or bad thing? Why?

A secret

Jhulan and Rahul, Suresh's parents

1 **3.2** Listen to part of a conversation between Suresh and Meninda.

1 Who has a secret? Who are they keeping the secret from?
2 What do you think it might be about?

2 **3.3** Listen to a conversation between Meninda and her sister Indra about Suresh, their cousin. Were your ideas in 1 correct?

Suresh   *Meninda*   *Indra*

3 **a** What can you remember? Who:

1 wants Suresh to take the job?
2 wants to go travelling for a year?
3 tells Suresh to talk to his parents?
4 has turned down a job?
5 is going to be upset?
6 is going to talk to Suresh?

3.3 Listen again to check.

b What do you think about Suresh's plan? Do you think he should tell his parents?

Relating a conversation

4 Look at the sentences from the conversation and discuss the questions.

Say is the most common word used to report direct speech.	1 He **said**, "You know I've been offered this great job …"
	2 Then I **said to him**, "Have you found something better?"
	3 He **says**, "Look, I want to tell you something, …"
	4 … and then he **says to me**, "Well, I said no!"
Meninda also uses these very informal expressions to report direct speech.	5 And he **goes**, "No, I've got a more interesting plan."
	6 I **went**, "You can't do that! You've got to tell them!"
	7 So I'm **like**, "Yeah! So what are you going to do?"
	8 I **was like**, "When are you going to tell them?"

1 Do the highlighted words and expressions report:
   • the exact words people say? • a summary of what they say?
2 Do they introduce:
   • only statements? • only questions? • both statements and questions?
3 When the speakers use the present tense, is this:
   • to show when something happened? • to make a story more dramatic?

Quoting

5 **a** When you quote someone's exact words, you pause and your voice goes up.
3.4 Listen to these extracts from Meninda and Indra's conversation:

MENINDA So then he said, // ↑ "You know I've been offered this great job by that law firm?" So of course I say yeah, and then he says to me, // ↑ "Well, I said no!"

I said, // ↑ "You're mad!" Then I said to him, // ↑ "Have you found something better?" And he goes, // ↑ "No, I've got a more interesting plan!"

b **3.4** Listen again, then practise saying the sentences.

6 **a** Meninda and Indra persuade Suresh to tell his father about his plans. In pairs, discuss these questions.

1 How do you think Suresh and his father will feel?
2 What do you think the result of the conversation will be?

b Write the conversation between Suresh and his father.

Suresh: "Dad, there's something I need to tell you." …

So, I say, "Dad, there's something I need to tell you." So he goes, …

c Imagine you're Suresh. Work with a new partner and relate the conversation to Meninda. Use some of the highlighted expressions in 4.

7 **3.5** Listen to the actual conversation between Suresh and his father. Were your conversations similar or different?

The lie detector

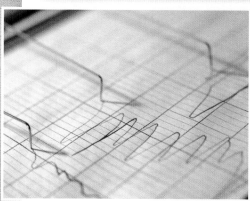

READING

1 Talk together.

1 What's a white lie? Do you have a similar expression in your language?
2 Do you think it's OK to tell white lies?

2 a 3.6 Listen to Jamie and Emma talking about lies.
Are their opinions similar to yours?

b They invent the expressions *black lie*, *grey lie* and *charcoal lie*. What do you think they mean?

3 Read the newspaper article about a new piece of software to detect written lies. Do you think it will work? Why? Why not?

File Edit View Favorites Tools Help

Address [   ] ✓ → Go Links »

New computer software to catch email liars

1 RESEARCHERS in the United States are planning to create lie-detection software for emails and text messages. The new software is being developed by a team led by Jeff Hancock at Cornell University in New York State.

2 "We asked people to come into the labs and write lies and we had other people come in and write the truth," says Hancock. "Using this method, we've built up a database of tens of thousands of emails."

The scientists have analysed the data and identified a number of simple tests to predict whether or not a person is lying.

3 One of the most important tests is the length of a message. Lying emails have, on average, 28% more words than truthful messages. Another sign is the overuse of sense words, such as 'see', 'feel' and 'touch'. "When you're lying, you want the other person to believe you, so you give more details," says Hancock.

4 Liars also tend to use pronouns like 'we' and 'they' rather than 'I' as a way of distancing themselves from a lie because they feel guilty. "People often use negative emotional words too, because they feel uncomfortable when they're lying," says Hancock. "So they'll use terms like 'sad', 'angry', 'unhappy' and 'stressed'."

5 Previous research has shown that up to one third of communications at work involve lying of some sort. The most common workplace lie is pretending to be sick to avoid going to work.

6 But Peter Collett, a psychologist who has written a book on lying, is sceptical about Hancock's work. "You can see if somebody is lying by looking at their body language, how fast they talk, and how they speak," he says. "How can a computer program see all this? They've clearly done a lot of research, but with emails all you have is words."

4 Read the article again.

1 How did Jeff Hancock's team collect the information?
2 What four things can suggest that someone is lying in an email?
3 Why does Peter Collett disagree with Hancock's method?

5 **a** Read two emails from different employees to their boss, Kyoko. Who do you think is telling the truth? Who do you think is lying? Why?

Hi Kyoko, Sorry but won't be able to come to work today. We had chicken last night and I think it was bad. Woke up at three this morning and felt awful. Was sick for four hours. Saw the doctor but he wasn't any help. Am exhausted. Feel stressed out because I'm not at work. Anyway, really sorry. I should be back at work tomorrow. Best wishes, Maya

Hi Kyoko, I'm really sorry but I can't come to work today. I've been sick all night. Anyway, I'm really sorry. I should be back at work tomorrow. Best wishes, Simon

b Compare your ideas in groups.

SPEAKING

6 Discuss the questions.

1 Are you good at telling lies?
2 Can you tell if someone is lying? How?

> Everyone knows when I'm lying because of the expression on my face.

But he said ...

LISTENING

1 🔊 **3.7** Listen to Kyoko talking to her friend, Naomi. What two lies do they talk about? Do you think each lie is serious? Is Kyoko's story surprising?

GRAMMAR

Reporting speech

2 **a** When we relate a conversation we often summarise what people say with reporting verbs. Complete the sentences from the conversations with these reporting verbs in the correct form.

| say   ask   promise   tell (x3)   agree   explain |

A	**C**
He _____ that he wasn't really sick. He _____ me that he just needed to see his brother.	I _____ him to tell me the truth. I _____ him to look in the mirror.
B	**D**
I _____ him what Anra said. He _____ why he did it.	He _____ not to do it again. I've _____ to let it go this time.

Grammar reference and practice, p142

b 🔊 **3.7** Listen again to check.

3 **a** Which verbs in A–D are followed by:

1 a question word? 2 *to* infinitive? 3 *that* ...?

b Which two verbs are followed immediately by an object pronoun?

SPEAKING

4 **a** Think about conversations you've had recently. Complete the sentences with your ideas.

• work • relationships • gossip about friends

1 My friend told ...
2 At work recently, I promised ...
3 A colleague asked ...
4 I explained ...
5 In a recent phone call, I said ...
6 My ... has agreed ...

> Barbara told me that she's pregnant!
>
> Really? That's exciting ...

b Compare your sentences with a partner. Ask questions to find out more.

Chat about friends

11.3 goals
- relate a conversation ♻
- summarise what people say ♻
- find out news about people you know

Uri   Mel   Hakim

TASK LISTENING

1   **Talk together.**

1   If you have a problem, who do you talk to?
2   If a friend of yours has a problem, what do you do?

2   •◗ **3.8** Listen to Uri, Mel and Hakim talking about another friend, Hussein.

1   What was Hussein's problem?   2   What happened in the end?

TASK VOCABULARY

Exchanging news

3   **a** Complete the highlighted expressions from the conversation with the correct forms of these verbs:

hear (x4)   tell   speak   say (x2)

1   Did you _____ about Hussein?   5   Have you _____ to Hussein lately?
2   Has anybody _____ from Mehmet?   6   That's not what I _____.
3   Who _____ you that?   7   I _____ his plane was cancelled.
4   Who _____ that?   8   Someone _____ he's got a new girlfriend.

b •◗ **3.8** Listen again to check.

4   **a** Work in A/B pairs. You're going to write a conversation together. Complete the sentences with your own ideas. Then choose conversation 1, 2 or 3.

Conversation 1   Did you hear about _____'s new _____?
Conversation 2   Have you spoken to _____ lately?
Conversation 3   Has anyone heard from _____ ?

b A, write one more sentence to continue the conversation. Then pass the paper to B. B, write the next sentence and pass it back to A. Use a highlighted expression from 3a in each sentence.

c Work in groups. Act out your conversations.

TASK

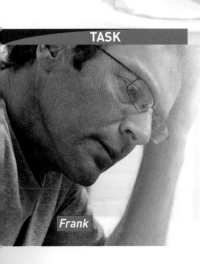

Frank

5   Work in groups of three. You're all friends of Frank. You're going to meet in a café and talk about Frank's problem at work. Read your role cards: A p123; B p128; C p132, and think about how to:

1   talk about people you know.   *Did you hear about Frank?*
2   summarise what people say.   *He told me that he wants to ...*
3   report speech directly.   *So she said, "What do you mean?"*

6   Have your conversation. Listen to what other people say. What do you think Frank should do?

7   Read Frank's email to his friends on p125. What did he do?

Across cultures Attitudes to family

LISTENING

Quang from Vietnam

1 ◖ **3.9** Listen to Patty, Quang and Çigdem talking about attitudes to family where they've lived. Who talks about:

a   looking after parents in their old age?
b   moving in with a partner before marriage?
c   growing up with different ideas about family?

2 ◖ **3.9** Listen again and answer the questions.

1   What does Patty say about children in Italy?
2   What does she say about children in Britain?
3   What does Quang say many Vietnamese families do?
4   What couldn't his friend Xuân do?
5   When do people leave the family home in Turkey?
6   What does Çigdem say many of her friends do?

Patty from Italy

VOCABULARY

Upbringing

In 1, Patty's talking about southern Italy, where her father's from.

3 **a** What country are the people talking about in each sentence?

Çigdem from Turkey

1   I was brought up to do things in his way.
2   Children ... are expected to take part in most family activities.
3   Children are encouraged to be more independent.
4   He was forced to spend his time and income supporting his elderly parents.
5   They're happy to follow in their parents' footsteps.
6   It's OK for them to go off and do what they want more.
7   In some circles it would be unacceptable to live with your partner before you get married.

b Check your ideas in the script on p159.

c Talk together about these questions.

1   As a child, what were you:
   • brought up to believe in?   • forced to do?
   • expected to do?   • encouraged to do?
2   As an adult, is there anything that is OK now that was unacceptable ten years ago?

SPEAKING

4 **a** Think about attitudes to family in your country and talk together.

1   Are children encouraged to be independent? In what ways?
2   Are children expected to take part in family activities?
3   Do teenagers spend more time with their family or friends?
4   When do most people leave the family home?
5   Is it acceptable to live alone if you're not married?
6   Are children expected to live near to their parents as adults?
7   Are adults happy to be told what to do by their parents?

b Do you know about attitudes to family in any other countries?

Goal

◎ write a factual report

1 a Look at these aspects of daily life. In your country, which do you think men usually spend more time on? Which do women spend more time on?

- commuting
- domestic chores
- social life
- relaxation
- work
- childcare
- appearance
- sleep

b Look at the table in figure 1 below. Do you think the statistics would be similar or different for your country? If you're from Japan, do you think things have changed since 2001?

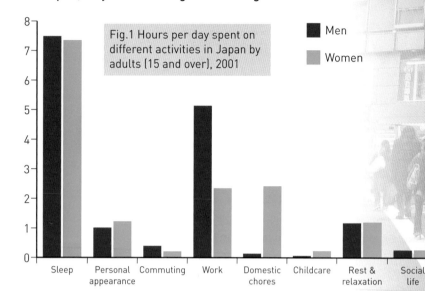

Fig.1 Hours per day spent on different activities in Japan by adults (15 and over), 2001

■ Men
▨ Women

2 Read the report describing the table. Match a–d with the four paragraphs.

a time spent on responsibilities
b a description of the table
c a summary of the main findings
d time spent on leisure and personal needs

3 a Find expressions in the report to:

| refer to the table (x3) |
| refer to topics (x2) |

| approximate figures (x4) |
| compare and contrast (x4) |

b Cover the report. In pairs, try to describe the table using expressions from 3a.

4 a Work in groups. You're going to write a report based on a class survey. Choose a topic and write seven or eight questions for other students.

Lying *Is it OK to tell white lies?*
Family *Do you have children?*
Gossip *Is gossip a good thing?*

b Ask people in the class your questions and make a note of their answers.

c Look at the information you've collected with your group. Plan your report together.

1 Organise your information into three or four paragraphs.
2 Think about the expressions in 3a you can use.

5 Write your report.

1 Figure 1 shows the hours per day that men and women spent doing different activities in Japan in 2001.

2 According to the table, men spent around twice as much time working and commuting to work as women. Men spent nearly six hours per day while women spent just under three hours. However, this pattern is reversed when it comes to housework and childcare, with women looking after the home and family for around three hours per day compared to only around fifteen minutes for men.

3 As the table shows, men and women spent about the same amount of time relaxing and socialising. However, women spent almost one and a half hours on personal appearance in contrast to just over an hour for men. As far as sleep is concerned, men slept for seven hours and forty-nine minutes per day with women sleeping, on average, fourteen minutes less per day.

4 In conclusion, there are still significant differences between how men and women spend their time, particularly when it comes to the key areas of work, home and family.

6 Read each other's reports. Which do you find the most surprising? Why?

11 Look again ♻

Review

1 a Add vowels to these verbs.

> wh_sp_r   c_mpl__n   scr__m
> b__st   _rg__   g_ss_p   sh__t

b Work in pairs. Choose a verb from 1a and write a short conversation to show its meaning.

Complain:
A The bus was late this morning.
B Was it? The buses are terrible, aren't they?

c Read your conversations to each other. Can you guess what the other pair are doing?

You're complaining.   Yes, that's right.

GRAMMAR Reporting speech

2 a Put the words in order to make sentences.

1   explain / my mum / used to / always / we couldn't do something / why
2   but / promised / I / for a friend / a favour / I forgot / to do
3   what to do / always / me / my boss / tells
4   don't like / friends / for me / to do favours / I / asking
5   what I'm thinking / a friend / I'm with / I / always / when / say

b Are the sentences true for you? If not, change them so they are.

c Talk together. Are your ideas the same or different?

CAN YOU REMEMBER? Unit 10 – Remembering an event

3 a Complete the questions with these verbs in the correct form.

> forget (x2)   ~~remember~~   remind (x2)
> recognise   notice

1   Do you _remember_ ever missing more than a month at school or work? Why did you have the time off?
2   Have you ever _____ someone's birthday? Were they upset?
3   Is there any food or drink which _____ you of a certain time or place?
4   Have you ever failed to _____ someone you know? What happened?
5   Do you usually _____ when a friend has a haircut?
6   Would you _____ someone that they owed you money?
7   How often do you _____ to lock your door?

b Ask and answer the questions. Ask questions to find out more.

Extension

SPELLING AND SOUNDS /juː/

4 a 🔊 **3.10** Listen and underline the letters in these words which make a /juː/ sound.

human   university   argue   computer   new   future   due   communication   knew   few   barbecue   usually

b Find words in 4a to match spelling patterns 1–3. /juː/ is usually spelled:

1   u at the start of words.
2   u in the middle of words.
3   ue or ew at the end of words.

c Complete the spelling of these words. Then check in a dictionary.

1 __seful	4 comm__nity	7 resc__
2 contin__	5 h__ge	8 attit__de
3 ren__	6 neph__	9 val__

d Spellcheck. In pairs, take turns to choose ten words and test your partner's spelling.

NOTICE Science and research

5 a Find nouns in the article on p88 which mean:

1   a computer program (**paragraph 1**)
2   rooms used for scientific work (**p2**)
3   lots of information stored on a computer (**p2**)
4   facts or information (**p2**)
5   studies to find out new information (**p5**)

b Complete the questions with words from 5a. Then discuss them.

1   Do you use any _____ at home, school or work? What is it? Is it useful?
2   Do you have _____ at your school, university or workplace? What are they used for?
3   Do you think the government should keep a _____ about its citizens? What _____ should it include?
4   Have you ever done any _____? What was it about?

Self-assessment

Can you do these things in English? Circle a number on each line. 1 = I can't do this, 5 = I can do this well.

⊚ relate a conversation	1	2	3	4	5
⊚ talk about truth and lies	1	2	3	4	5
⊚ summarise what people say	1	2	3	4	5
⊚ find out news about people you know	1	2	3	4	5
⊚ write a factual report	1	2	3	4	5

• For Wordcards, reference and saving your work → e-Portfolio
• For more practice → Self-study Pack, Unit 11

Any questions?

Stuntman

READING

1 You're going to read an article about a stuntman who does fire stunts. What would you like to find out about him and his job? Write three questions.

2 Read Rocky Taylor's description of his career. Were your questions answered?

How to set yourself on fire

1 My stunt career started in 1961. There was no training in those days. I was a black belt in judo, and went down to teach an actor in a big film. That's how I got into it.

2 When you do a fire stunt, you put a special gel on your skin, and then you wear a fireproof suit under your clothes. Your clothes are set on fire and normally stay alight for about 15 seconds. Fire goes upwards so it's always up around your face and the back of your neck. If it starts to hurt, then you're in trouble.

3 It does get very hot, and you have to do it with two or three people ready around you, so if you have a problem you can fall down on your hands and knees and they will put you out using fire extinguishers, spraying you headfirst all the way down to your feet. Then they wrap a big wet towel around you because sometimes you're so hot that you can re-ignite. You're

in control and you know that if you've had enough, or if it gets too hot, you can just lie flat down and they will put the fire out. If you're going to do a longer fire-burn, you need some breathing apparatus, so you wear small bottles called 'breathers' inside your suit so you can last a bit longer. The air gets burnt around you during a fire stunt, using up the oxygen.

4 Over the years, I've done about nine or ten fire jobs. They're special, not an everyday occurrence in a stuntman's career. You might have to do one every couple of years. For my first fire job, I was very anxious – and very pleased when everything was all right. It was in a film called *The Last Valley*, where I was set on fire and thrown onto a bonfire – a full body burn. I had a very nasty accident while filming Michael Winner's *Death Wish 3* in 1985, when I was seriously injured due to a mistake by the crew.

It was a big fire job, jumping out of an exploding building, and I got badly burnt because I wasn't actually supposed to be on fire.

5 My family are always anxious and want to make sure I'm all right. I have to phone them before and after a job so they know I'm OK. They never try to talk me out of it – after all, I've been doing it for over 40 years. Anyway, I'm now a stunt co-ordinator, so I don't do as many stunts. It's a young man's job being a stuntman.

▲ Rocky Taylor has been a stuntman for more than 40 years, working on almost all of the James Bond films and, more recently, *The Da Vinci Code* and *Stormbreaker*.

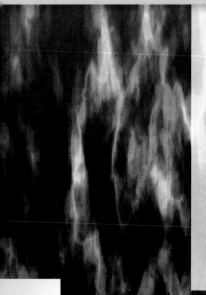

3 Read the article again and answer the questions.

1 How did Rocky get into the film industry?
2 How are the stuntmen protected from injury?
3 How did he get injured?
4 How does Rocky's family feel about the job? How does Rocky feel about it now?

4 Find words and expressions about fire with the following meanings in the article.

1 protected against fire (*adj*, 2)
2 made to start burning (*expression*, 2)
3 on fire (*adj*, 2)
4 equipment for putting out a fire (*noun*, 3)
5 start burning again (*verb*, 3)
6 to stop a fire (*multi-word verb*, 3)
7 an outdoor fire for pleasure (*noun*, 4)
8 damaged or destroyed by fire (*adj*, 4)

5 Discuss the questions.

1 Why do you think people do jobs like this?
2 What do you think would be the pros and cons of the job?
3 What sort of person would be good at it?

Giving a talk

Mike Caxton is an instructor at the Stunt Training Centre in Vancouver, Canada.

1 **3.11** Listen to Mike Caxton talking to stuntmen and stuntwomen about fire stunts. What does he say about:

- performing safely? • fire? • the course?

2 a **3.12** Now listen to the rest of the talk. How many parts of the course are there? What questions do people ask?

b **3.12** Listen again and make notes about the important details of each part of the course.

c Would you like to do the course? Why? Why not?

3 a Mike Caxton uses expressions to organise his talk. Put sentences 1–8 in the order that he says them.

1 Any further questions?
2 Secondly, fire is like wind: if there's an opening, it will find a way in.
3 And finally, you need to know that the fire course is our most challenging course.
4 Today, I'm going to talk about the fire courses at our training centre.
5 To start with, there are three things you need to know.
6 Before I move on to enrolment, are there any questions?
7 First of all, it's important to remember that when you watch a movie …
8 I'm going to move on now to talk about the different parts of the course …

b Check your ideas in the script on p159.

4 a Look at these sentences from the introduction to Mike Caxton's talk. He talks in groups of words to make it easier for listeners to understand. **3.13** Listen and notice the groups of words.

1 Today, // I'm going to talk about // the fire courses // at our training centre …
2 To start with, // there are three things // you need to know.

b Practise saying the sentences.

c Look at script 3.14 on p159. Where do you think the groups of words are? In pairs, mark the groups of words with //.

d **3.14** Listen to check. Practise saying this part of the talk.

5 a You're going to give a short talk about a course. Prepare in A/B/C/D groups.

As – look on p120. Bs – look on p125. Cs – look on p131. Ds – look on p133.

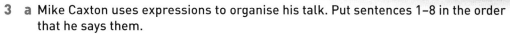

Technical mountaineering course (TMC)
- alpine mountain climbing course
- very popular training centre in New Zealand

Web design courses
- perfect for those who wish to learn the skills to progress into the world of web design

Photography courses
- learn how to get the most from your camera

Bungee jumping
- an unforgettable experience!
- bring friends, good opportunity for photos

b Organise the information into three or four sections and decide which expressions from 3a to use.

c Get into new groups, with one person each from A, B, C and D. Listen to each other's talks and think of questions to ask at the end.

6 Which activity would you most like to do? Why?

Talking to strangers

1 a ● **3.15** Listen to Mariama and answer the questions.

1   In her experience, is it easier to talk to strangers in Nigeria or the UK? Why?
2   What places and situations does she mention?
3   What would be a strange thing to do in Nigeria, according to Mariama?

b Discuss the questions.

1   Where you live, how often do people talk to strangers in these situations?
    • in a queue   • on public transport   • in the street   • in shops
2   Do you think things have changed in the last 20 years?
3   Do *you* ever speak to people in these situations? Why? Why not?

Mariama, who is British Nigerian, lives in England.

2 a ● **3.16** Listen to five short conversations, A–E. Which conversation is about:

1   global warming?   2   a form?   3   a suitcase?   4   litter?   5   a credit card?

b What does each speaker ask the other person to do? ● **3.16** Listen again to check.

Polite requests
and questions

3 a Look at the highlighted expressions from the conversations. Which questions 1–8:

a   ask for an opinion or information? (x2)
b   do you say before you ask someone to do something? (x2)
c   ask someone to do something? What? (x3)
d   ask for permission to do something? (x1)

Would you mind	[1]if I opened the window? [2]sending it to me? [3]answering some questions?	People often begin a conversation with these polite expressions, but usually continue with direct questions:
Could I ask you	[4]a favour? [5]to do something for me? [6]to look after my case?	**A** Could I ask you to do something for me? **B** Sure.
Could you tell me	[7]your views on that, please? [8]a little bit about your background?	**A** Can you fill that in for me?

b How do the strangers respond in each situation? Talk together, then check in the scripts on pp159–60.

4 a Work alone. Look at the situations below and think about what you want to say.

1   You're on a plane. You need a pen to fill in your landing card. Ask another passenger.

2   You're interviewing a candidate for a job. You want to know about his/her qualifications.

3   You're out, and you think you've forgotten to lock your front door. Phone your neighbour to check.

4   You're at a meeting. You want to know what your boss thinks about plans to cut jobs in the company.

b Work in pairs. Take turns to start a conversation.

Survey

GRAMMAR

Indirect questions

1 Which questions, A or B, do you use if you want to be more polite?

	A Direct	B Indirect
Yes/no questions	Have you applied for any other jobs?	I was wondering if you've applied for any other jobs.
	Do you use public transport?	Could I ask you if you use public transport?
Wh-questions	How do you get rid of your rubbish?	Could you tell me how you get rid of your rubbish?
	Why are you cancelling your order?	Could I ask you why you're cancelling your order?

2 Look at A and B and answer the questions.

1 What happens to word order in indirect questions?
2 What happens to auxiliary *do* in indirect questions?
3 What word do you need to add to indirect yes/no questions?

Grammar reference and practice, p143

3 Look at these opening questions from different surveys about local issues. Make them into indirect questions using: Could I ask you ...? Could you tell me ...?

shopping
1 Do you go shopping alone or with someone else?

Public transport
1 Have you had any problems with public transport?

Food and drink
1 What's your favourite café or restaurant in your area?

Entertainment
1 Where do you go in your area for entertainment?

Parking
1 Have you used the local parking facilities?

Cleanliness
1 Are you happy with how clean your area is?

SPEAKING

4 You're going to do a class survey. In groups, choose one of the topics from 3. Write another indirect question and three or four direct questions. You can ask questions about:

- habits
- preferences
- experiences
- good points
- bad points
- ideas for improvements

5 a Do your survey. Ask different people in the class your questions. Remember to start your survey with indirect questions, then continue with direct questions.

> Would you mind answering some questions?

> No problem.

> Thanks. Well, to start with, could you tell me ...

b Work in groups again. Gather your findings together and plan how to tell the class the results of your survey.

6 Tell the class what you found out.

> About half the class go shopping for food with their families. Most people go shopping for clothes with their friends.

12.3 Target activity

Deal with questions in a talk

12.3 goals
◉ give a talk about an interest or activity ♻
◉ ask polite questions ♻
◉ take questions in a talk

TASK LISTENING

1 Talk together.

    1 Have you ever found something old, valuable or interesting?

    2 What kinds of things do you think treasure hunters look for? Where might they look for them?

2 a ● ▸ **3.17** Martin Silva has been giving a talk about treasure hunting at a local college. Listen to the audience's questions and put the topics in the correct order.

    a the value of a vase
    b the law about treasure hunting
    c where to look for gold
    d why Martin started treasure hunting
    e finding valuable things
    f where to start

b ● ▸ **3.17** Listen again.

    1 Which two questions can't he answer? What does he suggest?
    2 How does Martin answer the other questions?

Martin Silva

TASK VOCABULARY

Answering questions at a talk

3 Look at Martin's answers to the audience's questions. Which highlighted expressions, 1, 2 or 3, does he use:

    a when he wants to answer later?
    b before he gives an answer?
    c when he isn't sure how to answer?

> 1 That's a good question.
> That's an important point.
>
> 2 I'll find out for you.
> I'll get back to you as soon as I can.
>
> 3 Well, it depends what you want to find.
> All I can say is that you will definitely find something of interest.
> To be honest, I don't know the answer to that.

4 a Work in pairs. Prepare two or three general knowledge questions.

b Ask and answer your questions together. Use the highlighted expressions in 3.

TASK

5 You're going to give a short talk about an interest or activity of your own.

    1 Choose a topic.
    2 Make a list of ideas.
    3 Organise your ideas. Use expressions from the vocabulary on p95.
    4 Prepare to give your talk.

6 Take turns to give your talks. For each talk:

    • Audience: Listen and write two questions to ask during the talk.
    • Speaker: Give the talk and deal with the questions at the end.

7 Afterwards, talk with a partner.

    1 Which questions were difficult to answer? Why?
    2 Which questions were the most interesting? Why?

Keywords *other, another*

Uses of *other* and *another*

> I think we're going to see another photo soon ... I hope...

1 a Look at the things people said at different presentations. In which cases is the presenter having problems?

1 And this is the other photo. Oh, that's not the right photo! I'm very sorry.

2 I'm afraid we've got another problem here. This video projector won't turn on.

3 Some thought it was an 'OK idea', but other people thought it was a 'very good idea'.

4 This laptop doesn't seem to be working. Does anyone have another one?

5 Here are some photos of the new factory in Sweden. There are others in the pack on your chairs.

b Look at the sentences in 1a again, then answer these questions.

1 Look at another/other + noun in sentences 1–3. Which is always singular? Which can be singular or plural?
2 What do another one and others refer to in sentences 4 and 5?

For a/an + other we say another. (*an other*)

2 a Add these expressions to sentences 1–5:
other   others   another   another one

                                other
1 Where I live now is much nicer than /\ places I've lived.
2 My job doesn't challenge me. I need to look for.
3 I always wear the same shoes. I haven't got any.
4 I never do sport or fitness classes. I've got things to do which are more interesting.
5 I don't worry too much about failing things. There's always chance to do better.

b Are the sentences true for you? Talk together.

Linking expressions

3 a (**3.18**) Listen to Juan Carlos and Kana talk about whether presentation skills should be taught in schools. Who thinks it's a good idea? Who doesn't?

b Complete the sentences from the conversation with expressions a–e.

a To put it another way
b Another point is
c Another thing is that
d on the other hand
e in other words

1 JUAN CARLOS   It's an important part of learning to communicate.
KANA   Yes, but _____, it's not really a subject, is it?

2 K   It's not like history or maths.
JC   So, _____, we should only teach academic subjects at school?
K   Well, yes. _____, education is about learning how to think.

3 JC   What about how to get on in the world of work? _____, it teaches kids an important life skill.

4 JC   You need to be able to communicate effectively. _____ it builds confidence.

c Which highlighted expressions are used to:

1 contrast ideas? (x1)
2 add ideas? (x2)
3 summarise or interpret ideas? (x2)

4 a What do you think about these topics? Work alone, choose one topic and make notes. Think about how to use the expressions in 3b.

- Do women make good drivers? What about men?
- Should extreme sports be taught in school?
- Should all children be taught to cook?
- What do you think education is for?

b Discuss your ideas. Do you agree?

> So, in other words, you think that women make good drivers, but ...

12 EXPLORESpeaking

Goal
- give yourself time to think

1 🔊 **3.19** Listen to Jasmina talking to her husband Rick about her presentation tomorrow.

1 How does she feel about it? Why?
2 What three things does she think help to give a good presentation?

2 a You can use different sounds, words and expressions in normal conversation to give yourself time to think. 🔊 **3.19** Listen again and tick (✓) 1–6 each time you hear them.

1	er	3	like	5	kind of
2	erm	4	sort of	6	you know

b Take turns to talk about these topics for 30 seconds each. Use the sounds, words and expressions in 2a when you need time to think.

- where you live
- your work or studies
- your interests
- last weekend

> Erm, I love my flat, you know, but I'm not very happy about my street because it's, er, it's sort of changed a lot recently.

3 🔊 **3.20** Listen to Jasmina's presentation. What points does she need time to think about?

4 You can use different expressions to give yourself more time. Complete 2–6 with expressions from Jasmina's presentation. Then read conversation 2 to check.

1 Just give me a second.
2 _____ a minute.
3 _____ a moment.
4 Let _____ .
5 Let _____ .
6 Let _____ .

5 a Work alone. You're A or B. Add two more questions about texts in this unit to your section below.

A	1	*What films has stuntman Rocky Taylor been in?* (Reading, p94)
	...	
B	1	*What does Mariama say is a strange thing to do in Nigeria?* (Listening, p96, 🔊 **3.15**)
	...	

b Work in A/B pairs. Take turns to ask your questions and try to answer. If you can't remember, have a look in the unit. Try to use the expressions in 2a and 4.

> What films has stuntman Rocky Taylor been in? Let me think. Er, just give me a second. No, no idea. Let me check.

Jasmina has to give a presentation to colleagues.

1

RICK	How are you feeling about the presentation tomorrow?
JASMINA	Erm, OK, I suppose. You know, I'm a bit nervous because all the senior management will be there, but, er, I think it'll be fine. I'm well prepared.
RICK	You said it was a bit of a disaster last time.
JASMINA	Yeah, well, before … you know, like, I didn't really prepare or practise, and then I got really nervous. I've got to sort of … I've just got to not get too nervous. I think if I kind of, er, look people in the eye at the start then it'll be easier.

2

JASMINA	I'm going to move on now to talk about the European results.
TONY	Sorry, can I ask something else about Japan? How many people did we recruit last month?
JASMINA	Erm, just give me a second. Let me check … erm, yes, here we are. Eighteen people overall.
TONY	Oh right. Er, thanks.
JASMINA	So, er, as you can see, the European results have been very good indeed.
TONY	What about last month's results?
JASMINA	I'm afraid the figures for last month aren't on the graph. Let me just have a look here. Erm, bear with me a moment. … Yes, I have the figures here, but unfortunately, you can't see them. OK, erm, let me think … I'll tell you what I'll do, if you hold on a minute … I'll read the figures to you and then you can ask me about them.
TONY	Thanks, erm, that would be very helpful.

12 Look again ♻

Review

1 **a** Write indirect questions for 1–7.

1 Which bus should I take for the station?
2 Where's the nearest bank?
3 Is there a post office near here?
4 When do the shops normally close?
5 What's the best way to get to the town centre?
6 Do you have a map?
7 Where can I buy a guidebook?

b Imagine you've just moved to this area. What do you need to know? Think of more questions.

c Ask each other your questions.

VOCABULARY Polite requests and questions

2 **a** Complete the highlighted expressions with words from the box.

mind   favour   ask   something   to   sending

	a 2_____?
Could I 1_____ you	to do 3_____ for me?
	4_____ wait here?
Would you 5_____	if I had another biscuit?
	6_____ me a form?

b Work alone. Write four or five questions to ask other people.

Would you mind passing me that dictionary?

c Ask your questions. Respond and have brief conversations.

CAN YOU REMEMBER? Unit 11 – Exchanging news

3 **a** Match 1–5 with a–e, then continue the conversation between three friends.

1 A Have you spoken to Ros lately?
2 A Well, someone said she's cancelled her party.
3 C What? Who said that?
4 C Well, that's not what I heard.
5 C Well, did you hear about Ros's new boyfriend?

a B No. Who is he?
b B No, she's always out when I phone her.
c A Tim did!
d B Oh no! I was really looking forward to that.
e A What do you mean?

b In pairs, write a conversation between friends using the highlighted expressions in 3a.

c Listen to each other's conversations. What was the news?

Extension

SPELLING AND SOUNDS /ɔɪ/

4 **a** ● 3.21 In most words, the /ɔɪ/ sound is spelled oi or oy. Listen and complete the spelling of these words. Then check in a dictionary.

p__nt   destr__   r__al   __l   j__nts
n__se   empl__er   av__d   enj__   v__age

b Which spelling pattern do you use:

1 before a consonant?
2 before a vowel?
3 at the end of a word?

c ● 3.22 Spellcheck. Listen and write ten words. Then check your spelling on p160.

NOTICE Patterns with *in*

5 **a** Which highlighted expressions below are:

a adjective + in   b in + noun

1 If you're interested in historical artefacts … you could start in your own home. ● 3.17
2 If it starts to hurt, then you're in trouble. p94
3 You're in control and you know that if you've had enough … they will put the fire out. p94
4 Personally, I'm not involved in looking for gold. ● 3.17
5 I'm experienced in sales.
6 My bedroom's in a mess. There are things everywhere!

b Discuss the questions.

1 What are you:
• interested in?
• experienced in?
2 Is your room or home often in a mess?
3 Have you ever been in trouble while travelling? What happened?
4 Do you know anyone who loves being in control?
5 Are you involved in any clubs or interesting activities? What?

Self-assessment

Can you do these things in English? Circle a number on each line. 1 = I can't do this, 5 = I can do this well.

◉ give a talk about an interest or activity	1	2	3	4	5
◉ make polite requests	1	2	3	4	5
◉ ask polite questions	1	2	3	4	5
◉ take questions in a talk	1	2	3	4	5
◉ give yourself time to think	1	2	3	4	5

• For Wordcards, reference and saving your work → e-Portfolio
• For more practice → Self-study Pack, Unit 12

13.1 goals
- talk about mistakes
- criticise past actions
- suggest alternatives

Looking back

Big mistake

1 Look at the book cover. What do you think the book is about?

2 Read the article about Gerald Ratner. How does the book title describe what happened to him?

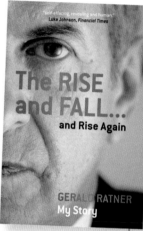

Doing a Ratner

Gerald Ratner will never get over his big mistake. In 1991, the then-head of the hugely successful Ratners Jewellers experienced one of the speediest downfalls in corporate history. While making a speech to the Institute of Directors, he said some of his products were rubbish and made a joke that his customers could buy "a pair of earrings for under a pound, which is cheaper than a prawn sandwich, but probably wouldn't last as long". Share prices fell dramatically and he was fired from the family business he'd started working for at 16, taken over from his father and built up into a global success.

He went bankrupt and had a nervous breakdown. The experience still hurts. "I did offer to resign within 48 hours of that speech," he says, adding, "And I wish now I had, rather than stay around for another 18 months for everything to fall apart."

Since then, he has struggled to make a comeback. He set up a health club in 1996 and made a good profit when he sold it five years later. He then set up an online jewellery business called Gerald Online (he was not allowed to use the name Ratners). He runs the business with only six people, compared with the 27,000 employed at his old company. "I do a lot more things myself," he says. He also spends two nights a week giving speeches at business events and he has written an autobiography, sales of which have been "not great".

Ratner is philosophical about his past, saying, "I made a huge mistake, which I regret, and I have to live with that fact. The good thing was I got into the habit of cycling 28 miles per day." When asked how he would like to be remembered, he says, "I know I'll be remembered, sadly, as 'doing a Ratner'" – an expression which became widely used for making big mistakes in business. "But what people forget is that before that speech, we had transformed a small family company into a global business. That's how I'd like 'a Ratner' to be remembered."

At 60, though, Ratner is back in business and excited about the future. He says, "People often ask me, 'Why didn't you write a book before?' And I reply, 'Because it wouldn't have had a happy ending.' "

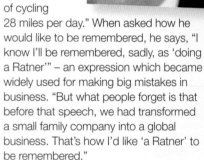

3 What kind of person do you think Gerald Ratner is? Why?

Events in business

4 a Cover the article and complete sentences a–h about Gerald Ratner's career with the expressions in the box in the correct form.

take over resign fail set up fire run go bankrupt build up

a He made a joke and as a result his business _____ .
b He _____ and struggled to get his life back on track.
c He _____ his father's jewellery business.
d He now _____ Gerald Online with a staff of six.
e He offered to _____ straight away.
f He _____ a health club, then another jewellery business.
g He _____ the company into a global success.
h He was eventually _____ a year and a half later.

b Put the events into the order in which they happened. Then read the article again to check.

5 Discuss the questions.

1 Look at the expressions in 4a. Do you know anyone who's done these things? What happened?
2 Who are the most famous business people in your country? What do you know about them?

He shouldn't have ...

LISTENING

1 a 🔊 **3.23** Listen to Debbie and Steve talking about the article.

Debbie and Steve

1 Who feels sorry for Ratner? Who is critical of him?
2 What similar story do they talk about?

b Whose opinion about Ratner do you agree with? Why?

GRAMMAR

should have, could have

2 a Complete the sentences from the conversation with: could, should or shouldn't.

> modal + *have* + past participle
> 1 He _____ have kept his mouth shut.
> 2 He _____ have said it in public.
> 3 He _____ have just apologised.

b Answer the questions about the highlighted expressions.

1 Are they about the past or the present?
2 Which can be used to: a criticise? b suggest alternatives?

3 a Read about four different situations. What was the problem in each?

"I decided to leave my job after just a month. I was really excited about it, but people were so unfriendly! Nobody tried to get to know me at all. DEREK"

"I packed beach clothes for my holiday in New Zealand, but it was freezing! I had to spend loads of money on some warm stuff. ALIJA"

"I was supposed to be giving this presentation at work, but I couldn't work out how to turn the screen on, and I totally forgot what I was going to say. KAREEM"

"I got these cheap DVDs from the market, but none of them will play, and the stallholder won't give me a refund. IAN"

b Work alone. Write two sentences for each situation.

1 What should the people have done? What shouldn't they have done?
2 What could they have done differently?

Grammar reference and practice, p144

c Talk about your ideas for the situations together.

PRONUNCIATION

Common pairs of words 3

4 a When we say past modals, we usually link the words and use the weak form of have, e.g. in should've. We don't write them in this way.

🔊 **3.24** Listen to sentences 1–3 in 2a and practise saying them.

b Practise saying the sentences you wrote in 3b.

SPEAKING

5 a Have you ever regretted something that you've said or done? Think of three or four stories about:

Things you've said to: • a friend • a colleague • a stranger • a teacher
Things you've done: • buying things • education • work • friends and family

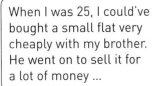
When I was 25, I could've bought a small flat very cheaply with my brother. He went on to sell it for a lot of money ...

1 What did or didn't you do?
2 Why was it a mistake?
3 What should or shouldn't you have done?
4 What could you have done differently?

b Talk together. What do you think your partner should or could have done?

A good deed

13.2 goals
◉ talk about acts of kindness and bravery
◉ speculate about the past

READING

> I'd probably shout so the person would realise someone was stealing their bag.

1 a Talk together. What would you do if you saw someone:

1 stealing someone's wallet or bag?
2 in trouble in a river or the sea?
3 pushing an old man in the street?
4 robbing a shop or bank?

b Tell the class. Would you do the same or different things?

2 Read three news stories. Which are about acts of kindness? Which are about acts of bravery?

①

A man who rescued a driver from a car that had been driven into Lopez Lake on Friday was fired because he could not make it into work after the rescue.

David Warne, a 29-year-old father of two from San Luis Obispo, California, risked his life by diving into the lake, braving sharp rocks to save a 40-year-old man whose car had broken through a guard rail into the water.

Mr Warne was only three days into his job with Paradise Pool Interiors, but when he phoned his boss to tell her he could not work due to the deep cuts on his feet and arms, he was told he no longer had a job. "I rang her and said, 'I've saved a guy from drowning and I've got to go to hospital to get stitched up,'" Mr Warne said.

Owner Lesley Burke was not impressed by the good deed. A spokesman for the company said: "If Mr Warne had worked here longer, it would have been different." However, San Luis Obispo Police have recommended Mr Warne for a bravery award.

②

A small village in Mexico is richer than it was, thanks to a wealthy widow who died recently and left all her money to the village. She wanted to thank everyone for the welcome she received when she moved there. Everyone over 60 received 10,000 pesos, while other gifts included 200,000 pesos to the local church. "She was a lovely lady who was always thinking of others," said a neighbour, 63, about Rosa Flores. "She helped me with my household chores when I was sick. She was always doing favours for people. But I think she was lonely after her husband died because she had no children. If she'd had a family, she probably wouldn't have left all her money to the village. We're very, very grateful to her."

③

"Seriously, I've got a gun. Give me the money." So shouted robber Robert Hendry as he burst into a bank in Portsmouth in England, his gun hand hidden in a bag. Terrified staff were about to do what he'd asked, when a customer who'd been quietly reading his paper walked up to Hendry and said, "You're joking, aren't you, mate?" and took the empty bag. Then Terry Parker sat down and went on with his reading. Hendry ran away. "If Mr Parker hadn't got involved," said John Anderson, the bank manager, "then I'm sure the man would have robbed the bank."

3 Cover the stories. Are 1–6 true or false?

1 David Warne was fired because his injuries stopped him going to work.
2 David had worked with Paradise Pool Interiors for a long time.
3 Rosa Flores left money to everyone in her village.
4 Rosa didn't have family in the village.
5 Robert Hendry tried to rob a bank with a gun.
6 Terry Parker didn't believe the robber had a gun.

Read again to check.

> David Warne was unfortunate to get fired.

4 How would you describe these people? Give reasons.

David Warne   Lesley Burke   Rosa Flores   Robert Hendry   Terry Parker

5 a Complete the facts from the stories with these verbs in the correct form.

> thank   ~~rescue~~   do   leave   save   help   risk   think

1 A man who _rescued_ a driver from a car that had been driven into Lopez Lake on Friday was fired.
2 David Warne _____ his life by diving into the lake.
3 I've _____ a guy from drowning and I've got to go to hospital.
4 A wealthy widow _____ all her money to the village.
5 She wanted to _____ everyone for the welcome she received.
6 She was a lovely lady who was always _____ of others.
7 She _____ me with my household chores when I was sick.
8 She was always _____ favours for people.

b Read the stories again to check.

6 a Cover 5a. Add prepositions to sentences 1–7. Then ask and answer the questions.

Acts of kindness:
1 Do you think it's important to thank people _____ helping you?
2 Do you ever help other people _____ their English?
3 Do you try to think _____ others before yourself?
4 Do you do a lot of favours _____ your friends?

Acts of bravery:
5 Have you ever saved someone _____ a difficult or dangerous situation?
6 Would you risk your life _____ diving into a river to save someone? What about other situations?
7 Would you rescue an animal _____ danger?

b Talk together. Who's the kindest person in the class? Who's the bravest?

I wouldn't have …

1 Look at the sentences from the stories. Answer the questions.

1 Are the situations: • real or imaginary?   • about the past or now?
2 Complete the form: if + had + _____ , would + have + _____

Situation	Result
If Mr Warne had worked here longer, If she'd had a family,	it would have been different. she probably wouldn't have left all her money to the village.

We can also say: It **would have been** different if Mr Warne **had worked** here longer.

2 a ● 3.25 Listen to situations 1–6. After each situation, work in pairs to discuss what happened and complete the sentences.

1 If he hadn't crashed … he wouldn't have …
2 If she'd … she would've …
3 If he hadn't seen … , he probably wouldn't …
4 She wouldn't have become …
5 She wouldn't have …
6 If he'd known …

If he hadn't crashed into the car in front, he wouldn't have met his wife.

b Compare your sentences with a new partner. Did you have the same ideas?

3 a Draw a timeline for your life and mark key events and decisions you've made.

b Show a partner your timeline and explain it.

2005	*left university*	*went travelling for a year*	*met my girlfriend in China*	2010

4 a Now prepare some questions about the choices your partner made.

If you hadn't gone travelling after university, what would you have done?

b Ask and answer the questions.

Target activity

Discuss what went wrong

TASK LISTENING

1 a Talk together.

1 Do you have a good sense of direction?
2 Do you ever drive when you're abroad? Do you find it stressful?
3 What do you do when you're lost?

b Look at the picture of Debbie and Steve. What do you think they're saying?

2 ● **3.26** Listen to Debbie and Steve driving in Athens.

1 What two things didn't they bring?
2 What's Steve going to do?

TASK VOCABULARY

Evaluating past actions

3 a ● **3.26** Listen again. What are Debbie and Steve talking about in sentences 1–5?

1 You could've told me sooner.
2 It would've been better to bring our own.
3 If you'd asked me, I could've told you exactly where it is.
4 If I'd known we were going to get lost, obviously I'd have brought it.
5 We should've known, really.

> It would have been more sensible to ...

Check your ideas in the script on p161.

b Can you think of different words or expressions to replace better in sentence 3?

Debbie and Steve are on holiday in Athens in Greece. They're lost.

TASK

4 a Work in groups, A and B. Imagine you're on a weekend break with friends. Choose one of the following situations or your own idea.

- a cottage in the countryside
- a hill-walking holiday
- a resort by the sea
- a sightseeing trip

b What kinds of things could go wrong on your holiday? Make a list of five things.

bad weather, not enough warm clothes ...

c You're going to have a conversation about the things that have gone wrong. Think about what you can say.

It would have been better to ...
If I'd known, I wouldn't have ...
You could have ...

5 Work in A/B pairs. Take turns to make a phone call and tell your friend about the things that have gone wrong on your holiday. What did you decide to do next?

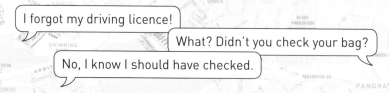

I forgot my driving licence!

What? Didn't you check your bag?

No, I know I should have checked.

6 Have you ever been in situations like these? What did you do?

Across cultures Rules and risk

LISTENING

1 Where you live, what are the laws about these things?

road rules   speed limits   buying cigarettes or alcohol   smoking in public

2 ● 3.27 Listen to Patrizia and Jon talking about attitudes to rules and risk in Italy and Britain. Which topics in 1 do they talk about?

3 **a** ● 3.27 Listen again. Who says these things?

Attitude to the law
1 There are rules, but they are followed in a loose manner.
2 People make a big fuss if you're doing something you're not supposed to do.
3 People are very aware of the rules.
4 A law is a law, but laws can be interpreted differently.

Smoking
5 If you were smoking in a non-smoking café, they'd ask you to stop.
6 If a policeman or passer-by approached, they'd be friendly to you.

Traffic
7 If you're cycling the wrong way down a street, people always complain.
8 A driver might bend the rules to get from A to B.
9 It looks chaotic, but actually it's quite controlled.
10 It's about how you can take a risk without hurting yourself or other people.

b Where are attitudes to the law more flexible, according to Patrizia and Jon: Italy or Britain?

4 Look at 1–10 together. Are things the same where you live?

VOCABULARY

make, let, be allowed to, be supposed to

5 Look at sentences 1–4 below from the conversation. Which highlighted expression do we use to say someone:

a is forced to do something?
b is expected to do something?
c has permission to do something? (x2)

1 If you were smoking in a non-smoking café …, they'd make you leave.
2 It sounds like in Italy people let you do what you want more.
3 There are rules for what you're supposed to do, but often people don't follow them exactly.
4 People are very aware of what they're allowed to do.

SPEAKING

6 **a** Think of places you spend a lot of time. How are you supposed to behave?

• a workplace   • a library   • at home
• a university   • a place of worship   • a café or canteen

b Discuss the questions.

1 In your country, what laws are there to protect people's health and safety? Think about the places in 6a.
2 Do you agree with the laws? Why? Why not?
3 Do you follow these laws? Give examples.
4 What do you do if other people don't follow the laws?

We're not allowed to smoke indoors in public places. I think it protects people's health and also their safety.

1 Discuss the questions.

1 What do you need to think about when you're organising a trip abroad?
2 Have you ever organised a trip for someone or had a trip organised for you? Did everything go well?

2 Read the information Barbara has researched for Zoë's trip to Kraków. Circle the information you think will be important or interesting for Zoë.

Goals

⊙ write a summary of information from different sources
⊙ write an email giving information

Barbara works in Poland. She's organising a trip to Kraków for a colleague, Zoë from Ottawa, Canada.

	27.10.2010	28.10.2010	28.10.2010
direction	Ottawa (YOW) – Toronto (YYZ)	Toronto (YYZ) – Warsaw (WAW)	Warsaw (WAW) - Kraków (KRK)
departure time	<u>13:00</u>	18:25	11:35
arrival time	14:05	09:00	12:30
flight aircraft	L04120	E90	LO0042

two changes

Wierzynek Restaurant

With a tradition going all the way back to 1364, it's hardly surprising to find that Wierzynek Restaurant has become something of a landmark in its own right. Its location on the corner of the Rynek and Grodzka Street places it right in the heart of Kraków's Old Town, and makes it a favourite for visitors who want to watch the world go by from their tables overlooking the Market Square. Thanks to its exquisite traditional Polish cuisine, perfectly trained staff, elegance and timeless charm, Wierzynek was named the best restaurant in Kraków by the prestigious Michelin Red Guide.

7:30pm with Stefan Daszkiewicz + Ela Górska

Hotel Bronislaw Kraków

☆☆☆

Saint Bronislaw's Hill was chosen as the site for the memorial mound in honour of the military hero, Tadeusz Kościuszko, because of its picturesque setting. In the middle of the nineteenth century the mound was surrounded by fortifications, which still exist today. It is a beautiful, historical and quiet location where guests can rest in real comfort.

The journey by car from the airport takes 15 minutes (Bus no. 100). Our guests are a step away from the centre and at the same time in a quiet corner far away from the noise of the city.
Meeting room for 40 people.
To assist with your meeting the following equipment and services are included: · flip chart and pens · data projector · TV · internet access.

2:00 meeting

3 **a** Read the first three paragraphs of Barbara's email to Zoë. Find and <u>underline</u> all the information in 2 that Barbara mentions in the email.

b Complete the rest of the email with information about the restaurant and Barbara's notes.

4 You've organised a weekend away for you and a group of friends to celebrate your birthday. In pairs, look at the information and notes on p132. In each section, circle one or two important points to tell your friends.

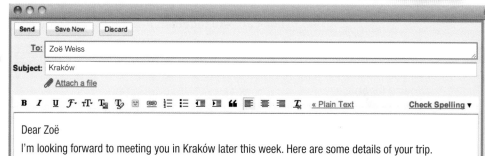

Send | Save Now | Discard

To: Zoë Weiss
Subject: Kraków
📎 Attach a file

B *I* <u>U</u> ... « Plain Text   Check Spelling ▼

Dear Zoë

I'm looking forward to meeting you in Kraków later this week. Here are some details of your trip.

Your flight isn't direct, I'm afraid. You have two changes, in Toronto and Warsaw. It leaves Ottawa at 13:00 on the 27th and you finally get to Kraków at 12:30 the next day! I've booked you into the Hotel Bronislaw. The hotel is in a beautiful historical location which is only 15 minutes from the airport.

The meeting will take place at 14:00 in the meeting room at the hotel. The meeting room has everything you'll need: flip chart and pens, data projector and internet access.

I've booked a table at ... for dinner at .... We're meeting ... there. It's right in the centre ... with tables overlooking .... The food is ... – it's one of the ... in Kraków.

So, have a good journey. I'll be at the hotel to meet you on the 28th.

All the best

Barbara Koch

5 Write an email to your friends explaining what you've organised.

6 Read another email. Does it sound like a good trip?

Review

VOCABULARY Events in business; Acts of kindness and bravery

1 a Match the verbs with the prepositions.

risk (your life) set thank do favours build take rescue help resign	for (x2) up (x2) with from (x2) over by

b Complete these sentences with expressions from 1a in the correct form.

1 My brother's really selfish. He never _____ anyone.
2 I've never _____ a job. I've worked for the same company for years.
3 I think it's crazy to _____ your life _____ not wearing a seat belt.
4 I enjoy listening to people and _____ them _____ their problems.
5 I would love to _____ my own business.

c Change the sentences in 1b so they're true for you. Then compare with a partner.

GRAMMAR Unreal conditionals: past

2 a Work alone. Think about a situation from your past in which something unexpected happened:

- a chance meeting
- a lucky coincidence
- an avoidable problem
- a happy ending

b Prepare to tell a partner about the situation.

1 What happened?
2 Why did it happen?
3 How could things have been different?

c Talk together. What would you have done if you'd been in your partner's situation?

CAN YOU REMEMBER? Unit 12 – Polite requests and questions

3 a Complete the questions with the expressions in the box to write a music survey.

- Could I ask you ...
- Would you mind ...
- Could you tell me ...

kind of music taste in music favourite singer/group sing me something prefer radio/MP3 player/Internet song lyrics

b Ask and answer your questions. Did you find anyone with the same taste in music as you?

> Could you tell me who your favourite singer is?

> I'd say my favourite singer of all time is Jacques Brel.

Extension

SPELLING AND SOUNDS /aʊ/

4 a In most words, the /aʊ/ sound is spelled ou or ow. ▶ 3.28 Listen to these words.

1 crowd powder owl 4 out south count
2 drown down town 5 towel vowel coward
3 sound found around 6 how now allow

b Which spelling pattern do you usually use:

1 before d, l or n? 3 before a vowel?
2 before nd, t, th and nt? 4 at the end of a word?

c Complete the spelling of these words. Then check in a dictionary.

1 ab__t 4 m__th 7 br__n
2 r__ 5 r__nd 8 cl__n
3 c__ncil 6 d __ bt

d Spellcheck. In pairs, take turns to choose ten words and test your partner's spelling.

NOTICE Expressions with *make*

5 a Complete the sentences from the article *Doing a Ratner* with these words. Then check on p102.

joke mistake speech comeback profit

1 While making a _____, he said some of his products were rubbish.
2 He made a _____ that his customers could buy "a pair of earrings for under a pound ..."
3 Since then, he has struggled to make a _____.
4 He set up a health club in 1996 and made a good _____.
5 I made a huge _____, which I regret, and I have to live with that fact.

b Try to think of more expressions with make.

make a decision, make a fuss, ...

c Choose five expressions with make and write questions to ask a partner. Then ask and answer your questions.

Self-assessment

Can you do these things in English? Circle a number on each line. 1 = I can't do this, 5 = I can do this well.

◉ talk about mistakes	1	2	3	4	5
◉ criticise past actions	1	2	3	4	5
◉ suggest alternatives	1	2	3	4	5
◉ talk about acts of kindness and bravery	1	2	3	4	5
◉ speculate about the past	1	2	3	4	5
◉ write a summary of information from different sources	1	2	3	4	5
◉ write an email giving information	1	2	3	4	5

- For Wordcards, reference and saving your work → e-Portfolio
- For more practice → Self-study Pack, Unit 13

14

14.1 goals
- understand news stories
- react to the news

In the news

Local news

LISTENING

1 What kinds of news stories do you find most interesting? Why?

- political stories
- crime stories
- business news
- health stories
- funny stories
- disaster stories

2 a ●3.29 Listen to the headlines of five news stories on a local radio station in North Queensland, Australia. How do you think each story will continue?

b ●3.30 Listen to the news stories. Were you right?

VOCABULARY
Understanding news stories

3 Can you remember the answers to the questions in boxes 1–5?
●3.30 Listen again to check.

1	Which residents were evacuated from their homes? How many firefighters were at the scene? What are police asking motorists to do?	3	What new law has been introduced? What do you now need if you want to cut down trees? Which organisations oppose the new laws?
2	How many police were involved in the incident? What did the police officers arrest the boy for? How many offences was the family charged with?	4	How many people currently live to 100 in Australia? What population change is predicted to happen?
		5	How was the crocodile injured? Who rescued it?

4 Match the highlighted expressions with the four categories below.

People	Emergencies	Crime	Politics
residents	evacuated from their homes	police	law

5 Are stories on the local news where you live similar to these?

What's interesting is ...

LISTENING

1 🔊 **3.31** Listen to two colleagues, Abby and Joe, talking about the news. Which two stories do they talk about? Had they both heard about the stories?

2 🔊 **3.31** Listen again and answer the questions.

1 What reminds Joe of a news story?
2 What are they shocked by in the story?
3 In the second story, what is Joe worried about?
4 What does Abby think is surprising?
5 What does Joe feel is important?

VOCABULARY

Reacting to the news

Luke Price, 14, from Townsville

3 **a** Complete the sentences from the conversations with the adjectives or verbs.

interesting   worries   funny   bothers   makes   important

What's
1 _____ is it's a grass fire, not a forest fire.
2 _____ is no one gets hurt.
3 _____ is the officers were going to arrest the boy ...

The thing that
4 _____ me angry is that normal kids can't have parties any more.
5 _____ me is how it started.
6 _____ me is the parents' attitude, not the boy!

b Which events are Abby and Joe talking about in sentences 1–6?

c Which adjective means *strange*? Which verb means *irritate* or *worry*?

> The thing that annoys me is ...

d Can you think of more verbs and adjectives to replace 1–6?

4 **a** Think about the other stories in the news report. Write one or two sentences about each one. Use the highlighted expressions in 3a.

b Talk about the stories together. Do you have the same opinions?

> What do you think about the tree clearing story?

> The thing that worries me is the environment.

PRONUNCIATION

Groups of words and linking

5 **a** 🔊 **3.32** Listen to this sentence from 3a. Practise saying it.

What's funny // is‿it's‿a grass fire // not‿a forest fire.

Notice how:
1 the groups of words make the sentence easier to understand.
2 words inside each group are linked.

b Look at sentences 2–6 from 3a and decide:

• which words form groups   • which words are linked

c 🔊 **3.33** Read the script on p162 and listen to check. Practise saying the sentences.

SPEAKING

6 Think of two or three interesting news stories. Make notes. Think about:

• who?   • what?   • where?   • when?   • other interesting information

7 In groups, talk together about your news stories. What do you think about each other's stories?

> Did you hear about that climber who was found three weeks after he went missing?

Fair play?

READING

1 Discuss the questions.

1 Do you think fair play is important in sport? Why? Why not?
2 Read the dictionary entry. How do you think genetic engineering could be used in sport?

> **genetic engineering**
> ▶ *noun* changing the structure of the genes of a living thing in order to make it healthier or stronger or more useful to humans. *Scientists have used genetic engineering to create two sheep that are exactly the same.*

2 a Do you think these statements are true or false? Talk together.

1 More and more drugs are being banned by sports authorities.
2 Scientists believe genetic engineering may become an alternative way to improve athletes' performance.
3 Professional athletes have never been permitted to use drugs.
4 In the future, researchers may be able to correct weak genes to make people healthier.
5 Genetic engineering is already a major problem in sport.

b Read the article to check.

Genetic engineering for athletes

1 Cyclist Alain Such has been suspended from the Ingotel cycling team for two years after a positive drugs test at the Institute of Drug Free Sport. "I am still in shock," said Didier Garcia, from Team Ingotel. "Alain joined our team last month and we had no idea that he was being investigated."

2 It's a story that has become more and more familiar in recent years, with the list of illegal drugs becoming longer and athletes continuing to look for legal and illegal ways to improve their performance. So it's no surprise to find that scientists are considering the possibility of using genetic engineering to further develop athletes' abilities. Dr Mohammad Farnood, a leading sports scientist from Cairo, Egypt, said: "It is thought that some athletes will look for other ways to improve performance apart from using drugs."

3 The use of drugs in sport has not always been illegal. In the Olympics in 1904, Thomas Hicks won the marathon after receiving an injection of strychnine (and some brandy) in the middle of the race. In fact, the first dose didn't revive him for long, so he was given another and, as a result, he collapsed soon after finishing. Another dose may well have killed him. Things are very different today. Drug tests and bans for athletes are becoming more and more frequent and some academics believe athletes may turn to genetic enhancement. "If genetics can improve performance with no risk of discovery," said Dr Farnood, "then it's likely to become common practice for athletes."

4 So, how would it work? Researchers are looking at the possibility of identifying 'athletic' genes and correcting weak ones. Put into practice, this would make a person healthier and, potentially, more capable of being athletic. Once scientists understand what the genes of top athletes look like, it might even become possible to identify 'athletic' genes in young people, and then money could be invested in children who have the most promising genes.

5 The fact that WADA (the World Anti-Doping Agency) is taking it seriously shows that genetic engineering in sport could become a major problem. However, there is another view in the genetic engineering debate.

6 "People are beginning to recognise that genetics can be used in many ways to benefit society, for instance in saving lives and in creating better-quality food for more people," Dr Farnood says. "Sport is only one example. So, those who offer themselves to be genetically engineered may be considered – in one sense – to be helping science and technology to move forward. Is it fair to use genetic engineering in sport? You could ask if it's fair for some runners to use the latest scientifically developed footwear. The key question is whether it's available to everyone."

3 Read the article again and answer the questions.

1 What happened to: Alain Such? Thomas Hicks?
2 What does the article say about:

- athletic genes?
- genetic engineering in sport?
- drug testing in sport?
- fairness in sport?

4 Talk together. Do you think that the use of genetic engineering in sport would be fair? Do you think it could benefit society? Why? Why not?

GRAMMAR
Passives

5 a Which sentences, A or B, are used in the article? Which are active? Which are passive?

> A The Institute of Drug Free Sport **has suspended** cyclist Alain Such from the Ingotel cycling team.
>
> B Cyclist Alain Such **has been suspended** from the Ingotel cycling team.
>
> A People **can use** genetics in many ways to benefit society.
>
> B Genetics **can be used** in many ways to benefit society.

b Why does the writer use the passive? Is the focus on:

a Alain Such or the Institute? (paragraph 1)   b genetics or people (p6)

6 Complete the sentences with the correct forms of be.

be + past participle	
The present simple: **The past simple:** **The present perfect:** **Modal verbs:**	It _____ thought that some athletes will look for other ways to improve performance. The first dose didn't revive him for long, so he _____ given another. Cyclist Alain Such _____ suspended from the Ingotel cycling team. Money could _____ invested in children who have the most promising genes.

7 Complete the sentences about news stories by choosing the active or passive past simple form of the verbs in brackets.

1 Apparently, the dinosaurs _____ (kill) off by a huge asteroid.
2 Did you hear that our hockey team _____ (win) gold?
3 I heard Meyer _____ (rob) of $7,000 after leaving the awards ceremony.
4 You know that journalist? He _____ (free) yesterday by the kidnappers.
5 It was a terrible match – we _____ (deserve) to lose.
6 The bank is saying that details of 24,000 clients _____ (steal) in the raid.
7 I'm reading about these sisters who _____ (separate) at birth.

Grammar reference
and practice, p145

Talking about news stories

LISTENING

1 **3.34** Listen to Melek and Tom talking about one of the news stories in 7.

1 Which story is it?
2 Tom mentions another article. How is it linked to the first story?

VOCABULARY

Talking about
news stories

2 Complete sentences 1–7 from the conversation with a–g. Then check in the script on p162.

1	Did you hear that thing	a	a while ago.
2	Was it the one about	b	these twins were part of an experiment.
3	I heard something about that.	c	in the news about the twins?
4	I read a similar article	d	Weren't they from New York?
5	It was talking about	e	the parents didn't know about it.
6	It actually said	f	the identical twins?
7	Yes, but apparently,	g	whether it's nature that makes us the way we are …

SPEAKING

3 You're going to discuss two articles about drugs in sport. Work in A/B pairs.

1 A, read the article on p122; B, read the article on p128. Underline the main ideas.
2 Think about your own opinions on the topic.

4 a Talk about your articles together. Do you agree with each other?

b Should drugs be allowed in sport? Why? Why not?

Choose a story for a news programme

TASK READING AND LISTENING

1 Read the advert. Why does NBS want a focus group?

Site map / Contacts / Useful Links / NPL

NBS is developing a new weekly programme called *The World This Week* covering interesting and entertaining stories from around the world. We need television enthusiasts aged between 18 and 65 to attend a meeting in order to share their views on what makes a good TV news programme today. During the meeting, we will ask you to discuss current stories in the news and to select one of the stories as the starting point for a half-hour programme.

If you're interested, please email Jennie asap at: jen@NBS-marketing.com

2 Read the summaries of two news stories provided by NBS for the focus group. Do you think either of the stories would make a good starting point for the programme? Why? Why not?

A

A gang of men have been arrested after kidnapping a Shanghai businessman from outside his home. The men, who demanded a huge ransom, are believed to have copied the idea from a TV show.

B

A new study claims that physically interactive computer games, such as Guitar Hero, are not just good entertainment. They can also help people with brain injuries and reduce obesity in children and adults.

3 a ● **3.35** Listen to three people discussing which story should make it onto the programme. Do they agree?

b ● **3.35** Listen again. What do they find most interesting about each story?

TASK VOCABULARY
Evaluating and selecting

4 a Which story are they talking about, A or B?

1 This one looks <u>good</u>. *promising*
2 I don't really <u>get it</u>.
3 Yeah, that <u>makes sense</u>.
4 Hm, I'm not <u>convinced</u>.
5 Personally, I'd <u>go for</u> this one.
6 That sounds <u>interesting</u>.
7 OK, so it's <u>got potential</u>.

promising ...

This one looks promising.

Yeah, that's right.

b Replace the <u>underlined</u> words and expressions in sentences 1–7 with these words and expressions with a similar meaning:

~~promising~~ possible entertaining choose understand sure seems reasonable

c Cover 4a. In pairs, look at 4b and try to remember the complete expressions.

TASK

5 Work in A/B/C groups. You're going to choose a story for NBS's new programme. Read your story and prepare to explain it: A, p122; B, p124; C, p126. Think about the language you need to:

- tell your group about a news story. *Apparently ...*
- react to a news story. *The thing that's interesting is ...*
- evaluate and select a story. *This one looks promising.*

6 Talk together about your stories. Choose one story for the programme.

7 Talk with other groups. Explain why you chose your story.

Keyword *see*

Meanings of *see*

1 Match the uses of see in the sentences with meanings A–D.

1 Anyone who saw the incident is asked to call Crime Stoppers. U14	A understand
2 You can see if somebody is lying by looking at their body language. U11	B find out / check
3 I can see why you're upset, but I don't think you appreciate how lucky you've been. U9	C notice with your eyes
4 The last time I saw you, you were going to study finance. U5	D meet up with

Did you see the news last night?

Yes, I did.

Did you hear about the ... ?

2 Find someone who:

1 saw the news last night.
2 sees their family most days.
3 prefers DVDs to seeing films at the cinema.
4 can always see how to put flat-pack furniture together.
5 likes to see what friends are doing online.
6 looks at the end of a book first to see if they want to read it.

Ask questions to find out more.

3 a How do you feel about adverts on TV?

b ● **3.36** Listen to Meninda and Richard talking about TV adverts. Who likes them? Who doesn't? What reasons do they give?

Patterns with *see*

4 a Look at the sentences from the conversation. In which pattern can see mean:

a understand, check or notice with your eyes?   b check?   c notice with your eyes?

A see someone do something	B see + if	C see + wh- word
I saw her drive past here the other day. I saw her come out of the supermarket yesterday.	If you give me the remote I'll see if I can find it. I'll just see if it's on another channel.	I'll see when it's on. I see what you mean. You can see what new stuff to buy.

b Discuss the questions.

1 What would you do if you were in the supermarket and you saw someone steal something?
2 When you watch TV, do you look at the guide to see what's on first?
3 When you're shopping, do you ever see if you can find things you've seen in adverts?
4 When's the last time you saw a friend do something silly, risky or funny? What was it?

Expressions with *see*

5 a Which meaning in 1 does see have in these expressions?

1 TV reality shows are stupid. I just don't see the point of them.
2 Personally, I don't see the problem of violence on TV. It just reflects real life.
3 I don't see the need for more TV channels. We already have enough.
4 I definitely see the attraction of not having a TV.
5 Children love a good story, whether it's in a book or on TV. I don't see the difference.

b Work alone. Do you agree or disagree with the opinions? Think about how to use the highlighted expressions to give your opinions.

c Discuss your ideas. Do you agree with each other?

Celia is leaving the NBS Marketing team, after five years.

1 Do you like surprise parties? Why? Why not?

2 a **3.37** Listen to Anya, Nadia and Jim arranging a leaving party for a colleague, Celia. What arrangements do they make?

b **3.37** While they talk about Celia's party, they also discuss other things. Listen again and make notes about:
1 Jim's party   2 DJ Carlos   3 the group Felony

c Read the conversation to check.

3 Look at highlighted expressions 1–10 in the conversation. Which of the expressions are used to:

1   interrupt?   2   return to the main topic?
3   change topic?

4 Complete these conversations with expressions from 3. There may be more than one possibility.

> **ANYA** Can I ask you about tickets for Felony, Jim?
> **JIM** Yeah, let's look on the website.
> **A** Oh, ¹…, do you think Nadia's OK?
> **J** Yeah, she seemed a bit stressed, didn't she?

> **NADIA** Are you coming to Li's party tonight, Jim?
> **JIM** Yeah, definitely. Oh, ³…, I booked The Meeting Point for Celia's party.
> **N** Oh, that's great! ⁴…, did you speak to Carlos?

> **JIM** Are you OK for tonight, Celia?
> **CELIA** Yes, thanks. It's just I'm feeling really sad about leaving. ²… , I'm looking forward to a nice dinner.
> **J** Oh, is there food? I thought …

> **MARK** OK, so, the room's booked for 30 people from 8.00 till late. And remember, it's a surprise!
> **JIM** Erm, ⁵… ?
> **M** Yeah, what's up?
> **J** Oh, nothing. It's just that I may be a bit late.

5 a You're going to arrange a party with a group. Choose one of these options:

- a birthday party   • a leaving party   • an end-of-term party   • a surprise party   • something else

b Work alone.

1   Decide when, where and what type of party you'd like it to be.
2   During the conversation, you must interrupt once. Think of a question you can ask when you interrupt.

c Talk with your group and arrange the party.

6 Tell the class what you've organised. Whose idea sounds the best?

ANYA Hey, everyone. We need to talk about Celia's leaving party.

NADIA Yes. Maybe we could book the Strada for dinner. Shall I give them a ring?

JIM Yeah, good idea.

NADIA Er, sorry, er, but ¹can I just say something?

ANYA Yeah, go on.

NADIA Well, dinner's OK, but Celia loves a good party. I think we should tell her it's a dinner but organise a surprise party.

JIM Yes, that's a great idea. Oh, ²by the way, I'm having a party this weekend, and you're all welcome to come.

NADIA Oh no, I can't. You should have told us earlier!

ANYA ³While we're on the subject of parties, did you hear what happened … ?

NADIA Look guys, I'm ⁴sorry to interrupt, but I've got to go in a minute.

ANYA Yeah, sorry. ⁵So, shall we organise a party then?

NADIA I think it's a good idea, yes. Who could we get to do the music?

JIM I know a good DJ, Carlos. Lovely guy. He's Mercé's boyfriend.

NADIA Really? I didn't know she was seeing someone.

JIM Yeah, they've been together a while now. But ⁶that's beside the point. He's a good DJ.

NADIA OK, then. Let's see if he's free.

JIM Oh, sorry, ⁷this is nothing to do with Celia, but did you know Felony is going to play at the Drill Room on the 19th?

ANYA Really? I'd love to go. Do you think there are any tickets left?

NADIA ⁸Excuse me, guys, but please ⁹can we keep to the point?

ANYA Oh, yeah, sorry, I just want to know if there are any tickets. Jim?

JIM Yeah, I think so. Let's talk about it later. ¹⁰Anyway, what about a venue?

ANYA There's a nice place upstairs at The Meeting Point.

Review

GRAMMAR Passives

1 a Put the words in order to make passive sentences.

1 built / <u>my home</u> / in the / was / <u>1970s</u>
2 by / given / me / my / my / to / was / <u>watch</u> / <u>wife</u>
3 are / made / my / of / <u>plastic</u> / <u>shoes</u>
4 was / <u>dad</u> / born / <u>1939</u> / in / my
5 completely / replaced / by / have / <u>email</u> / <u>letters</u> / been
6 used / <u>computers</u> / since / been / 2000 / have / <u>in my school</u>

b Change the <u>underlined</u> words to make the sentences true for you. Then compare with a partner.

VOCABULARY Understanding news stories

2 a Choose words from the box to complete the sentences about different news stories.

> evacuated   firefighters   arrested
> ~~residents~~   scene   motorists   opposed

1 Flooding in the north has forced hundreds of _residents_ to be _____ from their homes.
2 The Liberal party has _____ the new laws to ban street noise after midnight.
3 Police are advising _____ to avoid driving this morning.
4 A 21-year-old woman has been _____ for assault after she attacked a police officer this morning.
5 Fire has broken out at a warehouse in the Freshfield Business Estate. 50 _____ are at the _____.

b Write five sentences like 1–5 about news stories. They can be true or not.

c Take turns to listen to each other's sentences. Which stories do you think are true?

CAN YOU REMEMBER? Unit 13 – Acts of kindness and bravery

3 a Choose the correct preposition in each question.

1 Do you think parents should leave all their money to/for their children?
2 Do you think it's important to thank people of/for helping you?
3 How often do you ask people to do favours to/for you? What kind of favours?
4 Do you think parents usually think with/of their children before themselves?
5 Do you think parents should help their children about/with homework?
6 Do you think children should help their parents about/with the rent when they're earning money?

b Ask and answer the questions.

Extension

SPELLING AND SOUNDS /aɪ/

4 a ⏺3.38 Listen and use i, y or igh to make the /aɪ/ sound in these words. Then check in a dictionary.

1 cr__me   dec__de   t__me   outs__de
2 __dea   __cy   __rish   __sland
3 b__   cr__   fr__   Jul__
4 fl__t   f__t   l__t   br__t

b Which spelling pattern, i, y or igh, do you usually use:

1 at the start of words?
2 in the middle of most words, often with e at the end?
3 in the middle of some words, before t?
4 at the end of most words?

c ⏺3.39 Spellcheck. Listen and write ten words. Then check your spelling on p163.

NOTICE Common passive expressions in the news

5 a Choose the correct past participles in sentences 1–5 from news stories in the unit.

1 We had no idea that he was being revealed / investigated. p112
2 The family was arrested / charged with 10 offences. ⏺3.30
3 There was a story on the news this morning of a 14-year-old who was attacked / arrested for assault. ⏺3.31
4 Two police officers were involved / made in an incident yesterday morning. ⏺3.30
5 She said that 'drug-cheats' should be given / charged huge financial penalties. p128

b Work in pairs. Think of crime stories in the news that you've heard about recently. Prepare to talk about them using some of the passive expressions in 5a.

c Change partners. Tell each other about the crime stories. Have you heard about each other's stories?

Self-assessment

Can you do these things in English? Circle a number on each line. 1 = I can't do this, 5 = I can do this well.

◎ understand news stories	1	2	3	4	5
◎ react to the news	1	2	3	4	5
◎ tell someone about a news story	1	2	3	4	5
◎ evaluate options and choose one	1	2	3	4	5
◎ participate in a discussion	1	2	3	4	5
◎ interrupt politely	1	2	3	4	5

• For Wordcards, reference and saving your work → e-Portfolio
• For more practice → Self-study Pack, Unit 14

Activities

Unit 1, p12, Explore writing 3b

KEY: L A Seadan ★★★★★   Aliya Bakaev ★★★☆☆

Unit 8, p65, Lost 4a

B You finally come to a road. It's not a big road, but every few minutes a car comes past. There's a path leading away from the road and a hill on the other side. There are some cows with horns on the hill. Or are they bulls? Discuss what to do.

- **E** (p121) go towards the path • **T** (p133) try to get a lift from a passing car • **N** (p127) walk up the hill

Unit 9, p76, Explore writing 5

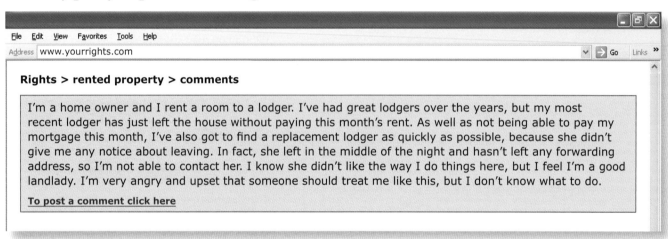

File Edit View Favorites Tools Help

Address | www.yourrights.com   ✓ | → Go | Links »

Rights > rented property > comments

I'm a home owner and I rent a room to a lodger. I've had great lodgers over the years, but my most recent lodger has just left the house without paying this month's rent. As well as not being able to pay my mortgage this month, I've also got to find a replacement lodger as quickly as possible, because she didn't give me any notice about leaving. In fact, she left in the middle of the night and hasn't left any forwarding address, so I'm not able to contact her. I know she didn't like the way I do things here, but I feel I'm a good landlady. I'm very angry and upset that someone should treat me like this, but I don't know what to do.

To post a comment click here

Unit 4, p30, Accident-prone 1a

A = 1 point   B = 2 points   C = 3 points   D = 4 points

If you scored ...

7–10 You must spend a lot of time feeling anxious. You should relax and enjoy life more.

11–16 You're generally a careful person. You aren't likely to have many accidents.

17–23 Think about what you're doing. You're likely to cause an accident if you're not more careful.

24–28 You obviously enjoy living dangerously, but you need to take care.

Unit 8, p65, Lost 4a

C There are lights on in the house, but there's a sign on the garden gate saying 'Beware of the dog'. Discuss what to do.

- **K** (p125) go back and follow the river • **R** (p131) knock on the front door • **H** (p123) shout from the gate

Unit 3, p22, Great ideas 2 (Student B)

His goal was to make it simple to use and beautiful to look at. The result was the iPod.

1 There are two things you need to know about Jonathan Ive, inventor of the iPod music player and the iMac computer. First, he changed the way we listen to music and made computers much more attractive. Second, he may be one of the most important industrial designers of our time, but he is rather shy and he does not usually do interviews.

2 It is all a bit odd really. But then Ive is no ordinary designer. In 1998, as head of design at Apple in San Francisco, he changed the way we see computers with the original iMac. And then came the iPod. In 2000, Ive and his team of designers realised you can fit a computer hard drive into a box the size of a deck of playing cards and use it to store thousands of songs. For the first time it was possible to carry your music collection in your pocket. Today, there are 30 million iPods out there. Its success was not just about clever electronics. Critics said it looked fantastic and was surprisingly easy to use.

3 After all the pre-interview warnings, it is a bit of a shock to meet Jonathan Ive. He is a charming and relaxed figure in his late 30s and he obviously believes he has the best job in the world. 'Our goals are simple,' he says. 'We genuinely try to make the very best product that we can. We have a belief that we can solve our problems and make our products better and better.' Ive says he is inspired by the everyday stuff that surrounds him. The aim, he says, is to create beautiful gadgets that can be used without looking at the instruction book.

4 You can sense that he is delighted – if a little surprised – by all the praise. But what gives him the most pleasure is when people tell him their iPod stories. 'What's really great is when someone you don't know comes up and wants to talk about what the iPod meant for them. That's really fantastic,' he says. 'At the end of the day, it's all about the music.'

3 a Complete the summary of this article.

1 Ive invented ... and the ... but he is ...
2 The iPod made it possible for people ... for the first time.
3 Ive's aim is ...
4 He loves it when ...

Unit 5, p42, Target activity 4a (Student A)

1 At school you wanted to become a lawyer. But you didn't. Why not?
2 Now, you're a/an _____ and you live in _____ with _____ .
3 You've just _____ and you plan to _____ .
4 You remember that B wanted to learn Japanese when he/she was at school. Ask B if he/she did it and what he/she is doing now.

Unit 3, p26, Target activity 5 (Student A)

Your product	Complete with your ideas
Name – 'Easy umbrella' *Idea* – sell cheap umbrellas at train stations *Market* – people who forget to take their umbrellas in the morning, and then find it's raining. They can buy a disposable cheap umbrella from the machine at the station.	*Your experience:* ... *Why you're optimistic about the product:* ... *Your concerns about the product:* ... *Hopes, dreams and ambitions:* ...

Unit 8, p66, Target activity 5 (Role play 1: Student A)

Unit 8, p66, Target activity 6b (Role play 2: Student A)

Unit 8, p65, Lost 4a

D The road is further away than you expected. You pass a sign for a campsite. You can still see the river as it bends around the hill. Discuss what to do.

• **K** (p125) go to the river • **B** (p118) continue looking for the road • **P** (p128) go towards the campsite

Unit 12, p95, Giving a talk 5a (Student A)

Technical mountaineering course (TMC)

- alpine mountain climbing course
- very popular training centre in New Zealand
- lots of famous climbers started career here
- previous experience not necessary
- participants must be fit and ready to learn
- participants must have basic rope skills (e.g. rock climbing, caving)
- learn new skills and practise in real alpine terrain
- at end of course, participants will be able to climb almost all alpine terrain safely and with confidence
- 10 day-course
- NZ$3150 per person
- includes all meals, transport, accommodation, technical gear

Unit 4, p33, Describing an experience 3 (Student A)

A volcanic eruption

"When I was still living in Mexico, in my town which is in the west of Mexico, there was a volcanic eruption one day. There had been some warning signs, but it was still a surprise when it erupted. I could actually see the volcano from my house. I could even see red lava coming out of it. My friends and I were all taking pictures and phoning each other about it. It was a big event. No one was hurt as the volcano was so far away from the nearest town, so it was just a really interesting experience for everyone who saw it." **ASTRID**

Answer these questions by making notes.

1 Where was Astrid at the time?
2 What could she see?
3 How did her friends react?
4 What were the effects of the eruption?
5 How did she feel about it?

Unit 8, p65, Lost 4a

E The path takes you along the side of a wood. There is a path through the wood, but you can't see where it goes. There is a sign pointing to a village, but you don't recognise the name. Discuss what to do.

- **Q** (p130) go into the woods   • **P** (p128) continue along the path   • **M** (p127) follow the sign to the village

Unit 5, p42, Target activity 4a (Student B)

1 At school you wanted to learn Japanese and move to Japan, but you didn't. Why not?
2 Now, you're a/an _____ and you live in _____ with _____.
3 You've just _____ and you plan to _____.
4 You remember that C planned to start a business after school. Ask C if he/she did it and what he/she is doing now.

Unit 9, p74, Target activity 6a (Student A)

1 **Rooms** You'd like to swap rooms with B. His room has a phone connection and you need the Internet to study.
2 **TV** Do you want a TV in the living room? Why? Why not?
3 **Shopping and chores** Is it best to share food? What about the bills? Should there be a rota for shopping, cooking and other household chores? If not, what's the alternative?
4 **Noise** How do you feel about noise and having parties? Should there be rules?

Unit 8, p65, Lost 4a

F The fields go on and on. You're getting tired. You think you can hear a road ahead, and you can see another house on the horizon. Discuss what to do.

- **D** (p120) carry on towards the road   • **S** (p132) go back and ask the man   • **C** (p118) investigate the house

Activities

Unit 14, p113, Talking about news stories 3 (Student A)

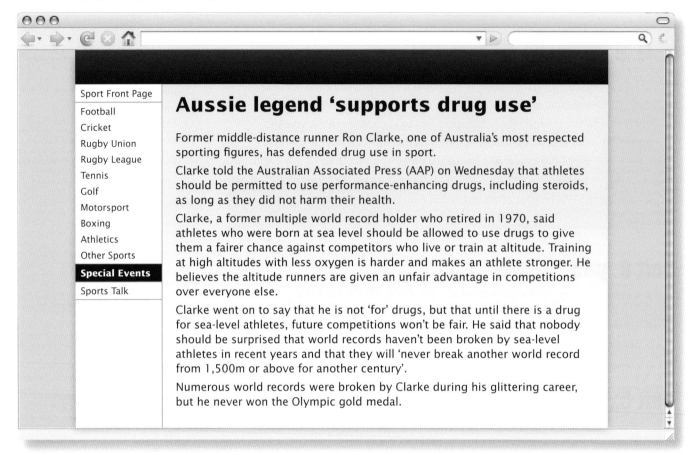

> **Aussie legend 'supports drug use'**
>
> Former middle-distance runner Ron Clarke, one of Australia's most respected sporting figures, has defended drug use in sport.
>
> Clarke told the Australian Associated Press (AAP) on Wednesday that athletes should be permitted to use performance-enhancing drugs, including steroids, as long as they did not harm their health.
>
> Clarke, a former multiple world record holder who retired in 1970, said athletes who were born at sea level should be allowed to use drugs to give them a fairer chance against competitors who live or train at altitude. Training at high altitudes with less oxygen is harder and makes an athlete stronger. He believes the altitude runners are given an unfair advantage in competitions over everyone else.
>
> Clarke went on to say that he is not 'for' drugs, but that until there is a drug for sea-level athletes, future competitions won't be fair. He said that nobody should be surprised that world records haven't been broken by sea-level athletes in recent years and that they will 'never break another world record from 1,500m or above for another century'.
>
> Numerous world records were broken by Clarke during his glittering career, but he never won the Olympic gold medal.

Navigation menu: Sport Front Page · Football · Cricket · Rugby Union · Rugby League · Tennis · Golf · Motorsport · Boxing · Athletics · Other Sports · **Special Events** · Sports Talk

Unit 8, p65, Lost 4a

G The man doesn't understand a word you're saying, and his language is unfamiliar to you. You write down the name of the place where you're staying, and he points towards the river. You can hear a road somewhere nearby. Discuss what to do.

- **K** (p125) go to the river • **D** (p120) go towards the road • **F** (p121) follow the footpath you're on

Unit 14, p114, Target activity 5 (Student A)

Is money in sport out of control?

This week saw the beginning of an unpleasant new development in the financing of sport.

Baseball star Dustin Pedroia signed a new six-year contract worth a record $40.5m, which will keep him at the Red Sox until 2014. Pedroia was quoted as saying, "I'm extremely excited – I definitely want to be here a long time."

With that sort of wage, I'm not surprised.

It was also reported this week that Manchester City, now the wealthiest football team in the world, offered £129 million for Real Madrid goalkeeper Ikar Casillias. And on top of this, they were willing to pay him £11 million a season to play.

What with the recent controversy surrounding cricket players joining the Indian Cricket League because of the vast sums of money available and the recent trend of Olympic (amateur) boxers to turn professional, I'm starting to wonder what sport really is about today.

Unit 8, p65, Lost 4a

H "Hello!" you shout, and a woman comes out of the house. You tell her the name of your holiday house and she points towards the river. "Right, then carry on," she says, and goes back into the house. You're not sure if she means you should go over the bridge you can see over the river. You can hear traffic in the distance. Discuss what to do.

- **K** (p125) go along this side of the river
- **M** (p127) go over the bridge
- **O** (p128) go towards the traffic noise

Unit 5, p40, Fate? 2 (Student B)

It was supposed to be this great party to celebrate my twenty-fifth birthday. We were going to have this big dinner and then clear the floor for some dancing. All my friends were coming and it was going to be just perfect. Anyway, on the afternoon of the party, we were getting everything ready when suddenly we heard this huge crash. At the same moment, the electricity went and suddenly we were all standing there in the dark. It was pouring with rain outside and we could hear thunder. I went outside to see if the rest of the street had had a power cut, but the street lights were on and everything. I looked back up at the building. The roof had caved in. I couldn't believe it. I went into the corner shop next door and asked what was going on.

"Did you see that?" the man said.

"What?" I asked.

"The hall was struck by lightning. There was this incredible bolt of lightning and it tore into the roof. Incredible."

I remember thinking: it's not incredible, it's ruined my party. Because now there was no way we could have the party in the hall. It didn't have a roof. I was really upset at the time, but it was no use ruining everyone's evening, so we ended up going to a nice restaurant in town and I soon cheered up. By the end of the night it just seemed really funny. Anyway, later that night at the restaurant, I got chatting to this guy in there and we hit it off straight away. Before we left he asked me out on a date. A year later he asked me to marry him and we've been married now for over fifteen years. I'm sure it's no coincidence that I met him on that day. That's when we always celebrate our 'anniversary' – not the day we got married, but the day the lightning struck.

Find answers to these questions in the story.

1 What had Maggie planned to do that evening?
2 What happened inside the building?
3 What was happening outside?
4 What did the man in the shop tell her?

5 How did she feel at the time?
6 How did she feel about it later that night?
7 What happened later that night?

Cover the story and think about how to tell A the story. Use the questions to help you.

Unit 11, p90, Target activity 5 (Student A)

You heard that your friend, Frank, might lose his job. You had a conversation with Frank's wife yesterday. She said:
- He can't sleep because he's worried he might lose his job.
- He's often late for work because he oversleeps. This makes his boss angry.
- She's met his boss. He isn't a very nice person.
- He's always worked really hard and done well in previous jobs.

Unit 8, p65, Lost 4a

I The woman laughs when you tell her where you need to go. "That's funny," she says, "that's my nephew's place. You must be the people he's got in this week." She draws you a map, going back and through the woods. You reach the house in just ten minutes. Well done!

Unit 7, p60, Explore writing 5a

Grand Hyatt Dubai
- 674 rooms and suites with oversized beds
- Airport limousine service
- 8 restaurants, 1 café and 2 bars
- MIX – Dubai's only super-nightclub
- 2 ballrooms
- 11 meeting rooms and 2 boardrooms
- Indoor and outdoor swimming pools
- Tennis and squash courts
- 450-metre jogging track

Mina A' Salam
- The 'gateway' property to Madinat Jumeirah, The Arabian Resort – Dubai
- Access to traditional souk and waterpark
- Dubai's only hotel in the authentic style of Arabian architecture
- Three superb restaurants and five bars and lounges
- Beautifully appointed in traditional Arabic style
- Large lounge areas with access to outdoor terraces
- Luxury spa with treatments
- Indoor and outdoor facilities for events

Unit 8, p65, Lost 4a

J You go up to the tent and say, "Hello, is there anyone there?" After a few seconds a sleepy-looking child comes out. You ask him if he knows the way to your holiday house. He points to a dark wood. You can hear a road nearby. Discuss what to do.

- **N** (p127) go back to the footpath • **O** (p128) look for the road • **Q** (p130) go into the wood

Unit 14, p114, Target activity 5 (Student B)

Russian and US satellites crash in space

NASA scientists are closely monitoring the skies after two satellites crashed into each other over Siberia in what experts have said is the first collision of its kind.

The accident, which took place more than 400 miles above the Earth's surface on Tuesday, has left a large cloud of debris floating in space. NASA officials are keeping watch to see if the debris could endanger other spacecraft, although they said it was unlikely that the International Space Station could be damaged.

"It will be weeks at least before the true size of these clouds is known," a NASA spokesperson said in a warning message. Air Force Lieutenant Colonel Les Kodlick, said, "We believe it's the first time that two satellites have crashed in space." Both satellites were used for telecommunications.

The crash has added some 500 to 600 new bits of debris (now being monitored by the command's Joint Space Operations Center) to the 18,000 or so other man-made objects already in space.

Unit 9, p74 Target activity 6a (Student B)

1 **Rooms** You'd like to swap rooms with C. He has the biggest room and you have a lot of stuff.
2 **TV** Do you want a TV in the living room? Why? Why not?
3 **Shopping and chores** Is it best to share food? What about the bills? Should there be a rota for shopping, cooking and other household chores? If not, what's the alternative?
4 **Noise** How do you feel about noise and having parties? Should there be rules?

Unit 12, p95, Giving a talk 5a (Student B)

Photography courses

- learn how to get the most from your camera
- learn how to adjust, edit and improve your photos
- we will help you turn good photographs into great ones
- one-day courses from €50, including field trips with transport provided
- no more than ten students per tutor
- access to your own computer and work area

- professional and passionate photographers to teach you all the skills you need
- learn about what camera equipment to buy
- never have a fuzzy picture again
- never have 'red-eye' flash photographs
- learn how moving just centimetres can turn 'dull' into 'drama'
- learn why moving yourself is better than moving your subject

Unit 11, p90, Target activity 7

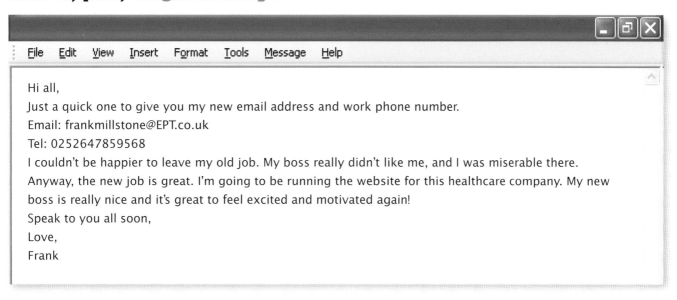

File   Edit   View   Insert   Format   Tools   Message   Help

Hi all,

Just a quick one to give you my new email address and work phone number.

Email: frankmillstone@EPT.co.uk

Tel: 0252647859568

I couldn't be happier to leave my old job. My boss really didn't like me, and I was miserable there.

Anyway, the new job is great. I'm going to be running the website for this healthcare company. My new boss is really nice and it's great to feel excited and motivated again!

Speak to you all soon,

Love,

Frank

Unit 8, p65, Lost 4a

K You follow the path along the river, past a bridge, until you come to a locked gate and a sign saying 'Private – Keep out'. Discuss what to do.

- **F** (p121) go back towards the fields   • **N** (p127) climb over the gate   • **P** (p128) cross the bridge

Unit 5, p42, Target activity 4a (Student C)

1   At school you wanted to start a business, but you didn't. Why not?
2   Now, you're a/an _____ and you live in _____ with _____.
3   You've just _____ and you plan to _____.
4   You remember that A planned to become a lawyer after school.
    Ask A if he/she did it. Ask about what he/she is doing now.

Unit 8, p66, Target activity 5 (Role play 1: Student B)

Unit 8, p66, Target activity 6b (Role play 2: Student B)

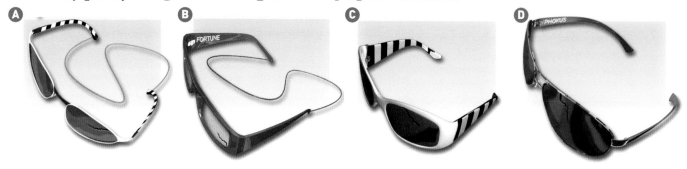

Unit 8, p65, Lost 4a

L   The map the man draws points you back the way you came, over the fields. You're still not sure he's understood you. You can hear what sounds like a road. The man is cycling away in the other direction. Discuss what to do.

• **F** (p121) follow the map   • **D** (p120) go towards the road   • **B** (p118) follow the man

Unit 14, p114, Target activity 5 (Student C)

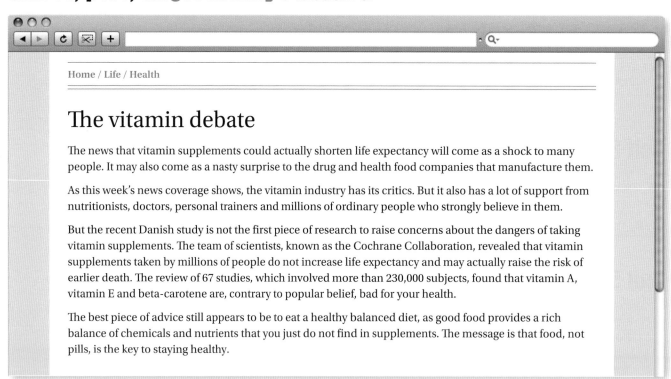

Home / Life / Health

The vitamin debate

The news that vitamin supplements could actually shorten life expectancy will come as a shock to many people. It may also come as a nasty surprise to the drug and health food companies that manufacture them.

As this week's news coverage shows, the vitamin industry has its critics. But it also has a lot of support from nutritionists, doctors, personal trainers and millions of ordinary people who strongly believe in them.

But the recent Danish study is not the first piece of research to raise concerns about the dangers of taking vitamin supplements. The team of scientists, known as the Cochrane Collaboration, revealed that vitamin supplements taken by millions of people do not increase life expectancy and may actually raise the risk of earlier death. The review of 67 studies, which involved more than 230,000 subjects, found that vitamin A, vitamin E and beta-carotene are, contrary to popular belief, bad for your health.

The best piece of advice still appears to be to eat a healthy balanced diet, as good food provides a rich balance of chemicals and nutrients that you just do not find in supplements. The message is that food, not pills, is the key to staying healthy.

Unit 8, p65, Lost 4a

M You come to a small village. A middle-aged woman is walking down the high street. Discuss what to do.

- **O** (p128) go through the village   • **D** (p120) go back to the main road   • **I** (p124) ask the woman

Unit 8, p66, Target activity 6c (Role play 3: Student A)

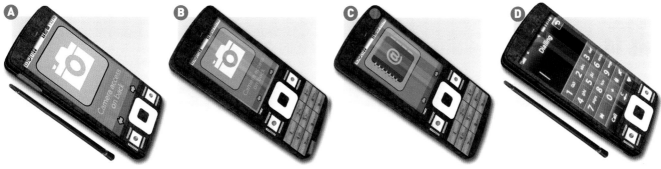

Unit 8, p66, Target activity 6c (Role play 4: Student A)

Unit 8, p65, Lost 4a

N The path takes you up a hill, from where you can see a small house and another footpath. There's a sign saying 'Private property' in front of the footpath. You think you can hear a road across the fields. Discuss what to do.

- **C** (p118) go towards the house   • **D** (p120) look for the road   • **E** (p121) follow the footpath

Unit 10, p81, Making a complaint 8a (Student A)

You call a helpline to complain about the _____ you bought from the website.
Before your call today, you …
- wrote _____ emails.
- called the helpline _____ times – no answer.
- waited _____ on hold.
Your order number is 9564R.
Ask for a new _____ .

Unit 10, p81, Making a complaint 8c (Student A)

Ask for the order number.
Tell the customer it takes _____ working days to receive replacement goods.

Unit 11, p90, Target activity 5 (Student B)

You heard that your friend, Frank, might lose his job. You spoke to Frank yesterday. He said:

- His boss isn't very nice. He gives Frank too much work.
- His boss also ignores Frank in meetings.
- Frank wants to find another job but doesn't have a lot of confidence because of his boss.
- Frank's got an interview for a job but doesn't want his boss to find out.

Unit 14, p113, Talking about news stories 3 (Student B)

Athletes need to speak out against drugs, says Ulmer

Sarah Ulmer, poster girl for Drug Free Sport NZ, has said that athletes need to do more in the fight against drug use in sport.

"I think we need more current athletes being more vocal about drug use and about how they feel competing against drug cheats."

Ulmer, an international athlete herself who has represented New Zealand on the world stage, said that the sport needed to create a stronger anti-drugs culture.

"If a drugs 'culture' exists in certain sports, then we as clean athletes should work to create a far stronger anti-drugs culture to oppose it. I think this is something that could have a huge effect." She said that 'drug-cheats' should be given huge financial penalties, and that more athletes should be banned for life "to really get the drug-takers thinking about what is at stake if they cheat". She said that similar campaigns could be adopted by other countries.

Unit 8, p65, Lost 4a

O   You still can't find a main road or a sign which leads to your village. The footpath forks, with left taking you into a wood, and right going up a hill. Suddenly you see a woman walking away from you across a field. Discuss what to do.

- **B** (p118) go right, up the hill   • **Q** (p130) go into the wood   • **I** (p124) ask the woman for help

Unit 3, p26, Target activity 5 (Student B)

Your service	Complete with your ideas
Name – www.cookshare.com *Idea* – launch a website which is like www.youtube.com, but for cooks. People can upload their videos about cooking and their recipes. *Market* – young people interested in cooking.	*Your experience:* … *Why you're optimistic about the product:* … *Your concerns about the product:* … *Hopes, dreams and ambitions:* …

Unit 8, p65, Lost 4a

P   You come to a small campsite with a tent and a caravan in it. You can hear two people shouting inside. Discuss what to do.

- **R** (p131) knock on the caravan door   • **J** (p124) try the tent   • **M** (p127) carry on through the site

Unit 10, p82, Target activity 4a (Student A)

Read about the problem and then do 1–4.

Your neighbour plays loud music in the evenings.
- Your children can't sleep.
- You can't hear your TV properly.
- The problem started a long time ago but is worse now.
- You made some helpful suggestions, e.g. that your neighbour should wear headphones.
- A month ago, your neighbour said: "I'm sorry. I'll turn the music down."
- You've knocked on your neighbour's door twice this week to ask him to turn it down, but he didn't answer.

Think about language from the unit you can use to:
1 talk about how long the problem has existed.
2 say how many times something has happened.
3 say if there have been any changes or results.
4 soften what you want to say.

Unit 10, p82, Target activity 4b (Student A)

Read about the problem and add your own ideas to 2–4.

Your neighbour's unhappy that you and your family and friends park your cars in front of her home.
1 It's a shared parking area.
2 Your neighbour doesn't need the space because …
3 You and your family and friends only park there when …
4 After your neighbour talked to you, you …

Think about <u>softeners</u> you can use in the conversation.

Unit 4, p33, Describing an experience 3 (Student B)

An earthquake

"The historical event I remember most vividly is a big earthquake in Mexico City in 1985. I was about five years old and I remember my mum was about to drive us to school, er, when I noticed that all the lamps were shaking and the furniture was moving. I didn't really understand what was happening. We went out of the house and stayed in the garden and we didn't go to school that day. Later on, we found out that our grandfather, who actually lived in the city centre, had gone out from his building early in the morning and when he came back everything was destroyed and he didn't have a house or neighbours or anywhere to go to, so it was very sad and shocking."
NURIA

Answer these questions by making notes.

1 What was Nuria doing at the time?
2 What could she see?
3 How did the earthquake affect Nuria's day?
4 What happened to her grandfather?
5 How did Nuria feel about the earthquake?

Activities

Unit 8, p65, Lost 4a

Q The woods are dark at first, but soon open out and the path takes you up a steep hill. As you get to the top and look down, you start to recognise the scene and realise that you're looking straight down at your holiday house. Well done, you made it!

Unit 10, p82, Target activity 4a (Student B)

Read about the problem and prepare to speak with your neighbour.

> **You listen to music in the evenings. Your neighbour doesn't like the noise. Think about softeners you can use to say:**
> 1   you're a musician. It's part of your job to listen to and learn new music.
> 2   you don't think it's a problem. It's nice to hear music. It's better than other types of noise.
> 3   you might be prepared to play music only during the day or stop playing it at a reasonable time.
> 4   you don't think your neighbour's suggestions are practical, e.g. that you wear headphones.

Unit 10, p82, Target activity 4b (Student B)

Read about the problem and add your own ideas to 1. Then do 2.

> **1   Your neighbour and his/her family and friends park their cars in front of your home.**
> - This means you …
> - You're annoyed because …
> - The problem started …
> - When it started, your neighbour said: …
> - You've talked to him/her about the problem …
>
> **2   Think about language from the unit you can use to:**
> 1   talk about how long the problem has existed.
> 2   say how many times something has happened.
> 3   say if there have been any changes or results.
> 4   soften what you want to say.

Unit 10, p79, False memories 6b

remind /rɪmaɪnd/
> ▶ *verb 1*: to make someone remember something, or remember to do something: ▷ [+ to do sth] *He reminded the children to wash their hands.* ▷ [+ question word] *Remind me what we're supposed to be doing tomorrow.* ▷ [+ that] *I reminded Jill that the conference had been cancelled.*

know /nəʊ/
> ▶ *verb 1*: to have knowledge or information about something in your mind: *'How old is she?' 'I don't know.'* ▷ [+ question word] *Do you know where the station is?* ▷ [+ that] *I knew that she was lying.*

understand /ʌndəstænd/
> ▶ *verb 1*: to know the meaning of something that someone says: *She explained everything and I understand now.* ▷ [+ that] *formal* used to say that you believe something is true because someone has told you it is: *I understand that you're interested in borrowing some money from us.* ▷ [+ question word] *I understand what you mean.*

find (sth) out /faɪnd aʊt/
> ▶ *phrasal verb*: to get information about something or to learn a fact for the first time: *How did you find out about the party?* ▷ [+ question word] *I'll go and find out what's going on outside.* ▷ [+ that] *She found out too late that the train had been cancelled.*

Unit 10, p81, Making a complaint 8a (Student B)

Ask for the order number.
Tell the customer it takes _____ working days to receive replacement goods.

Unit 10, p81, Making a complaint 8c (Student B)

You call a helpline to complain about the _____ you bought from the website.
Before your call today, you …

○ wrote _____ emails.
○ called the helpline _____ times – no answer.
○ waited _____ on hold.

Your order number is 2697K.
Ask for a new _____ .

Unit 8, p65, Lost 4a

R You knock on the door and hear a loud growl. A large dog is running straight at you. You need to get out of here fast! Discuss what to do.

• **F** (p121) run towards the fields   • **K** (p125) run towards the river   • **P** (p128) run towards the footpath

Unit 12, p95, Giving a talk 5a (Student C)

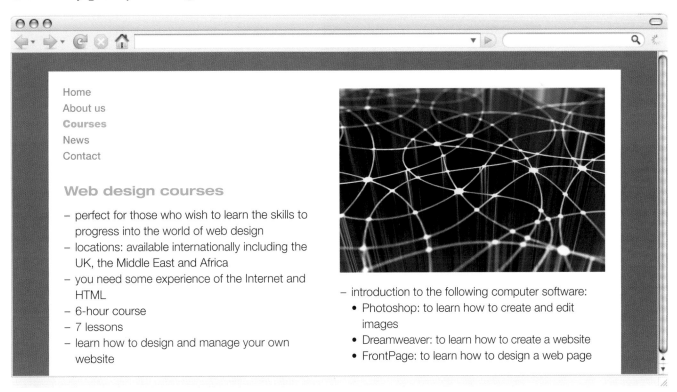

Home
About us
Courses
News
Contact

Web design courses

– perfect for those who wish to learn the skills to progress into the world of web design
– locations: available internationally including the UK, the Middle East and Africa
– you need some experience of the Internet and HTML
– 6-hour course
– 7 lessons
– learn how to design and manage your own website

– introduction to the following computer software:
  • Photoshop: to learn how to create and edit images
  • Dreamweaver: to learn how to create a website
  • FrontPage: to learn how to design a web page

Unit 9, p74, Target activity 6a (Student C)

1 **Rooms** You'd like to stay in your room. You don't need a big room but you enjoy the view.
2 **TV** Do you want a TV in the living room? Why? Why not?
3 **Shopping and chores** Is it best to share food? What about the bills? Should there be a rota for shopping, cooking and other household chores? If not, what's the alternative?
4 **Noise** How do you feel about noise and having parties? Should there be rules?

Unit 11, p90, Target activity 5 (Student C)

You heard that your friend, Frank, might lose his job. You had a conversation with Frank's friend, Penny, recently. She said:
- She knows someone who worked with him five years ago. He lost his job then too.
- Frank finds his job boring so he doesn't work very hard.
- He should find another job.
- His boss knows everyone in the business. It might be difficult for him to find a job.

Unit 13, p108, Explore writing 4

Friday / Saturday night + breakfast

Hotel du nord is located near the Notre Dame, between two famous streets, Saint Michel and Saint Germain. All the rooms facing the street have an incredible view of Saint-Severin, a Gothic church built between the 13th and 15th centuries. Those facing the courtyard have a view of the rooftops of Paris. The entire hotel is elegantly furnished, and the interior has real 17th-century decor. The rooms have all the modern amenities and are designed

Shopping!

Department store heaven:
Le Bon Marché

It is only in Paris that a department store can have hundreds of designer labels desired by thousands of shoppers, yet still feel like a boutique. Le Bon Marché (meaning cheap, though that's not entirely true) is an old Parisian institution in a modern building. There's also a cosmetics department, men's clothing and a gorgeous home section. Just can't get enough? The Galleries Lafayette and Le Printemps are only a Metro ride away.

After an early dinner, take advantage of the nocturnes; most museums have late openings once or twice a week until 9 or 10pm.

Louvre?

Techno on the river: Batofar

It's been going for years, but Batofar is still the place to go in Paris for techno fans. On a boat that is permanently moored, you won't go sailing down the river, but you will dance till dawn with a lot of Parisians.

+ Davide, Amelie, Jean-Marie and François. 10pm

Cultural wining and dining: L'Entrepôt

This hip arts centre feeds the mind with exhibitions, cinema and live concerts, and the body with delicious French cuisine. Listen to hot young bands over a plate of boeuf bourguignon, salmon with roasted courgettes or lamb with Provençal vegetables. Or choose a quieter meal and a cocktail in the romantic courtyard. On Sundays there are plenty of delicious sweets and savouries at the €25 brunch buffet. Reservations recommended.

Open: Daily 9am-12am (until 1am during concerts) Cost: €25 for Sunday brunch; €35 for à la carte

Sunday, 12.30pm

Unit 8, p65, Lost 4a

S   The man doesn't understand you. He is speaking a language which you don't know. Discuss what to do.

- **L** (p126) get him to draw you a map
- **G** (p122) try again to make him understand
- **F** (p121) go back towards the fields

Unit 8, p66, Target activity 6c (Role play 3: Student B)

Unit 8, p66, Target activity 6c (Role play 4: Student B)

A   B   C   D

Unit 8, p65, Lost 4a

T   After ten minutes, a car stops and picks you up. You tell the driver the name of your holiday house, and he types it into his sat nav. It's only five minutes' drive away. You're back at last. Well done!

Unit 12, p95, Giving a talk 4a (Student D)

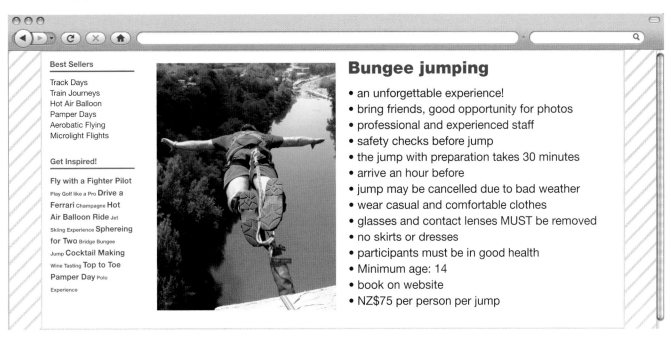

Best Sellers

Track Days
Train Journeys
Hot Air Balloon
Pamper Days
Aerobatic Flying
Microlight Flights

Get Inspired!

Fly with a Fighter Pilot Play Golf like a Pro Drive a Ferrari Champagne Hot Air Balloon Ride Jet Skiing Experience Sphereing for Two Bridge Bungee Jump Cocktail Making Wine Tasting Top to Toe Pamper Day Polo Experience

Bungee jumping

- an unforgettable experience!
- bring friends, good opportunity for photos
- professional and experienced staff
- safety checks before jump
- the jump with preparation takes 30 minutes
- arrive an hour before
- jump may be cancelled due to bad weather
- wear casual and comfortable clothes
- glasses and contact lenses MUST be removed
- no skirts or dresses
- participants must be in good health
- Minimum age: 14
- book on website
- NZ$75 per person per jump

Grammar reference and practice

1 TALKING ABOUT THE PRESENT

MEANING

Use the present simple to talk about things that are always true, or happen all the time.
She has two sisters.
I play football at the weekend.

Use the present progressive to talk about things happening now, or around now.
Can you be quiet please, I'm watching TV.
I'm studying French at university at the moment.

Use the present perfect to talk about life up to now.
I've lived here all my life.
I've seen this film recently.

For more uses of the present perfect, see unit 3, p25.

FORM

	Present simple	Present progressive	Present perfect
❓	How many sisters do you have?	What are you watching?	What countries have you visited?
➕	I have two sisters.	I'm watching a film.	I've visited lots of countries.
➖	I don't have any sisters.	I'm not watching TV.	I haven't visited many countries.
❓	Do you play football?	Are you working now?	Have you been to São Paulo?
✔	Yes, I do.	Yes, I am.	Yes, I have.
✘	No, I don't.	No, I'm not.	No, I haven't.

PRONUNCIATION

You usually stress question words, main verbs and nouns.

Where do you live? I live in Frankfurt.

In negative sentences and short answers, you also stress *do*, *have*, *be* and *not*.

She isn't waiting for an email.   Yes, she is.

No, I'm not.

PRACTICE

1 **a** Complete the sentences with the correct form of the words in brackets.

1 **A** What *do you do* (you / do) at the weekends?
   B I _____ (relax) at home.
2 **A** What _____ (you / do) right now?
   B I _____ (write) a report.
3 **A** _____ (you / be) anywhere interesting recently?
   B No, I _____ (not / be) away for ages.
4 **A** What _____ (you / do) to relax?
   B I usually _____ (watch) TV.
5 **A** _____ (you / do) anything interesting at school or work at the moment?
   B No, not really.
6 **A** _____ (you / hear) anything interesting on the news this week?
   B No, I haven't.
7 **A** _____ (you / read) a good book at the moment?
   B Yes, I _____ (read) a book about Darwin.
8 **A** How often _____ (you / see) your closest friend?
   B We _____ (not / live) near each other, so not often.
9 **A** _____ (you / do) anything exciting recently?
   B No, I _____ (not / had) any time off.
10 **A** What films _____ (you / see) recently?
   B I _____ (see) *Young Frankenstein* and a terrible comedy – I can't remember the name.

b Ask each other the questions and give your own answers.

134

2 *will, could, may, might*

MEANING

Use will to say you are sure about something in the future.
People will do most of their shopping online in the future.

You can also use will to talk about now, or about things in general.

A *Let's call Nathalie.*
B *No, she'll be in the car.*

He's always complaining so no one will listen to him.

Use might, may and could to say you're not sure about something now or in the future.

Chinese might / may / could become the most important language in the world. (future)

A *Where's Kimiko?*
B *I don't know. She might / may / could be at work.* (now)

There might / may / could be thousands of animal species we don't know about. (in general)

May is a little more formal than might. May is more common in formal kinds of writing, but might is more common in everyday speech.

There is an important difference between could and can.
The supermarket could be crowded on Saturday. (= It's possible that it will be crowded on Saturday.)
The supermarket can be crowded on Saturday. (= It is sometimes crowded on Saturday.)

Use will and may with other words to show that you are more or less sure.
+++ *Nathalie will definitely be there for the meeting.*
++ *Nathalie will be there.*
+ *Nathalie will probably be there.* Also: *Nathalie may well be there.*
? *Possibly / Maybe / Perhaps Nathalie will be there.*

You can also use be likely to and be unlikely to to express probability. Use more or less to <u>compare</u> probabilities.
Don't call Nathalie now. She's likely to be busy at work.
She's unlikely to have her mobile switched on.
Try her landline. She's more likely to be at home than at work.
She's less likely to answer if you call her mobile.

FORM

will / might / may / could + infinitive without *to*

❓	*Will it rain?*	➕	*It'll / It will rain.*
	–		*It might rain.*
	–		*It may rain.*
	Could it rain?		*It could rain.*
✔/✘	*Yes, it will. / No, it won't.*	➖	*It won't / will not rain.*
	It might. / It might not.		*It might not rain.*
	It may. / It may not.		*It may not rain.*
	It could.		–

PRONUNCIATION

Will is often contracted like this: 'll /əl/ and won't /wəʊnt/.

You usually stress the infinitive (main) verb but not will / might / may / could.

Will Kimiko pass her test next week?

I think she'll try her best.

But she might fail.

But you stress won't, not and will / might / may / could in short answers.

She won't pass.

She might not pass.

She might.

PRACTICE

1 **a Complete the conversations with will, won't or might.**

 1 A Kimiko's got her driving test tomorrow. Do you think she _____ pass?
 2 B Hm, she's not really prepared. She _____ pass if she gets a nice examiner.
 3 A Yeah, she's so nervous she _____ panic and make mistakes.
 4 A _____ it be hot enough tomorrow to have a picnic?
 5 B Well, the weather forecast says it _____ be 35⁰.
 6 A Yeah, but they _____ be wrong. They often are.

   A Shall we go to Luigi's for dinner?
 7 B Yes, but it _____ be fully booked; it's sometimes busy.
 8 A No, I'm sure it _____ be full on a Monday night.
 9 B Well, you _____ be right, but let's ring anyway.

 b Can you find one place in each conversation to use may well?

2 **a Rewrite the underlined parts of the conversation 1–8 using the modal verbs and expressions of probability.**

   A What do you think has happened to Monica?
   B ¹<u>Perhaps she's stuck</u> in traffic. might
   A Yeah, but the train leaves in ten minutes. I'll phone her.
   B ²<u>She probably won't answer</u> the phone if she's driving. be unlikely to
   A Let's phone Vijay. ³<u>He probably knows</u> where she is. may well ... OK. He says ⁴<u>he's sure she'll be here</u> soon. definitely
   B Will Elisa come, do you think?
   A Hm, ⁵<u>she'll probably</u> have a lie in! be more likely to
   B Yeah. What do you think the training will be like?
   A I haven't a clue. ⁶<u>Maybe it'll be interesting.</u> could
   B I hope so. Anyway, what are you doing this evening?
   A Well, ⁷<u>perhaps I'll have</u> a quiet evening in. I'm a bit tired. may
   B No, really? Come round to mine. ⁸<u>I know Jon's cooking!</u> will definitely
   A Oh look, here's Monica!

 b Practise the conversation with a partner.

3 PRESENT PERFECT AND TIME EXPRESSIONS

MEANING

You can use the present perfect to talk about unfinished actions or situations.
I've always known my best friend.
I've never been to Africa.
I've lived in my flat for five years.
I've been a teacher since 2006.

You can also use the present perfect to talk about finished actions which are important now.
I've just heard the news about the fire. Isn't it awful?
We've painted the house. It looks lovely.

Don't use the present perfect with finished times in the past. Use the past simple.
We painted our house last week.
He saw this film on Monday.
They went to Africa in 1999.

Time expressions

You often use these time expressions with the present perfect:
for   since   always   never   yet   recently   just   already

You can use:
– always and never to talk about the whole of your life until now.
– for and since to talk about part of your life until now.
– recently and just to talk about a short time ago.
I've just seen Maria. If you hurry, you can go with her.

– yet to talk about something you expect to happen.
Have you finished your homework? No, I haven't started it yet.

– already to talk about something that happened sooner than expected.
He's already seen this film.

ever in questions means 'at any time in your life'.
Have you ever had Thai food?

FORM AND PRONUNCIATION

For present perfect, see p134.

FORM

Present perfect + time expressions		
In mid position: auxiliary + time expression + past participle	for + period of time since + point in time	At the end of the sentence
• I've always known my best friend. • I've never been to Africa. • I've just heard the news. • I've already written the essay.	• I've lived in this flat for five years. • He's lived in his flat since 2005.	• I haven't written the essay yet. • We've seen her recently.

Note: Some time expressions can go in more than one position. Already can also go at the end of a sentence. *I've written the essay already.*

Recently can also go in mid position in positive sentences. *We've recently seen her.* It can't go in mid position in negative sentences. *We haven't recently seen her.*

PRONUNCIATION

You usually stress the adverb in mid position and at the end of a sentence.

I've always known my best friend.

I haven't written the essay yet.

But you don't stress *for* or *since*.

I've lived in this flat for five years. /fə/

He's lived in his flat since 2005. /sɪns/

PRACTICE

Add these time expressions to the sentences:
for   since   already   yet   just   never   always

1 You've done the homework, haven't you? Could you help me? ***You've already done the homework ...***
2 I haven't finished the report for today's meeting. I'm very worried.
3 He's lived in the same house. He was born there.
4 They've had that car ten years. It's broken down. (x2)
5 We've come back from safari in Kenya. It was an amazing experience.
6 We haven't seen each other university, but it seems like yesterday.
7 I've seen this film. I saw it years ago, when it first came out.
8 I've liked spicy food. It's too hot for me.

4 NARRATIVE VERB FORMS

MEANING

Use the past simple to talk about things that are in the past and finished.
I dropped your camera. I'm sorry.
I met my husband in 1989.

Use the past progressive to talk about an action that was in progress at a time in the past.
I was working in Spain in 1989.

You often use the past progressive to explain the background to another past event or action.
I was teaching in a primary school when I met my husband.

You can use the past perfect to refer to an earlier event in the past.
I went to the shop after work and bought loads of food for the weekend. I didn't realise you'd already done the shopping this morning.

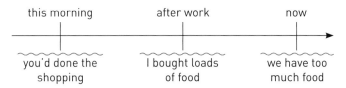

this morning	after work	now
you'd done the shopping	I bought loads of food	we have too much food

FORM

	Past simple	Past progressive	Past perfect
❓	Where did you go last night?	What were you doing?	Where had you been?
➕	I went to a party.	I was driving to work.	I'd been in a café.
➖	I didn't enjoy it.	I wasn't going fast.	I hadn't realised how late it was.
❓	Did you stay long?	Were you using a mobile?	Had you tried to ring?
✔	Yes, I did.	Yes, I was.	Yes, I had.
✘	No, I didn't.	No, I wasn't.	No, I hadn't.

PRONUNCIATION

You usually stress question words and main verbs.

Where did you go? What were you doing? Where had you been?

I went to a party. I was driving to work. I'd been in a café.

But in negative sentences and short answers, you usually stress did, was, were and had.

I didn't enjoy it.   I wasn't going fast.   I hadn't realised.

Yes, I did.   No, I didn't.   Yes, I was.   No, I wasn't.

Yes, I had.   No, I hadn't.

PRACTICE

1   **a** Complete the conversations with the correct verb forms.

> pick up   ring   put the phone down

1   **A** Where were you when I _____?
    B I was in the middle of washing up. When I finally _____ the phone, you _____ .

> not want   run   fall   break

2   **A** Why didn't you tell me you _____ your leg?
    B Sorry, I _____ to bother you. I'm fine.
    A So, what happened?
    B Well, I _____ for the bus and I _____ over.

> not have   have   go

3   **A** _____ you _____ a good holiday?
    B No, we _____ a very good time, actually.
    A Oh dear! Why not? You've been there before, haven't you?
    B Well, we _____ never _____ to that hotel before, and it was really unpleasant.

b Take turns to start conversations 1–3.

2   Put the words in the correct order to make sentences.

1   what / Later, / found / had / we / out / happened
2   didn't / was / I / what / going on / know
3   there / realise / been / We / had / didn't / an / earthquake
4   can't / I / what happened / remember / really
5   way / I / on / called / the / you / was / the station / to / when
6   trying / I / to write / the computer / was / an / email / when / crashed
7   started / went out / Everything / the lights / and / suddenly / shaking
8   heard / we / the / warnings / Unfortunately, / hadn't

5 FUTURE FORMS – *will, going to* AND PRESENT PROGRESSIVE

FUTURE IN THE PAST – *was/were supposed to, was/were going to,* PAST PROGRESSIVE

MEANING

You can use these forms to talk about the future:

Use will to talk about a decision made at the moment of speaking.
A There's someone at the door.
B OK, I'll get it.

Use be going to to talk about a future plan you've made before speaking.
A Do you want to go out tonight?
B Erm, I'm just going to watch TV tonight.

Use the present progressive to talk about something you're sure will happen, because it's been arranged.
I'm getting married on the 1st June.

You can use these forms to talk about past plans and arrangements.
I was meeting my friend at seven, so I left at six thirty.
I was going to eat dinner, so I said goodbye to my friend.
I was supposed to cook that night, so I left for home.

You can use *was/were supposed to* and *was/were going to* when the plan or arrangement <u>didn't</u> happen.
I was going to go to the cinema, but there was nothing on.
I was supposed to meet somebody, but he didn't turn up.

FORM

be going to
Use am/is/are/was/were going to with the infinitive.

❓ Are you going to see her again? Were you going to go to the cinema?	➕ I'm going to see her on my next trip to Malaysia. I was going to see my friend, but he's not around tonight.
✔/✘ Yes, I am. / No, I'm not. Yes, I was. / No, I wasn't.	➖ I'm not going to see her until next year. I wasn't going to fly there, but now I am.

Present and past progressive

❓ Are you having a meeting later? Were you meeting her last night?	➕ I'm having a meeting at 2pm. I was meeting her at 2pm.
✔/✘ Yes, I am. / No, I'm not. Yes, I was. / No, I wasn't.	➖ I'm not doing anything tonight. I wasn't meeting her last night.

will
Use will with the infinitive.

❓ Will you pass me the remote?	➕ I'll give you a lift.
✔/✘ Yes, I will. / No, I won't.	➖ I won't have a cigarette.

was/were supposed to
Use was/were supposed to with the infinitive.

❓ Were you supposed to be at home last night?	➕ I was supposed to be at work an hour ago.
✔/✘ Yes, I was. / No, I wasn't.	➖ You weren't supposed to write all the report.

PRONUNCIATION

be going to and be supposed to
We usually stress going and the infinitive. We say to with a schwa, /ə/.

I'm going to see a play with John on Saturday.

In fast speech we often say going to without stress, as /gənə/.

We're gonna /gənə/ watch a film tonight.

We usually stress supposed and the infinitive. We say to with a schwa, /tə/.

I was supposed to finish this essay last night.

In negative sentences and short answers with going to and supposed to, we also stress be.

We aren't going to have a holiday this year.
You weren't supposed to do that.
Yes, I am.
No, I'm not.

will
We usually stress the infinitive in positive sentences with will.

I'll get the phone.

You can stress will to express strong intention.

I will get the job!

We usually stress won't and the infinitive in negative sentences.

I won't go shopping until later.

Present and past progressive
Present progressive: See *Grammar reference* for unit 1, p134.
Past progressive: See *Grammar reference* for unit 4, p137.

PRACTICE

1   Choose the correct form to complete these conversations.

   1 **A** I have to be at work in five minutes.
     B Really? Don't worry. <u>I'll / I'm going to</u> give you a lift.
   2 **A** <u>I'll meet / I'm meeting</u> Amy tonight at the Café Bleu.
     B Oh, say hi from me.
   3 **A** Can we have pizza for dinner tonight?
     B Sorry, no. <u>I'll / I'm going to</u> make a curry.
   4 **A** Are you doing anything nice this weekend?
     B Yeah, actually, my brother <u>will come / 's coming</u> to stay.

5 A What are you doing for your birthday?
   B Oh, I'll / I'm going to meet up with some friends and go clubbing.
6 A I really want to go out tonight. Do you want to do something?
   B Actually, I'm really tired. I'm just watching / going to watch TV.
7 A I really can't carry all these bags!
   B Sorry, I'll / I'm going to take one for you.
8 A I can't do the homework. Have you done it yet?
   B No, I'll do / I'm doing it later with Juan. Why don't you come round too?
9 A We've run out of milk again.
   B OK. I'll go / I'm going to the shop in a minute to get some.
10 A Are you ready to go?
   B No, you go ahead. I'm calling / going to call Amy first to ask her if she wants to come round later.

2 **Complete the sentences with a correct form of the verb in brackets: past progressive, was/were supposed to or was/were going to.**

1 I _____ (finish) the report this morning but my computer crashed so I couldn't.
2 A Do you know where Jon is?
   B He _____ (eat) at Fernando's flat. Why don't you call him there?
3 I _____ (call) you but I completely forgot, sorry.
4 She _____ (get) the flight at ten, so she should be in LA now.
5 Ana and Carmen _____ (meet) in the café next door. They should still be there, I think.
6 I _____ (see) the doctor but he was ill.

6 VERB + -ing

MEANING and FORM

Some verbs can be followed by the -ing form.
I tried calling you but you were out.
Have you considered moving home?

These verbs are often followed by -ing:

admit, adore, appreciate, avoid, consider, delay, deny, detest, dislike, dread, enjoy, (can/can't) face, fancy, feel like, finish, give up, hate, can't help, keep, like, love, miss, recall, can't stand, suggest, think about

PRONUNCIATION

Both the first verb and the -ing form are usually stressed.

I avoid sleeping in the afternoon.

She finished decorating her room yesterday.

PRACTICE

1 **a Complete these sentences with your own ideas.**

1 I dislike ...
2 I finished ... last year.
3 I enjoy ...
4 I've never considered ...
5 I really want to give up ...
6 I fancy ... right now.
7 I can't stand ...
8 I really can't face ...
9 I miss ...
10 I try and avoid ... but ...

b Talk about your sentences together.

7 COMPARING

MEANING

You can use quantifiers to modify the meaning of a comparative form.
He's much more intelligent than I am. (a big difference)
He's a lot more intelligent than I am. (a big difference)
She's a little taller than me. She's a bit taller than me.
(a small difference)

You can also use adverbs to modify a comparative form in the same way.
It's far easier going by train. (a big difference)
It's slightly further away. It's marginally closer.
(a very small difference)

We can use some adverbs with the comparative expression as ... as to modify the meaning.
He isn't nearly as argumentative as he used to be.
(a big difference)
She isn't quite as grumpy as she was yesterday.
(a small difference)
He's almost as noisy as you. (a small difference)
They're just as bad as each other. (exactly the same)

PRONUNCIATION

Adverbs and quantifiers are usually stressed in comparative sentences.

He's much more sociable than I am.

She's much faster than you.

They're just as good as us.

PRACTICE

1 **Change the underlined adverbs and quantifiers so that the sentences have the same meaning.**

1 Please write your answers on a computer. It's far easier for me to read.
2 You're nearly as fast as him. He only beat you by one second.
3 Let's take the train. It's slightly quicker.
4 I find German a little more difficult than French.
5 I think these trousers will be fine for Jorge. He's only marginally taller than I am.
6 My wife's a lot more practical than I am. I'm not very good at fixing things at home.

2 **Choose an adverb or quantifier to complete these sentences.**

1 Why don't you apply for the job? You're _____ as experienced as he is.
2 Sally and Naomi are very similar but I don't think Sally is _____ as argumentative as her sister.
3 I don't think it matters which way we walk. It's _____ closer if we go by the river.
4 Bill's really changed. He isn't _____ as difficult as he used to be.
5 My brother's _____ more adventurous than I am. He's travelled all over the world.

8 MODALS OF DEDUCTION AND SPECULATION

MEANING

You can use must to say that you are sure about something.
That must be Laura. She's coming round for coffee.

Must is only used in this way in affirmative sentences. In negative sentences you use *can't* to say you're sure something is impossible.
She can't be here yet. She just texted me from the office.

Might and could are both used to say that you're not sure about something but it's a possibility.
That could be my cab. It's come really quickly.
My exam results might arrive today. I'm really nervous.

FORM

must / might / could / can't + infinitive without *to*

(sure +)	(not sure)	(sure −)
That must be Laura.	That might be Laura. That could be Laura.	That can't be Laura.

PRONUNCIATION

We often stress must, might, could and can't in sentences because these modal verbs express the speaker's attitude.

That must be my cab.

That might be for me.

This can't be your coat.

PRACTICE

Complete the sentences with must, might or can't.

1 This coffee _____ be yours. I asked for tea.
2 There _____ be a direct train soon. The timetable says there are four every hour.
3 This _____ be our bus. It isn't due for another 20 minutes.
4 That _____ be the postman. Will you go and check?
5 **A** Is this your file? There's no name in it.
   B It _____ be mine. My name's on the cover.
6 **A** Which way shall we go? Left or right?
   B It doesn't make much difference. Left _____ be a bit quicker.
7 **A** Where's Plinio? He should be here by now.
   B Well, he's not answering the phone, so he _____ be on his way.
8 **A** Here's your suitcase.
   B No, that _____ be mine. Mine doesn't have a red stripe on the side.

9 REAL AND UNREAL CONDITIONALS

MEANING

In real conditional sentences, the speaker thinks the situation in the if part of the sentence is realistic or possible.
If you're free tomorrow, we could go to the cinema. (I think you might be free tomorrow.)

You can use real conditionals to do a lot of different things. For example:
If Perfect Day is on, you should go and see it. (recommending)
If you like, I'll get you a ticket. (offering)
If you have time, we could get a coffee. (suggesting)
If you don't feel well, you should go home. (giving advice)

In unreal conditional sentences, the speaker thinks the situation in the if part of the sentence is unrealistic or impossible. These sentences use past verbs (*were, had*, etc.) but they are not about the past. They're about the present or the future.
If you were free tomorrow, I'd invite you too. (I know you aren't free tomorrow.)

FORM

Conditional sentences have two parts, the if clause and the main clause. You can change the order of the two clauses. When the if clause comes second, you don't need to use a comma.

Real situation	
If you're free tomorrow, ... We'll go to the cinema ...	... we'll go to the cinema. ... if you're free tomorrow.

Imaginary situation	
If you were free tomorrow, ... We would be able to go to the cinema ...	... we would be able to go to the cinema. ... if you were free tomorrow.

You can replace will and would with other modal verbs, e.g. can, could, may, might, should.
If Perfect Day is on, you should go and see it.
If you're free tomorrow, we could go to the cinema.
If your brother lived here, he might be able to help us.

In unreal conditionals, you can use was or were after *I, he, she* or *it*.
If your brother was / were here, it would be fantastic.

PRONUNCIATION

The sentence stress in real and unreal conditional sentences is the same as in other sentences.

The if clause and main clause are usually pronounced as separate groups of words.

If you're free tomorrow, // we could go to the cinema.

We could go to the cinema // if you were free tomorrow.

PRACTICE

1 a Complete the conditional sentences with the correct form of the verb in brackets and will or 'd where necessary.

1 If I _____ (have) a better job, I _____ be a lot happier.
2 If you _____ (go) to Paris, you should visit the Eiffel Tower.
3 If the weather _____ (be) bad tomorrow, we can just stay in.
4 I _____ talk to Felix if I _____ (see) him tomorrow.
5 I _____ be a lot healthier if I _____ (not / eat) so much fast food.
6 If he _____ (work) harder, he _____ probably do better in his job.
7 If you _____ (not / feel) well, you should go home.

b Say what you think the situation is for each sentence.

1 The person is unhappy because he/she doesn't have a very good job.

10 VERB PATTERNS

MEANING AND FORM

Verbs can be followed by different patterns.

Example	Pattern	More verbs which can be followed by this pattern
I got a newspaper this morning.	noun phrase	*bring, buy, cut, do, enjoy, find, give, help, know, like, love, make, need, offer, remember, take, want*
I remembered that I had to meet a friend.	*that* clause	*argue, believe, forget, hear, hope, imagine, know, realise, recognise, suggest, think, understand*
I reminded him that he had to see his friend tonight.	direct object + *that* clause	*convince, persuade*
I forgot what I had to do.	*wh-* clause	*check, consider, depend, guess, hear, imagine, know, learn, remember, see*
She showed me what I had to do.	direct object + *wh-* clause	*remind*
I love getting up early in the morning.	*-ing*	*dislike, enjoy, finish, mind, miss, practise, suggest*
They agreed to meet at 11 o'clock.	*to* infinitive	*arrange, begin, choose, forget, like, mean, need, prepare, remember, start, want*

See Unit 11, p142 for patterns following reporting verbs.

Some verbs change their meaning depending on whether they are followed by -ing or to infinitive.

Verb	*-ing*	*to* infinitive
remember and forget	I remember learning to swim when I was a child. I'll never forget meeting my best friend. (refers to the past)	I must remember to ask about the start date. You mustn't forget to post the letter. (refers to something you need to do)
stop	He stopped smoking a year ago. (He doesn't smoke now.)	He stopped to have a cigarette. (He stopped doing something in order to smoke.)
try	Try pressing the red button and seeing what happens. (experiment to see if something works)	I've tried to lift the suitcase but it's really heavy. (attempt to do something difficult)

PRACTICE

Complete the sentences with the right form of the verb, -ing or to infinitive.

1 Don't forget _____ (call) me later on.
2 **A** Why did you take so long?
   B Sorry. I stopped _____ (talk) to the new neighbour in number 26.
3 Have you tried _____ (talk) to him about the problem? That might help.
4 I stopped _____ (work) there ten years ago now.
5 We've been here ten years. Do you remember _____ (walk) into the house for the first time?
6 I know I'm going to forget _____ (tell) Jenny the news.
7 I must remember _____ (pack) the passports.
8 I've tried _____ (open) the window but I can't. I think it's stuck.

PRESENT PERFECT SIMPLE AND PROGRESSIVE

MEANING

You can use both present perfect simple and present perfect progressive to link the past and present.

Present perfect simple

Use the present perfect simple to emphasise the result of finished actions in the past.
I've finished painting the room. Do you like it?

You also use it to talk about the number of times something has happened.
I've only smoked five cigarettes today.

You usually use it with 'short-action' verbs, for example: start, lose, buy ...
I've just started an English course.

Present perfect progressive

You can use the present perfect progressive to talk about unfinished or recently finished activities.
I've been painting my room. Do you like it so far?

You also use it to emphasise how long something has been happening, or that it's been happening a lot.
I've been smoking for five years. (emphasise duration)
I've been smoking a lot today. (emphasise repetition)

You usually use present perfect progressive with 'long-action' verbs, for example: try, play, rain, learn ...
I've been learning English for a long time.

FORM

Present perfect simple
have/has + past participle
I've just begun decorating the front room.

Present perfect progressive
have/has + been + -ing
She's been playing tennis for an hour now.

PRONUNCIATION

You usually stress the past participle in the present perfect simple.
I've started a new class recently.

You usually stress the -ing form in the present perfect progressive. Been is often pronounced /bɪn/.
It's been raining all day.

PRACTICE

Complete the sentences with the present perfect simple or progressive of the verb in brackets.

1 I _____ (play) tennis all afternoon and I'm exhausted.
2 I _____ (have) five cigarettes today. I feel really guilty.
3 I _____ (look) for a birthday present for Carolina, but I can't seem to find anything.
4 We _____ (decorate) the front room and the kitchen. We just need to do the bathroom now.
5 I _____ (work) on this project for a couple of months.
6 I _____ (finish) the report and the presentation. Do you want to have a look?
7 I _____ (learn) English for three years now and I still can't have a conversation.
8 I _____ (cut) my finger. Have you got a plaster?

11 REPORTING SPEECH

MEANING

When we relate a conversation we often use reporting verbs to summarise what people say. The verbs describe the function of the person's speech.
"I'm sorry. I won't do it again."
He said he's sorry. He promised not to do it again.

FORM

Reporting verbs are followed by different patterns. Many verbs can be followed by more than one pattern.

Tell must be followed by a direct object. Ask is usually followed by a direct object.
She told me what to do. She asked me what to do.

Some verbs never have a direct object, e.g. say, explain, agree, lie.
They said they're on the way. NOT: They said me they're on the way.

	+ *that* clause	+ *wh* clause	+ *to* infinitive
say	He said that he's sorry.	He won't say what's wrong.	–
tell	She told me that she's got the job.	She told me what to do.	She told us to leave.
ask	–	She asked me what to do.	They asked us to leave.
explain	He explained that the figures were wrong.	They explained why we had to go.	–
promise	He promised (me) that he would help.	–	He promised to help.
agree	They agreed that it was a good idea.	They agreed where to meet.	They agreed to do it.
other verbs:	complain, decide, guarantee, mention, recall, suggest, warn	consider, decide, discuss	decide, offer, refuse

In reported speech, the verb can sometimes change 'one tense back'. This often emphasises that what you are reporting is not a fact but it's just what someone said. Compare these examples:

"I'm married." — He told me he's married.
or He told me he was married.

"I've been to Guatemala." — She said she's been to Guatemala.
or She said she'd been to Guatemala.

"The figures are wrong." — They explained that the figures are wrong.
or They explained that the figures were wrong.

PRACTICE

Complete sentences 1–7 reporting Anna and Bill's conversation.

ANNA I haven't made this soup before. [1]Do you know how to cook it?

BILL [2]Yeah, I make it all the time!

A [3]Can you help me?

B [4]Yes, of course. I'll make it, if you like.

A Oh thanks. [5]But I'd like to know how to do it. Maybe we could do it together.

B [6]Yeah, of course. So, first of all, you chop the veg. [7]Can you do that?

1 Anna asked Bill how to cook the soup.
2 Bill said that he …
3 Anna asked him …
4 He promised …
5 Anna said …
6 They agreed …
7 Then Bill asked Anna …

12 INDIRECT QUESTIONS

MEANING

Indirect questions are more formal and polite than direct questions. You often use them when you talk to strangers or people you don't know well. You tend to begin a conversation with indirect questions, then continue with direct questions.

A Could you tell me where the nearest bank is?
B Yes, it's on Grant Street, opposite the train station.
A Thanks. Can I walk there?
B Yes, it's only five minutes' walk.

There are many ways of introducing an indirect question. Some of the most common are:
Do you know what time the coach leaves?
Could you tell me if you're free tomorrow afternoon?
Could I ask you if you enjoyed the film?
I was wondering whether I could borrow your laptop.

FORM

Do you know when the banks open?
Could I ask you if you know when the banks open?

Where's the nearest cash machine?
Do you have any idea where the nearest cash machine is?

Have you talked to the manager yet?
Could I ask you if you've talked to the manager yet?

Yes/no questions	Direct
	Do you know when the banks open? *Are you waiting for a bus?* *Have you seen a wallet around here?*
	Indirect
	Could I ask you if you know when the banks open? *Could you tell me whether you're waiting for a bus?* *I was wondering if you've seen a wallet around here.*

Wh-questions	Direct
	When's the next bus? *Where's the nearest cash machine?* *What's the best way to get to Paris?*
	Indirect
	Do you know when the next bus is? *Do you have any idea where the nearest cash machine is?* *Could you tell me what the best way to get to Paris is?*
In indirect questions:	• use the same word order as affirmative sentences (e.g. subject + verb). • don't include do, does or did. But we do include other auxiliary verbs (e.g. be, have) and modals (e.g. could, should). • use if or whether in yes/no questions. We usually use whether … or to emphasise a choice of two.

PRONUNCIATION

You usually use indirect questions to find out something. So, the question normally ends with a falling intonation (↘).

Could you tell me when the next bus is?

You usually stress indirect questions in the same way as other questions.

I was wondering if you could answer some questions?

Could you tell me whether you're interested in becoming a member?

Do you know when the next bus is?

PRACTICE

1 a Make these questions into indirect questions.

A	B
Do you always eat breakfast?	Which meal of the day is the most important?
How do you get to school or work?	How long does it take?
What political party do you support?	Do you think it's OK not to vote in an election?
How many languages do you speak?	Should all children learn a foreign language?
Are you a member of a gym or leisure centre?	How much exercise do you do every week?

b Choose a topic from A to ask different people about. Then walk around and ask your questions. Ask questions to find out more information.

13 *should have, could have*

MEANING

Use should have and shouldn't have to evaluate or criticise past actions.
You should have turned left at the roundabout.
We shouldn't have left so late.

Use could have to talk about something that was possible but didn't happen. You can use *couldn't have* to talk about something that wasn't possible.
I could have done better in the exam.
They couldn't have done anything more.

FORM

modal + *have* + past participle
I could have done better in the exam.
You should have worked harder.

PRONUNCIATION

You usually contract have when using past modals in fluent speech. Where not have occurs, both words are often contracted in fluent speech (but not in writing).

You should've told me you were busy.

I shouldn't've gone out last night.

Modals are often stressed in these sentences.
We shouldn't have left so late.

PRACTICE

1   **a** Write the verbs in the correct form in the sentences and questions.

   1   I should (not go) to university. It was a waste of time.
   2   I could (try) harder to keep in contact with my old friends.
   3   I should (not stay up) so late last night. I'm really tired.
   4   I could (not work) any harder. I've always done my best.
   5   I should (tidy) my room at the weekend. It's a mess.
   6   Is there anything you should (do) before you left home this morning?
   7   Do you think you could (do) better at school?

   b Are sentences 1–5 true for you? Talk to a partner and ask questions 6 and 7.

UNREAL CONDITIONALS: PAST

MEANING

You can use unreal past conditionals to talk about past situations that are imaginary and didn't happen.

Real past situation	Imaginary past situation	
	Condition	Result
I didn't go to university. I didn't get a degree.	If I'd gone to university, ...	... I'd have got a degree.
I didn't learn languages at school. I didn't travel much.	If I'd learned languages at school, ...	... I would have travelled more.

FORM

If + had + past participle, would + have + past participle
If I'd worked harder, I'd have achieved more.
If I'd known sooner, this wouldn't have happened.

You can change the order of the two clauses. When the if clause comes second, you don't need a comma.
would + have + past participle if + had + past participle
We wouldn't have had a problem if you'd remembered to check in online.

PRONUNCIATION

Would, have, had and not are often contracted in fluent speech where two words occur together (e.g. *not have* or *would have*).

If I'd worked harder, I'd've achieved more.

If I'd known sooner, this wouldn't've happened.

In conditional sentences, you usually say the condition and result clauses as separate groups of words.
If I'd worked harder // I'd have achieved more.

PRACTICE

Complete the sentences with the verbs in brackets to make unreal past conditional sentences.

1   I _____ that if I _____ it would make you cry. (not say, know)
2   If you _____ me you wanted the job, I _____ you an interview. (tell, give)
3   If he _____ that mistake, he _____ his driving test. (not make, pass)
4   You _____ it easily if you _____ my instructions. (find, follow)
5   I _____ what to do if you _____ me. (not know, not tell)
6   If you _____ two more questions correctly, you _____ a distinction. (answer, get)
7   If I _____ my flat five years ago, I _____ a lot of money. (buy, make)
8   If you _____ to the party, you _____ it. It was really boring. (come, not enjoy)

14 PASSIVES

MEANING

In active sentences, the subject is the 'doer' of the verb. In passive sentences, the 'doer' of the verb is not the subject.

The teenager murdered the man. (Active sentence)
The man was murdered by the teenager. (Passive sentence)

We use the passive:
– to focus on the main topic of a text.

Active
Brazil won the World Cup in 1970.

Passive
The World Cup was won in 1970 by Brazil.

> In an article about the World Cup, the second (passive) sentence will keep the focus on the main topic.

– if the doer of the verb isn't important or is unknown.
My wallet was stolen last night. (I don't know who took it.)

– if the doer of the verb is clear or known by the reader, or is 'people in general'.
Several soldiers were killed. (It is clear that it was in a military fight.)

FORM

	be + past participle
Present simple	It's made in China.
Past simple	It was made in China.
Present perfect	It's been done really well.
Modals	It can be done again. It will be done again. It would be done again.
Present progressive	It's being published by CPS International.
be going to	It's going to be reviewed by *Time Magazine*.

PRONUNCIATION

Passive sentences have the same stress as other sentences. The past participle is stressed.

The World Cup was won in 1970 by Brazil.

In passive sentences, forms of be, modals and going to are not stressed. is and will are often contracted.
It was made in China. /wəz/
The cards were made by my friend. /wə/
It can be done again. /kən/
It's going to be published by CPS International. /gənə/

PRACTICE

1   a Complete the sentences with the correct form of the verb in brackets.

   1 The first McDonald's restaurant _____ (open) in Chicago, USA in 1956.
   2 About a billion cans of Coke _____ (drink) every day.
   3 Twenty-three Americans _____ (eat) by alligators since 1973.
   4 *Hamlet* _____ (write) by Shakespeare.
   5 Six hundred and three films _____ (make) in Hollywood in 2006.
   6 *Raja Harishchandra* _____ (make) in India in 1913. It was India's first silent film.
   7 *Les Miserables*, the musical, _____ (see) by 51 million people in 38 countries since 1980.

   b Which is your favourite fact? Do you know any more surprising facts? Write three or four sentences in groups. Then compare them together.

Unit 1

🔊 1.1

AIKO I love TV. When I wasn't so busy, I used to watch it all the time. I remember, when I was fourteen or fifteen, I used to love these drama shows, which were always on at 9pm on Monday nights on Fuji TV. They were called *getsuku*, which means, er, Monday at nine. I used to look forward to it all day. But these days I don't have time to follow any series. In fact, I hardly ever watch TV. I like to know what's going on in the world though, so I try and follow the news and when I'm travelling I watch BBC World News, which is really good, very informative.

JUAN I'm not a big fan of TV, to be honest. I find a lot of channels really irritating because there are so many ads. I can't stand watching the ads, so I tend to record the shows I like so I can fast forward through all the ads and then watch the shows over and over. I'm really into music and we have MTV América Latina in Argentina, which is really good. But I tend to listen to the radio a lot, mostly music stations. I prefer radio to TV actually, because you can do other stuff while you're listening.

YASIR I don't have a TV. I don't need one because I can watch everything I'm interested in on the Internet. I select the programmes I want ... usually the news and sport. I'm a big fan of all sports, especially football. So if there's something good on, I'll watch it on the Al Kass Sport Channel. I don't usually watch anything else, but recently I've watched *Chef Ramzi*, a cookery show, with my wife a couple of times. She wants me to improve my cooking.

CARMEN There are too many reality shows on TV these days, programmes where people become pop stars or change their houses or something. I'm not keen on them, to be honest. I'd rather watch documentaries ... at least you find out something new. I've just watched a very interesting series about some special natural areas in Spain. It's inspired me to go to places I've never been in my country. And when there's nothing on TV and I'm alone, I watch *CincoShop*, the shopping channel. I've bought so many things. It's a bad habit, but I enjoy it!

🔊 1.2

PAUL What are you doing?

REBECCA Hm? Reading. Another Agatha Christie ... *Murder is Easy*. Have you read it?

P No, no. Is it any good?

R Well, I've read it three times, so I know exactly what's going to happen. It's great!

P I don't know how you can read books again and again.

R At least I read. Your problem is you never read anything.

P That's not true. I read magazines.

R Yes, but do you read books?

P Sometimes, yeah. Anyway, isn't there anything good on TV?

R I don't know, I haven't looked. Why don't you read a book?

P I'm not reading anything at the moment. I don't have any new books to read. Can you pass the remote?

R Oh, please don't put the TV on, I'm trying to read.

P OK, but I want to watch something at eight. There's a film on. It's called *Sideways*.

R Oh yeah. We've seen it before. It's about those two guys on a road trip.

P Yeah, it's really good. Do you want to watch it?

R No, I'm going out with Carole at half eight, so I'll miss most of it.

P Oh, OK. Would you like me to record it?

R No, don't worry. I don't like watching films more than once.

P Really? Well, I'm going to watch it anyway.

R OK. Can I read now?

P Yeah, yeah, go ahead.

🔊 1.5

CARMEN I started reading *A Hundred Years of Solitude* recently. It's by someone called Gabriel García Márquez. Have you read it? It's quite a well-known book ... it's been made into a film, actually. It's about this family who have all these problems and about the history of this town called Macondo. I think I read that it's based on Márquez's own life. People say it's amazing, but actually I found it boring. It has hundreds of names and people and it just goes on and on. I won't spoil the ending because ... well ... I got half-way through and gave up.

AIKO I saw *The West Wing* for the first time recently. It's really well known – have you seen it? [No.] It's about the US president and his aides. It's based on what happens in American politics but it's a bit more idealistic and romantic than real life. [Oh.] I enjoyed it because it's very entertaining, but it's quite difficult to follow. It has Martin Sheen in it – he's the one who was in *Apocalypse Now*. [Oh, yes.] There's this one episode where the president, Martin Sheen, ...

REBECCA I'm not usually into autobiographies, but there's a book I read recently which is just brilliant. It's called *Born on a Blue Day* and it's by a man called Daniel Tammet. He's got this condition, it's called savant syndrome, which basically means

he's a genius but he also has some problems. Anyway, it looks at his life ... erm, he's an amazing guy. He can do enormous calculations in his head – in seconds – and he speaks loads of languages. Apparently, scientists have studied him to try to understand how his brain works. It's a really interesting book because it helps you understand how he thinks.

YASIR Recently, I've started watching *Chef Ramzi* on the Internet with my wife. It's a cookery show with this celebrity chef. Basically, it shows you how to cook great meals. The food is delicious and healthy and Chef Ramzi is famous because he talks about the cultural importance of the meals. I wasn't sure if I'd like the programme, but I've tried making one or two of the meals, and I have to say, the results were pretty good.

🔊 1.7

FEDERICO Some years ago, I worked for a company in Egypt, and on the first weekend we all went out for the day. Everyone else was Egyptian and we all spoke English together. We went to the beach in Alexandria – it was really beautiful. Everyone brought their families ... which, erm, surprised me, actually. We played games together, tennis, throwing a ball around, and we went swimming together. Er, some of my new colleagues kept asking me if I was having a good time. I told them I was. When it was lunchtime, we had a big picnic together. One of my colleagues, Manu, offered me some of his lunch. He insisted I took some. Basically, they did everything together and were incredibly hospitable.

I thought it was lovely, but I just didn't feel comfortable. Erm, you see, I'm not used to being so close to people all the time. So in the afternoon I went for a walk along the beach on my own. Looking back, it was probably a bit rude but I needed a bit of space. When I came back Manu looked really worried. He came over to me and asked me what the matter was. I said there was nothing the matter – I just wanted to go for a walk. He looked really upset and asked me what they'd done to upset me. I felt awful.

🔊 1.8

FEDERICO It was a really weird day. At work afterwards things were a bit strange. But after living in Egypt for six months or so I began to understand what had happened. That day at the beach ... erm ... I think maybe Manu was trying to make me feel like I was one of the family. I've noticed that welcoming a new individual is an important part of Egyptian culture – their fantastic hospitality is something they're really proud of. But for me, coming from Buenos Aires, a big city in Argentina, and living alone, I didn't feel comfortable. I wasn't used to spending so much time in big groups. Now I'm OK with it. I'm used to it now, but I found it quite difficult at first. Anyway, once I realised all this, things became easier and I slowly got used to being with a lot of people. I don't know that I've really changed that much now I'm back at home, but I really admire that aspect of Egyptian culture and I'll never forget my year there.

Unit 2

🔊 **1.10**

PAULA   I think Facebook is a waste of time. I'm totally addicted, I have to say. But, er, there really isn't much going on. You just spend hours just, sort of, making friends, checking other people's profiles, looking at the, erm, pictures they've, er, posted and it's just, I don't know, I mean, nothing happens. It's just that, I don't know, it's very voyeuristic and it, erm, really is a waste of time, I think.

MEGAN   I find myself wasting a lot of time on Facebook. I'm now back in touch with people I knew in primary school but we don't actually say anything to each other. You just go onto their page, look at their pictures and then that's it, but for some reason I still find myself checking it constantly.

P   Yeah, it's incredibly addictive. Erm, it's happened to me as well. Like, er, I was contacted by people I hadn't seen, er, in a very long time, and then you realise that you've changed a lot and you actually have nothing to talk about so there's no point in being friends, really. You know, all this, like, sort of, virtual friendship, it just leads nowhere, I think. It's not like a real friendship.

M   It's such a huge waste of time that I've heard that some workplaces are banning its use because so many of us are wasting so much time looking at it.

GRAHAM   How are you doing? Busy?

DENIZ   I'm so busy! It's great to get out and have some fun.

G   But you're always messing around with your phone when we're talking.

D   Oh, am I? That's terrible. I … I'm just trying to keep up with my emails.

G   Yeah, but they say you need to take breaks from work, in the evening and weekends and stuff. Apparently, if you don't it really affects your performance. I read it somewhere.

D   No, I don't think that's true.

G   Do you really have to answer everything straight away?

D   Yeah, it saves such a lot of time.

G   And do you ever turn it off? I mean, what do you do at night?

D   I screen my calls and if it's someone I need to talk to it pings, which wakes me up. Then I can call them back.

G   Couldn't they wait till the morning?

D   Well, the thing is, I have to talk to people in New York and Tokyo. So I have to be in contact during their work hours.

G   That must be hard. I reckon you must get tired.

D   Yeah, it's tiring being on call all the time. But you know, it's so interesting – I love the job.

G   And what about holidays?

D   Yeah, I know some people say you shouldn't take your work on holiday, but I take my phone.

G   Really?

D   Yeah. There's no harm in checking your emails from time to time, you know.

G   You couldn't leave it at home?

D   Er, no, no, I couldn't.

G   I'd say it must be impossible to relax, though.

D   Yeah, it's difficult to relax sometimes, but I love what I do … it's amazing how much I miss the buzz of work when I'm away, even for a few days.

G   Really? I don't have that problem.

🔊 **1.12**

2 I reckon you must get tired.

3 They say you need to take breaks from work.

4 Some people say you shouldn't take your work on holiday.

5 There's no point in being friends really.

6 There's no harm in checking your emails from time to time.

🔊 **1.14**

ERIC   It's mad banning the intranet. I mean, what about urgent emails and stuff?

GRAHAM   Well, I don't know, I reckon one day without it isn't going to make so much difference. At least it's only company emails.

E   I tell you, it's going to waste such a lot of time.

G   In what way?

E   Well, we'll have to walk around and talk to people. It'll take longer to do everything.

G   I don't know. I think it might actually help us to get things done quicker.

E   Eh? I don't get that. How?

G   Because you'll be able to make decisions immediately, instead of

sending emails back and forth for days. And it might be nice to have a chat sometimes.

E   Yeah, but it'll be really irritating when you need to speak to someone, and they're not there.

G   Yes, that's true. But you can use the phone, you know. I think we should use the phone more.

E   Yeah, but there's no record of phone calls. I just think it'll cause problems.

G   We might need to give it a chance.

E   Hm. What annoys me more, you know, is Rob's attitude.

G   What do you mean?

E   Well, he obviously thinks we can't organise our time properly.

G   Yeah, I guess so. I hadn't thought about it like that.

🔊 **1.16**

SYLVIA   I got a computer recently and I've just had it connected to the Internet for the first time. My grandson did it for me. I told him I was too old to change now – I'm seventy-nine – but he said he'd show me how to use it. He came round and I said if he set it all up for me then I'd make him a nice lunch. But he did it all so quickly that I didn't have time to make us a cup of tea. I thought it would take all day. And then he showed me what to do. I didn't know it was so easy to use. You just click on a couple of things and you write an email. And it's so cheap! It's made such a difference to my life. You see, my daughter Holly lives in Hong Kong, so phone calls cost a lot and she's not a good letter writer. But now we're constantly in contact. I can't believe I ever said I didn't want it. In fact, it's such an easy and cheap thing to use that I'm going to get an internet phone as well. Then I'll be able to call Holly and my grandchildren for free.

🔊 **1.18**

1 Asking for clarification

Do you mean people aren't working hard enough?

Are you saying I can't use my ticket?

What I don't get is, how can you fall in love when you've never seen the person …

What exactly do you mean?

So you're saying … ?

2 Clarifying what someone is saying

What I'm trying to say is people want to work.

No, I'm saying there are no trains going there from this station.

Well, how can I put it … I just *did*.

What I meant to say was …

No, I was trying to say …

🔊 1.21

1	chance	6	cultural
2	exchange	7	each
3	catch	8	achieve
4	tuna	9	touch
5	question	10	future

Unit 3

🔊 1.22

AMINATA   One day, I'd like to learn to swim because I'm not very comfortable in water. I'm thinking of taking some lessons because I end up looking like a fish that's about to drown. At some point, I'd absolutely love to be comfortable in the water.

EDUARDO   My dream is to be a guitar player in a rock band because I love playing guitar and I love rock music. I play in a band with some friends and we performed at an event in my village last year and it was the best night of my life. I'm considering doing a degree in music when I'm eighteen and that'll really help, I think.

ELISA   My ambition is to live in Tokyo for a year and learn karate there. I've always wanted to train at the JKA dojo in Tokyo – erm, the JKA is the Japan Karate Association. In my opinion, it's the best place to learn karate in the world. The training is very very hard but it would really help my karate. My aim is to go there next year – I'm hoping to go in the spring.

🔊 1.24

2 At some point, I'd absolutely love to be comfortable in the water.

3 I'm thinking of taking some lessons.

4 I'm considering doing a degree in music.

5 My dream is to be a guitar player.

6 My aim is to go there next year.

7 My ambition is to live in Tokyo for a year.

8 I've always wanted to train at the JKA dojo.

🔊 1.25

AMINATA   Do you know, one of the things I'm most proud of is that I've learned to ride a bike recently.

INTERVIEWER   Really? So, why now?

A   Well, all my friends can ride bikes, and I've never been able to go with them, and so I just thought it was time really.

I   Oh right. So how's it going?

A   Well, I've had the bike for about a year now and it took me about a month to learn. I've fallen off millions of times and had a lot of bruises, but I have finally learned to ride it.

I   That's incredibly brave.

A   Yes, it was brave and also slightly foolish! But I can do it now and hopefully I'll never forget.

MARGOT   The thing I'm most proud of, actually, is that I've just written a cookery book.

INTERVIEWER   Really? What kind of cookery book?

M   Well, it's about healthy food, I guess. Healthy but delicious, and it's called *Treat Yourself*.

I   That sounds good. Where can I buy it?

M   Well, it hasn't come out yet, but it should be in the shops in January.

I   Fantastic. And have you written anything else?

M   Well, I've already written a novel actually, but it wasn't published. I mean, I've always wanted to write.

I   Yeah? So what's next?

M   Well, I'm helping to run a restaurant at the moment, which is great but it's very hard work. So I haven't written anything since the cookery book. It takes me ages to write anything. But maybe I'll have another go at a novel one day.

CHARLIE   One of the things that gives me greatest pleasure, as an achievement, in the last, say, five, ten years, is I've learned to play drums – erm, not very well, but I've learned to play drums – and, erm, I never played music before, and I became part of a *samba* band, erm, a *samba* band in England, erm, which started from very small beginnings and grew till now we have 50 or 60 members, and we go off to Ireland and play in *samba* festivals and so on.

INTERVIEWER   So, you tour?

C   We tour, yeah, we tour.

I   That sounds very exciting.

🔊 1.26

INVESTOR   So, Olga, can you tell me a little bit about your idea?

OLGA   Yes, of course. My ambition is to make shopping easier for parents with young children. My bag – called the *easybag* – can be used with any pram or buggy. It sits behind the buggy like this. The two straps clip easily over the handles without getting in the way of your hands and it has its own set of wheels. [Right.] There's plenty of space in the bag for all your shopping, and as you can see, it's attractive, easy-to-use and environmentally friendly, of course.

I   Er, can you explain what the different parts of the bag are for?

O   Yes, of course. The top pocket is for your purse, your mobile phone and any other valuables, so you can find them easily. Then there's a side pocket for all the things your baby might need while you're out, and then

the main compartment is for all your shopping. [Oh, I see.] There's no need for a supermarket trolley and there's no need to try and carry plastic bags with you while you're trying to get your shopping home.

I   Oh, OK. Erm, in what way is it different from other products on the market?

O   Well, the really unique thing about this bag is that it works with or without the buggy because of the wheels. [Aha.] So once your child is walking, you can still use the bag. It really is a bag for life …

🔊 1.27

INVESTOR   OK. So, er, what are you hoping for from us?

OLGA   What I'm looking for is a £100,000 investment for marketing and materials in return for a 33% stake in my company. My aim is to sell the product in supermarkets in Europe and I'm thinking about the USA and parts of Asia, too. I'm really excited about the product and I feel very optimistic about its chances of success in the market.

I   Well, thank you, Olga. Erm, I have some doubts about selling the product outside Europe, to be honest. Can you give us a bit more information about your background?

O   Well, I've spent ten years working in product development and have helped to develop a number of children's accessories for the international market in that time. That's where this idea came from, really. During the research for my work, I spoke to lots of parents in shops and I've seen how difficult it is coping with prams, young children and shopping, so I feel very sure about the need for something like this. [Yes, I see.] What I'm more concerned about is the marketing, as I don't have much experience of that, so this is where I'd need your support and help. I'm very keen to hear your thoughts about the business plan.

I   Thank you, Olga. That sounds very interesting. Erm, are you a mother yourself?

O   Well not, not yet, erm, but I hope to be one day …

I   Well, er, you should be well prepared. OK, thank you, Olga, er, we'll get back to you later this week with our decision.

O   Thank you.

🔊 1.28

OLGA   Hello?

INVESTOR   Hello, is that Olga?

O   Yes?

I   It's John Simmons here. We had a meeting recently through *Connections*.

o Oh, yes, of course ...

I Well, I was very impressed by your interview. It's good to see someone so passionate about their product. So I'm phoning to say we would like to invest in your business ...

o Oh, that's great news. I'm very happy about that.

I Yes, but we have some doubts about a few things in the business plan and a couple of things about the design. We'd like to set up a meeting and ask you some questions about international sales and we'd like you to meet our design expert ...

🔊 1.29

INTERVIEWER Mariama, are you comfortable talking about your achievements and things you're proud of?

MARIAMA Absolutely not. I don't, I think ..., I think it's because, erm, it's hard to sound comfortable, erm, because you don't want to sound as if you're blowing your own trumpet and you don't want to sound pompous. So I'm not at all comfortable.

I Do you think that's personal or cultural? Do you think it's ...

M I think it's quite cultural. I think, erm, a lot of my American friends are much more confident about saying what they've achieved, for example if they're writing their CV, erm, they tend to put everything on there, and they're much more confident about coming forward. [Right.] But I think being, erm, British, it's a lot harder because you don't want to seem arrogant and, er, and you don't certainly want to seem as if you've done everything you could possibly have done in your life. [Yeah.] So I'm not at all comfortable talking about my achievements. [Right.]

INTERVIEWER So, Remco, would you say you're a competitive person?

REMCO I, I am very much. Er, I've always played sports and I've always tried to play sports at a very high level and it's, it's all about winning I'm afraid, er, which means that other people have to lose ... for me to win. Erm, I mean you'll find that most good sports, er, most good athletes are not very nice people at all. And, er, not that I was very good, I don't think I was, but, er, I wasn't very nice. I want to win, and I want to win at all costs.

I Wow!

R I know.

I What about outside sport?

R Erm, I tend to be a bit more relaxed outside sports, but sometimes the, er, the competitive edge gets the better of me. Erm, I don't try and bend the rules as I do, as much as I do in sports, erm, because there

... you know, in a game you have a referee to set you straight, whereas on the work floor you don't, so that's not necessarily fair to, you know, push colleagues ...

I So you play by the rules at work?

R Erm, most of the time, most of the time, because it means a lot more. I mean, a game is still just a game, whereas work is ... erm, it means far more to people.

🔊 1.30

INTERVIEWER Right, it's Olga, isn't it?

OLGA Yes, that's right.

I Right, now as you know, we're looking for someone with extensive experience for our product development manager post. I see you've got 12 years' experience in the field.

o Yes, that's right. I started out in finance, then moved into the development side about ten years ago. I've been at ICB for five years now and for much of that time I helped develop the new West range of children's accessories for ICB.

I OK, and what do you think you can bring to the job, Olga, from that experience? What are your strengths?

o Well, you know, ICB is one of the most successful firms internationally, so I feel my international experience can be of great benefit to your company. Another thing is that I actually worked with Ron West on the development of his range and that was an amazing experience.

I OK. That's very impressive.

o Yes, I learned so much from him and I would love to be given the freedom and responsibility to develop my own ideas.

I Right. Er, can you tell me a bit about the products you're most proud of?

o Yes, well I'm obviously proud of the fact that I helped develop the West range of products, but the thing I'm actually most proud of is the product I'm working on now, which will be released into the market in a few months' time. It's a 'drink pod' and it will completely change the way we carry drinks with us.

I Right. Erm, how is it different from products that are already available?

o Well, it's very light – only 75 grams – because it's made from a completely new type of material, that we've developed which will keep your drink at exactly the same temperature – from frozen up to 100°C – but it won't affect the outside of the pod or change temperature at all. School children, joggers, office workers – you know, they will be able to take homemade soup or coffee to work and it will still be hot at lunchtime. I really believe everyone will have one.

🔊 1.31

1 years	7 twenty-first
2 seventy-five	century
grams	8 and so on
3 eight o'clock	9 against
4 number	10 approximately
5 after midday	11 per week
6 with	12 please turn over

Unit 4

🔊 1.35

1

A Oh, I've dropped your camera. I think I've broken it. I'm sorry.

B Oh, I'm sure it'll be ok.

A I was trying to take a photo and it just slipped out of my hand. Sorry.

B Don't worry. It's fine. Look, it's working.

2

A Ow!

B What's the matter?

A I banged my head on the cupboard door. Ow!

B Oh, are you OK? Does it hurt?

A It's *really* painful.

B Let's have a look. Oh dear ...

3

A What happened to you?

B Oh, yeah, I broke my wrist.

A How did you do that?

B I was on the way to work and I slipped on the ice and fell over!

A Oh, that's awful!

4

A What have you done? ... Are you OK?

B Yeah, I've broken a glass. It was a nice one too.

A Oh no. What happened?

B I was in the middle of washing up and I dropped it. I'm really sorry.

A Oh, don't worry about that.

B And I've cut my finger on the glass.

A Oh, here, let me have a look.

5

A Aah!

B What happened? Are you all right?

A No. I've hurt my leg.

B How did you do that?

A I tripped over that stool.

B Oh, sorry. That's my fault.

A It doesn't matter.

B Sorry. Are you OK?

A Yeah, it's not serious. I'm fine.

🔊 1.36

FRAN Erm, I was living in Sri Lanka when the tsunami hit. Erm, I was actually living within two hundred metres of the sea, [Oh wow!] erm, but the water amazingly didn't come to the street that I lived in. Erm, just, I was actually at home when it happened, and of course I didn't ... I didn't hear it, I didn't know anything about it, and suddenly my landlady, she came upstairs and she was shouting "Seawater, seawater!" and, erm, then we ran onto, up to the roof and we could see into the next street and there were, like, what looked like canals of water between the houses. But … and nobody knew what had happened, of course, because nobody was expecting a tsunami to happen.

ASTRID You were very lucky.

F It was really scary.

A Did you have to move to a different town?

F No, we stayed because, erm, the water then subsided very quickly, erm, and then, it was quite soon that we found out what had happened, that there had been an earthquake and that it had caused a tsunami. Erm, there was a very small danger of another one happening, but it was so small that there was no real need to move elsewhere.

A Your family probably was very worried for you.

F Well, my parents were actually visiting me at the time, so …

A Oh, they had the full experience.

F But luckily we were able to contact our family back at home very quickly [OK.] and tell them that we were all OK.

A That's good. That's very good.

ANTÓNIO The day of the eclipse was interesting, erm, because everybody seemed to be on the beach. It was absolutely packed with people in the middle of a working day. Er, everyone just left their workplaces and they immediately headed down to the sea. It wasn't actually a total eclipse, but we all sat around on the beach waiting for something to happen. The sky just changed colour very slowly and there was a very strange quality to the light. And as soon as the light started changing the birds went silent. It was, er, very eerie.

There were lots of people on the street who were selling special sunglasses and, er, other things to watch the eclipse through and people were walking around with little bits of card, trying to look at the sun without damaging their eyes. The atmosphere was amazing. I remember thinking that it was really odd that the whole town had gone to the beach in the middle of a working day to see this strange event. I was really glad I went though. Obviously I'd have liked my kids to see it too, but unfortunately, they were at school so they missed it. It was definitely an interesting experience.

🔊 **1.37**

1 Obviously, // I'd have liked my kids to see it too.

2 But unfortunately, // they were at school // so they missed it.

3 The water // amazingly // didn't come to the street I lived in.

🔊 **1.38**

JANE My daughter's a little bit accident-prone. Luckily, she's never been seriously hurt, but her silliest accident was a couple of years ago.

She had a friend round to play and they were playing some kind of game on the stairs. I was working in my study at the time and I didn't know what they were doing. I could hear that they were having a very good time, laughing a lot, but then suddenly it all went very quiet and I got this horrible sense that something was wrong. So I went to find out what was going on and, er, sure enough Megan was lying flat on her back at the bottom of the stairs next to a surfboard. I immediately realised what had happened. Megan had tried to surf down the stairs on her surfboard! Her friend hadn't come to tell me what had happened. She was just sitting on the stairs looking really terrified. Megan couldn't breathe properly because of the fall, and she could hardly speak or move but I didn't know why at the time. Obviously, I was worried she'd done something terrible to her back or neck. So I called a health advice line and they said, "Look, I think you should call an ambulance." So, we got Megan to the hospital. Erm, I can't really remember what happened next, but fortunately, in the end, she was fine. She'd hurt herself a little bit, but her back was OK. She'd just scared herself so much that she couldn't move and she frightened the life out of me, but luckily, nothing much was wrong with her.

🔊 **1.39**

TOMOKO My husband and I redecorated the living room over the summer. And we decided to do it ourselves, which was a big mistake. We just thought it would be easier and cheaper. Er, the first problem was how much it all cost. We thought we'd save money on all the materials but it cost over 50,000 yen.

We had lots of different ideas for the room. We have planes that fly over our house, so we wanted to put in some special sound-proof windows. We also don't have a lot of space but we have loads of books, so we decided to put a shelf over the door to the living room. Anyway, we'd been working all day and I was getting really stressed so I went over the road to the local café to have a coffee. When I came back, I was just putting my key in the door when I heard a loud crash from inside. I rushed in and found my husband on the floor with the shelf and a pile of

books on him. I know it's terrible but I just burst out laughing! Luckily, he wasn't hurt. Anyway, a lot of other things went wrong, but we've finally finished. I'm so glad it's over.

🔊 **1.43**

1	cream	6	basket
2	clock	7	package
3	kiss	8	chicken
4	security	9	joke
5	fork	10	pocket

Unit 5

🔊 **1.44**

A

JON Hi, Rob. How are you?

ROB Erm, I'm OK. I need your help though.

J Oh right. What's up?

R Well, before I start, the batteries on my mobile are about to run out, so if it goes dead, that's why.

J OK.

R I've locked myself out of the house.

J Oh no.

R And I'm supposed to be picking my mum up from the train station, but my car keys and wallet are in the house. She's staying this weekend.

J Oh, right. Erm, can't you call her on her mobile?

R I've tried but it's not switched on.

J OK. Erm, why don't you get a taxi?

R I've tried calling one but there's no answer! And she's arriving in five minutes! Would you mind picking her up?

J I'm sorry, but I can't go to the station right now.

R What should I do?

J Let me think. What about Amy? She's at home today, I think. Maybe she can go and pick your mum up.

R That's a good idea. Do you think she'll mind?

J Look, don't worry. I'll call Amy now, then I'll call you back. OK?

R OK. Thank you.

B

AMY Hi Jon.

JON Hi Amy. You OK?

A Er, not bad. I'm supposed to be going on that bike ride today, but I'm too tired.

J Ah. Listen, Amy, sorry to ask, but I was hoping you could help. Rob's meant to be picking his mum up from the train station, but he's locked himself out of the house. And my car's at the garage.

A Oh! OK. Well, I'll pick her up.

J Would you?

A Yes, no problem. When does her train get in?

J Well, she's arriving soon, around now actually.

A OK, I'll go now.

J OK, great. Thanks, Amy!

A No problem. Bye.

J Bye.

C

ROB Hello?

JON Rob? It's Jon.

R Hi Jon.

J Listen, Amy's going to pick your mum up.

R Oh, that's great. Thanks.

J How are you going to get into your house?

R Er, well, I found a window open upstairs, so I'm going to find a ladder.

J Good idea. Listen, I should be at work, so I've got to go.

R OK. Thanks a lot, Jon. Listen, my phone's dying.

J OK. I'll speak to you later.

🔊 **1.45**

ROB Hi, Mum. Lovely to see you, sorry about the mess-up.

MARIA Hello, darling. Don't worry. I've had a lovely chat with Amy.

R Oh good. Thank you so much, Amy. You're a real star.

AMY No problem, it's nice to see your mum again. So, how did you get into your house? Did you climb in a window or something?

R Er, no. It's ... it's a bit embarrassing, actually. I found the keys.

A You're joking. Where were they?

R In my back pocket. I forgot I'd put them there.

A So, you could've driven to the station, then?

R Er, yes, I suppose so. I'm really sorry.

A I don't believe this!

R I said I'm sorry.

M Useless boy. Oh well, it was good to see you again, Amy ...

🔊 **1.47**

1 What are we going to see?
2 Do you want to do anything later?
3 I have to buy some food.
4 I need a few things at the shops.
5 We're going to the theatre.
6 I'll look for the theatre programme.

🔊 **1.48**

MUNIZHA So, do you think everything happens for a reason?

PIERRE I feel there is a reason behind things happening the way they do sometimes, although I still believe there is also control over that, and how you react to certain situations, definitely. What about you, Munizha?

M I'm ... I'm exactly the same, actually. I used to think everything happened for a reason, but I realise now that things are quite random really and it's how you interpret them, or use them or react to them like you say. But sometimes it is nice to think of something like fate, particularly when you're in love, or ... You feel like something was meant to happen, it kind of makes it special, doesn't it?

P Oh yeah, absolutely. I think if the word 'fate' is mentioned, the first thing you think of is love ...

🔊 **1.49**

MAGGIE It was my husband's birthday, his fortieth, so I wanted to do something special for him. But I'd been away on a business trip and hadn't had time to plan anything, so I decided to surprise him when he got home from work. Well, my plan was this: while he was at work I was going to cook his favourite dinner – Moroccan chicken and rice – and make a beautiful chocolate cake. Then I was going to take him to the theatre and then on to a nice little club to listen to some jazz. Well, it was getting quite late and I'd just started the cake when I realised I didn't have enough eggs. So I went to the corner shop to get some, but when I got back to the flat I realised I didn't have my keys. I'd locked myself out of the house. I sat down on the doorstep and waited for my husband to come home from work and let me in. It started to rain. It was a disaster!

🔊 **1.50**

MAGGIE When my husband came home from work I was soaking wet from the rain. I told him what had happened and said I was sorry about his birthday being ruined. He looked at me like I was completely mad, then started laughing. I'd got the day wrong. It wasn't his birthday till the next day!

🔊 **1.51**

IQBAL Is that you, Carolina?

CAROLINA Iqbal? Look at you! How are you?

I I'm OK, thanks. You're looking well.

C Thanks. And you haven't changed a bit.

I I'm not sure that's true but thanks.

C It's been a long time ...

I Yeah, I know ... but seeing everyone, it ... it seems like only yesterday.

C Really? It seems a long time ago to me. Isn't it great to see everyone again?

I Yeah, it's amazing. Now, er, when we were at university, you were going to be a doctor. So, er, what happened?

C Oh, I'm not a doctor, no. That didn't work out. I just, er, didn't have the energy for all that study. I'm an office manager for a law firm. It's ... What about you? The last time I saw you, you were going to study finance.

I Yes, well, er, I did study finance, and I did quite well and, er, now I live in Kuala Lumpur.

C Kuala Lumpur's a great city.

I Yes, I'm going to buy a house there this year actually. I love my life over there.

C Oh, that's fantastic. So what do you do?

I I'm still in finance. Erm, I have one of those jobs that's really difficult to describe. I move the company's money around, basically.

C Oh, that's ... good. I was never very good with maths.

I Did you ever travel around Europe? I remember you always wanted to do that.

C I did actually. It was great. That was a long time ago though. I should do some more travelling really. I'm a bit bored with my life at the moment.

🔊 **1.52**

MARK I used to work in telecommunications in Paris and once I had to go to Japan to discuss a contract. So, at the end of the meeting I asked if they were interested, and they nodded and then stood up and came over and shook my hand. [Right.] I was happy that everything had gone well. Anyway, I flew home and the next day I checked my emails and there was one from the Japanese company I'd just been talking to the previous day, right? It said thanks very much for coming to see them and sorry they couldn't agree on a deal, but they'd like to keep in touch in the future. I couldn't believe it. I thought they'd said 'yes' but actually they'd said 'no'. Since that time, I've realised that it's a cultural difference and that, in Japan, it's not polite to say no directly. [Oh, I see.] You can say something is difficult or that it's a problem, and that, to a Japanese person, clearly means no. But at that time, I didn't think beyond my own experience in England and France, where saying no is not a problem.

VICTOR I'm Brazilian, but I've lived in the States for five years now, in Boston. A friend of mine, José Carlos, also a Brazilian guy, he got married last spring to an American woman, Sarah. I already knew her quite well – we would all go out dancing and stuff, and she speaks good Portuguese, actually.

Anyway, when they said they were getting married, I was really happy for them, and I said I would love to come to their wedding. I wasn't completely sure at the time that I could go to their wedding, but I didn't want to say no because it would seem rude, you know? [Sure.] So, I think José Carlos knew that I wouldn't come, but Sarah was sure I'd said that, yes, absolutely, I could come, and she got really upset when I said, a couple of weeks before the wedding, that actually I couldn't come. She took it, like, "He doesn't care about us", which is obviously not true at all.

We're friends again now, but it made me think about how we say no in Brazil, in a subtle way, not direct, with body language perhaps, or something in the tone of voice, which Brazilian people hear and understand. Americans don't have the same difficulty in saying no, and so for them it's much more rude to cancel something at the last minute. It's something that, now, I'm much more careful about.

Unit 6

2.1

HELPLINE If you're not an existing customer, press one. If you're phoning about a technical problem, please press two. Due to the high number of calls today, you will have to wait in a queue to be answered. You are currently number three in the queue. We are sorry for the delay. You are still in a queue.

TECHNICIAN Hello. How can I help you?

VISHAL Oh hello. I'm having problems with my computer. I haven't been able to get online today.

T Right. Have you tried switching everything off and on again?

V Yes. I've already tried that. I still can't get online. Er, and this isn't the first time – it keeps happening.

T OK. Do you have a router? [Mm-hm.] Have you turned it off and on again?

V Yes. I have. That didn't work either. My router keeps going wrong.

T Well, there may be a problem with it. Have you considered getting a new one?

V This one is brand new. It's the third one I've had.

T OK, I understand. Well, try and avoid leaving your router on all the time if you can. You should think about turning it off at night.

V Oh, OK. I didn't know about that.

T If you hold on a minute I'll check your signal … Hello, are you there?

V Yes, I'm still here.

T Well, you've got a signal this end, so it's not the line. You'll need to check your internet connection. Have you done that?

V Er, no, not yet. Can you tell me how to do that?

T Yes, of course. If you go to Start – that's the button in the bottom left corner of your screen.

V OK, right. What do I do next?

T Click on Control Panel and open Network Connections and tell me what it says.

V Sorry, hold on a minute, I don't know where that is.

T OK, can you see the Control Panel screen?

V Yes. There are a lot of icons. Which one should I open?

T Network Connections.

V Oh right, I can see it now. OK, I've opened it.

T What does it say?

V Oh. It says the Local Area Connection is unplugged. But it's not. I've checked and I've plugged everything in.

T OK. You'll have to shut everything down, unplug your router and computer and try opening the Internet by using the main socket.

V So, you're saying I've got to take everything out of my office and set it up in another room? I did that a few months ago. I can't face moving everything again.

T I'm sorry, but I'm afraid you'll have to test each piece of equipment separately to see where the problem is.

V So, this will show me if it's the router that's the problem?

T Yes, or if it's the socket you're using.

V OK. And there's nothing else you can do to help me?

T Not until you've tested the equipment. I mean, we can send an engineer out to test the line but that will cost you £50. And if they come out for nothing, that's a waste of money.

V OK. I'll give it a go then. Thanks for your help and advice.

T No problem. Do give us a call back if that doesn't work.

V Thanks. Bye.

2.4

First, you need to turn it on and plug it in to the computer. Then load it with all the sound files you want. Some of them, you can put photos on too. Then, when everything's finished loading, unplug it, and check that it's worked. Then plug in the headphones, press 'Play', sit back and enjoy.

2.6

JÖRG Well, we know that many marriages break down because of financial issues, so it's important to manage money in the right way because the consequences can be very serious. There are a few simple rules that can make a big difference.

Since it's such a big issue, you need to make sure you're always open about your finances, about how much each of you earns and spends. We all know that money can be a source of conflict. So, we should all be honest and open about money with a partner.

Second, it's a very good idea to have a joint account. Due to the fact that many couples share the payment for lots of things, their finances can become confused. You'll have to pay for your household expenses – the bills,

your rent or mortgage, your car and anything else you use as a couple or family. It's extremely time-consuming to negotiate these payments every month, so it's a good idea to pay bills from one joint account. You should both agree on a fixed amount to pay into that account every month.

Then thirdly, you need to know how to budget. You must put enough money aside each month to cover the bills and a bit extra for emergencies and holidays. It's easy to find out how to budget as there's a lot of advice online; for instance, one good site is yourbudget.com. Once you've decided on a budget, you have to work out together how to keep to it. As this is not always possible, you'll also need to agree on what to do when you go over your budget.

Finally, if you both work, it's important to each have your own account as well as a joint account. Couples who argue a lot – well, it's often due to disagreements about money. It's important to have your own money, so that you can buy yourself – or your partner – something nice from time to time. It's helpful to recognise that we are all individuals financially as well as personally.

2.7

SABRINA It's great to see you, Felipe. It's been too long.

FELIPE Yes, I know. Seven years! I meant to call you last week to say I was coming, but I've been so busy.

S Don't worry. It's lucky I'm not away.

F I wish I was a student here again. I mean, it's too bad I've got to work.

S Yes, but not until Monday. You can enjoy your weekend in Arezzo first. Where are you staying?

F I'm at the Arezzo Palace, no, sorry, I mean the Arezzo Hotel.

S Right. What's it like?

F It's OK. It's a bit quiet. I mean, there's nobody else staying there!

S Oh, that's strange. So, what's happening on Monday?

F Well, my conference starts at 9.00, so that means leaving here on Sunday night.

S Oh, we haven't got long then. What do you want to do with your weekend? I can show you around …

F Er, well, we've got the whole afternoon … I mean … we could just walk around. It's so great to be here.

S Yeah. That sounds nice.

F Oh, by the way, I found an old photo of us as students. Here, do you remember that day?

S Wow! We look so young.

F I know, this photo means a lot to me.

2.8

S Hey, can I look at your passport photo? Look at that beard!

F Hey! It's an old photo, you know?

S Oh, I didn't mean to upset you. It was just funny seeing that beard again. You look so young! Actually, it brings back great memories. Erm, Felipe, I don't mean to worry you, but your passport's falling apart. Oh no! I'm really sorry ... look what I've done!

F Oh! Could you grab that page quickly before it flies away? [Got it.] ... Thanks. [Sorry.] Er, don't worry. I keep meaning to fix it. It's been like that for ages. Well, not quite like that, but ...

S Sorry. [It's OK.] Er, do you want to go out for a meal tonight? I mean, it's your last night, isn't it?

F Good idea. Where shall we go?

S I was thinking about Burger King ... no, I mean Burger World.

F Er, I don't mean to sound rude but I'd rather go somewhere more ... I mean ... er, it would be nice to go somewhere more Italian. What was that place we used to go to? I mean, the small place in the main square.

S Oh I know. Loggia Vasari. I haven't been there for years. It may not even be there any more.

F Shall we go and see? Oh, by the way, I've been meaning to ask you, could you give me Marco's phone number? I'd like to get in touch with him while I'm here.

2.10

1 say you don't understand
Sorry, I'm lost.
I don't get it.
2 say you partly understand
I get that bit.
3 explain something
It just means you mix all the tiles up.
It's like a card game with tiles.
The idea is to collect sets.
I meant to say the aim is to get rid of all the tiles in your hand first.

2.12

1 organise	6 corner
2 lawn	7 reward
3 explore	8 adore
4 towards	9 warning
5 courtroom	10 important

Unit 7

2.13

INTERVIEWER   So, Anne, what do you need to succeed in the dancing world? What kind of person do you need to be?

ANNE   You need to really really want to be a dancer. You need to be the sort of person who never gives up. It's surprising how many people grow up with 'dance mums', with parents who really push them to be dancers and to be successful. But often with people like that, they grow up and one day they suddenly say: "Actually I really don't want to be a dancer." So you have to really want to do it yourself. Erm, you have to have discipline to keep going, mentally as well as physically. A lot of people sort of give up and leave the profession when it just gets too much psychologically, but you really have to be the kind of person who keeps going; you have to just train, train, train.

I Yeah, I'm sure it's the sort of thing that needs a lot of discipline. I mean, it must be really difficult keeping in shape and everything.

A Actually, that's something that people don't really understand. People think that dancers are all the same, that you have to be really skinny and really flexible and all that, but actually people want dancers who are different. I mean, when I started out I tried to be the same as the other young dancers. But as you get older and more into the profession, you realise that people want to see dancers who are unique. For me, as I got older and I became more comfortable with myself and I let my own personality show in my dancing, I started to get jobs. It's the kind of job that requires a lot of confidence actually. You have to have the confidence to be yourself.

I OK, OK. Er, what are some of the obstacles dancers can come up against?

A The main obstacle is the competition; it's fiercely competitive. And it's not just about having talent. You need to be lucky, too. There's always someone that can ... that *is* a better dancer than you out there. You just have to be in the right place at the right time.

I Erm, do you have to be good at dealing with disappointment then?

A Yes, definitely. You have to be someone who can take rejection well. It wasn't till recently when we were leaving college that my friends first started to be turned down for auditions. I've been turned down for auditions right from the beginning. It's really hard. But then something you don't expect will often come up. You really have to have an open mind about where your career will go. For me, that's what makes it exciting.

2.14

1
I just sit in my armchair and watch him swirl around. Watching him is far better than watching television. He's much friendlier than a lot of the ones you see, like those in big office aquariums. He comes up to the glass to say hello when I come in the room. He's a great character. Am I happier because of him? I think I probably am.

2
Tim's a bit unusual so I'm not really surprised that he wanted an unusual pet, like a reptile. I was horrified when he first brought her home though, because she sometimes behaved like an absolute lunatic. Apparently, if their owner gets stressed, then they get stressed too. But Tim's generally a calm person, so she tends to be calm now too.

3
My friends tell me I'm an eccentric and a bit unusual – just like my five feathered friends. It's true that the way I talk sometimes and the way I bob my head is just like them. They all have individual traits I see in myself. Molly loves people. At times she's a little bit of a show-off, too.

4
I think we are growing even more like each other as we get older. We are both becoming a lot more grumpy. We certainly aren't quite as tolerant as we used to be. I enjoy my food just as much as he enjoys his, although I am a little more fussy. But we have our good times still. When I'm in a good mood I often notice him wagging his tail, which means he's happy, I think. Other than that I think I am slightly more intelligent than him.

5
Are we alike? Hm, I think so. I mean, I'm a nice guy, and he's really nice too. You can hold him for hours and he just walks around your hands and arms and shoulders, looking around. But when he's left in his cage he always manages to find a way out and gets into all sorts of trouble. He's a strange creature, but I'm very fond of him.

2.16

Tim's generally a calm person, so she tends to be calm now too.

I enjoy my food just as much as he enjoys his.

If their owner gets stressed, then they get stressed too.

2.17

TARA   I had a teacher when I was at secondary school, erm, who was a big influence on me. She was a really nice woman, and she was just really passionate about her work. She taught physics, and she really got me interested in the subject. She had a great way of explaining things by using examples from everyday life. Like, for example, she'd use sports like athletics events or, erm, figure skating to explain rules of motion, that kind of thing. The rest of my teachers didn't really think much of me, but she inspired me to do better. She really had faith in me, and she encouraged me to go on to university. And, well, I did, I went on to do physics at university, as a result. I'm now working in space science, and if it wasn't for her, I think my life would be very different now. Erm, another person who's influenced me was my best friend at high school. I met her when I was sixteen and she was completely different from me. She was a really clever girl, and really confident and just said exactly what she thought. Her confidence made a huge impression on me. I was quite shy at that age, and she really helped me to be myself, I suppose. She made me much more confident.

2.18

HAYES   It's difficult to say what I define myself as first. I'm a mother and have a son but I'm divorced. And, erm, I don't see my parents very often either so maybe family isn't such a big thing for me. When I meet people I usually say: "Hi, I'm Hayes, website designer", just to get the conversation going really. And I suppose that means my job is a big part of who I am. I'd describe myself as a hard-working person with my own business and, yeah, I'm very proud of the work I do. Work is seen as a big thing here. People don't have much holiday, sometimes only a couple of weeks a year, and, erm, people retire later and later. In fact, retirement is perceived as a bit lazy really. I think that's true. Erm, at least, it isn't strange to still be working in your seventies. My dad really struggled to know what to do with himself when he retired. He still seems a bit lost. I guess I'll be the same. I know it's not the same in Europe. Maybe work isn't regarded as so important over there.

ALEX   Er, probably I would say I see myself as a father first, then as a friend. But, erm, I also think of myself as a colleague to people at work. I take that responsibility quite seriously. Erm, but in terms of what's most important to me that would be my family. Family ties are very important in Greece, in terms of support, what people would expect, and your family would expect you to be able to look after them if need be. I mean, my family aren't typical, but generally speaking I think my parents would be quite unhappy if they had to go into an old people's home. They would expect to be somehow supported by their children. My

brother actually lives with my parents at the moment. That's another thing that's very different in terms of family ties. He has lost his job, he's nearly forty now, my brother, and he lives with them and is supported by them. People tend to live with their families a lot longer in Mediterranean countries than elsewhere, I think.

2.19

1   He's a really charming guy.
2   She's a great character.
3   He's such a calm person.
4   She can be a bit difficult.
5   He's a bit miserable sometimes.

Unit 8

2.21

A (12pm)

ALICE   The train must go from here. This is platform 1, isn't it?

JAVIER   Yes, platform 1.

A   Yeah, come on. It'll be great to see Sue.

J   Does she know what time we get in?

A   Yeah. I told her we'll arrive at two.

J   Is she coming to pick us up?

A   No, she said to get a cab. It's her birthday party. Anyway, she's got to look after the barbecue.

J   Why are we leaving? The train doesn't leave for another fifteen minutes. What's going on?

A   Are you sure we're on the right train?

J   Oh, no. This can't be our train! Excuse me, excuse me. Sorry. Is this the train to Beauville?

STEWARD   No, sir. This train is going to Newmont. It doesn't stop in Beauville.

J   But it said platform 1 on the board.

S   Yes, but there are three sections to platform 1: 1A, 1B and 1C.

J   Oh no! What are we going to do?

B

JAVIER   Can we get off at the next stop? Maybe change trains and get one to Beauville from there?

PASSENGER   This train goes direct to Newmont. It takes an hour and a half to get there. Then you can catch the train to Beauville from there.

ALICE   Oh no! What a nightmare! We're going to be late.

C (2.30pm)

JAVIER   Here we are. Let's ask when the next train to Beauville is. Excuse me! Can you tell me when the next train to Beauville is, please?

OFFICIAL   Er, there are no more trains to Beauville today, I'm afraid. They've all been cancelled. There's been an accident down the line. There's a replacement bus service, though.

ALICE   Oh, that's just great! How long does that take?

O   It'll take a couple of hours to get to Beauville.

A   That can't be the only way, surely!

O   I'm afraid so. The next bus goes in five minutes though. You'll find it round the back of the station. Just show your train ticket.

J   This bus is just awful! It's so uncomfortable.

A   What's that noise?

J   No idea, but it doesn't sound very good.

D (3.10pm)

ALICE   There must be a problem with the engine. Listen to it!

JAVIER   We're stopping.

A   This is unbelievable.

BUS DRIVER   I'm afraid we have a problem. Would you all please get off? I've been informed that there will be another bus along shortly.

A   Do you know how long the next bus will be, please?

BD   Well, it could be an hour before it gets here. Maybe sooner, but …

E (3.25pm)

JAVIER   Now what?

ALICE   I don't know. There might be a local bus that goes past.

J   There aren't any bus stops.

A   No. I suppose there could be one further along. We might be able to hitchhike.

J   Hm. There aren't many cars. Maybe we should just wait for the next bus.

A   No, I'm not going to wait here for an hour. Let's start walking and try to get a lift.

J   OK.

F (6.40pm)

SUE   Alice, Javier! Where have you been? Why didn't you phone me?

ALICE   Yeah, sorry, Sue. I lost my phone and Javier doesn't have your number.

S   Who was that woman in the car?

JAVIER   Oh, she drove us here. It's a long story.

A   Where is everyone?

S   They've all gone home. What happened?

2.24

1

LOST PROPERTY   Hello, Lost property.

PETE   Oh, hello. I lost my wallet, last week.

LP   OK. What does it look like?

P   Well, it's a small, brown, leather wallet, quite plain. It's got some cash inside, about 20 dollars, and some cards.

LP   OK, we've got quite a lot of those. One of them might be yours.

P   And, also, one of the credit cards is a Visa, gold and black. It's got my name on it.

LP   OK, I'll just make a note of this. Would you hold the line, please?

P   Of course …

LP   Erm, no, nothing like that has been handed in.

P   Oh, OK.

2

LOST PROPERTY Hello, Lost property.

SALLY Hi there. I've lost my mobile.

LP Er, OK. Can you describe it for me?

S Erm, it's a Motorola. And the most obvious thing about it is that it has pink stripes on the outside. It also has a little silver stripe on the bottom and there's a heart design on the front.

LP OK. It's a Motorola, you say?

S Yes, that's right.

LP Would you hold the line, please?

S Sure. …

LP Yes, hello?

S Hello?

LP Yes, this one must be yours. A silver stripe on the bottom, you say?

S Yes, that's it. Oh fantastic!

3

LOST PROPERTY Hello, Lost property.

JAVIER Oh, hello. I've lost my bag. I left it on the number 48 bus this morning. It's a black and grey sports bag, mostly black, with a shoulder strap.

LP OK. I've got one right here. It hasn't got much in it.

J That can't be mine. It's full of clothes and other stuff. It's got pockets on the side, and there's a blue water bottle in one of them.

LP OK. Would you hold the line, please? I'll see if we've got anything like that.

J Right, thanks. …

LP Erm, no, nothing like that has been handed in. But you could try again tomorrow. Sometimes it takes a little time for people to hand things in.

J Oh, OK. Thanks. I'll try again tomorrow then.

🔊 **2.25**

SALIL I still haven't found my phone.

MANI Oh, what a nightmare! Maybe you left it at work. That reminds me, I can't find my coat.

S Didn't you take it to have it cleaned or something?

M Yeah, I had it dry cleaned, but I picked it up at lunchtime yesterday. I've left it somewhere probably.

S When did you have it last?

M Yesterday afternoon. I had to go into town for a meeting.

S And did you take it off at any point?

M Maybe, yeah. Oh, what did I do? I'd just been to the dry cleaners and then I had some food at the café and then I caught the bus to go to work …

S Ah, maybe you took it off on the bus. Were you talking to someone?

M Well, I had a chat with this old lady at the bus stop. Maybe I left it there. Bet it's not there now though. I'll give lost property a call.

S Yeah, good idea.

🔊 **2.28**

1	dance	6	palm
2	market	7	half
3	calm	8	example
4	father	9	target
5	start	10	bath

Unit 9

🔊 **2.29**

LIDIA Are you ready? My parents will be here in an hour.

BEN Yeah. What are we going to do about lunch?

L I've got no idea. We could all go out, I suppose.

B Oh no! I think you should come down here a second. There's water everywhere.

L Oh no! Where's it all coming from?

B I've no idea. What shall we do?

L We'll have to call someone.

B Hold on a second. Where's it coming from?

L I don't know.

B Maybe it's the washing machine.

L Turn it off then.

B I'll give it a try, but I'm not sure it …

B No, that's not it. You know my shirt is in the washing machine.

L Well, wear another one.

B But I don't have any others. They're all in the wash.

L Well, you can pop out and buy one. We need to stop this flooding first. Have you turned off the water at the mains?

B I don't know where the tap or switch thing is.

L You're useless. It's under the stairs, I think. Here, I'll have a go.

B OK?

L Er, no. The handle's come off in my hand.

B We're going to have to call a plumber to sort this out.

L Who's that?

B That can't be your parents. They're early!

L Typical. Where are those kids? Downstairs now! Your grandma and grandad are here!

🔊 **2.30**

SIMON Hi everyone. Isn't it great that it's going so well? We've had more people coming in than I ever expected so soon after opening.

YELENA Yes, it's fantastic. What do you think, Lidia?

LIDIA Yes, it's crazy, but it's great.

S Yeah, but of course this means we're much busier than we expected. In fact, we could do even more business if we had a bigger place. But we can't afford it.

Y Well, what about opening a terrace? We've got the space and that would attract even more people.

S Yes, that's just what I was thinking, Yelena. If we open a terrace, we'll be able to serve a lot more people.

L But it's too expensive. And if we did that, it would take a lot longer to serve people outside.

S Well, maybe. I'm afraid we're all going to have to work more hours anyway, because we're so busy.

L Hm, that's a problem for me. I mean, if I didn't have three children, I'd do it, no problem. But I know I won't do a good job if I'm exhausted.

Y Well, I'm sure we can cover it with the people who want more work. I'm more than happy to take on extra hours.

S Well, er, have a look at this timetable here and you can see what I have in mind. The names I've put in are just suggestions, so don't panic, Lidia.

Y OK, this is very useful, Simon. But it does mean everyone would have to do more hours. So, I wonder if there's another way round it?

S Yes?

Y Well, I suppose this is impossible, but if we employed another person, we wouldn't have to do so many hours.

L That's not a bad idea. But if we employ another person, we'll take home less money.

S Yes, but it would solve the problem, and when we get the terrace, we'll need someone else anyway. I think it's a good idea. If we cover everything for this week, then we can advertise in Friday's local paper.

Y OK, but maybe we could just think of people we know.

S Good idea, let's make a list of possibles. Lidia, any thoughts?

🔊 **2.32**

b But it's too expensive. // And if we did that, // it would take a lot longer to serve people outside.

c Hm, // that's a problem for me. // I mean, // if I didn't have three children, // I'd do it, // no problem.

d Well, // I suppose this is impossible, // but if we employed another person, // we wouldn't have to do so many hours.

e That's not a bad idea. // But if we employ another person, // we'll take home less money.

🔊 **2.33**

BRAD OK, guys, I can't stand this kitchen any more. I can't even find a plate to eat off. Nobody does the washing up apart from me!

NASSER OK, Brad, how about if we take turns to do it?

LUIS But Nasser, that would mean making a rota.

B We could do that, I suppose. Or we could just do our own stuff. Since we don't often eat together, that would make more sense.

N Yes, you're right. Would you do your own washing up, Luis?

L Yes, OK, but if I agree to do that, could you please do something for me?

B What do you mean?

L Well, the bathroom. Erm, it's always busy. I can't ever get in there. I missed my first lecture the other day.

N Yes, actually, Brad, you do take an awful long time in the bathroom.

B Me?

N Yes, sorry.

B That's not true. Maybe there's just not enough time for everyone to have a shower in the morning. Nasser, what if you had your shower in the evening?

N I need to have a shower before I go out, thanks. In fact, Brad, you don't have to be at college first thing in the morning, do you? Maybe you could use the bathroom later, when we've gone. That way, you can take as long as you like.

B Yeah, I suppose I could do that. But while we're talking about these things, Nasser, if I use the bathroom later, would you mind not having the radio on all the time? It drives me crazy.

N Really? But it's interesting.

B For you, maybe, but that talk radio on all the time, it makes me feel stressed.

L Well, maybe you could listen to it in your room.

N But I like listening to it while I'm eating.

L OK, let's say you can listen to it in the kitchen if the door's shut.

N Yeah, yeah. OK, OK.

2.34

ÇIGDEM

1

If I have a client who is unhappy with the treatment I'm proposing, I would probably be quite direct and ask them what the problem is. If someone is behaving oddly, I would probably leave it for a while, but if it carries on, I would ask them very directly what they are unhappy about. And often that resolves it. If there's still an issue, I'll discuss it with them and usually we'll reach a compromise.

2

I find that in particular in England, families are very hush-hush. If someone's done something which causes tension, nobody says anything. They often don't try to resolve the conflict. They tend to leave it. With my husband, when there is tension with his siblings, I'll say "Can't you just phone them and talk about it and ask them what's wrong? I would to my brother." And he says, "No, no, it'll all be OK if we just leave it." That's not the Turkish way.

3

I have disagreements with my father but I would still always show him respect. I mean, I wouldn't shout or swear at him, but I would argue my case. Even now, *benim annem*, my mother will still tell me what to do and tell my brother what to do and she still interferes in our lives. And actually, I listen to her now. We still have quite angry rows though, and my daughter and I will have fiery arguments as well because we are much more Turkish like that.

4

I think in England people do a lot of talking behind the scenes, talking about each other. There's that typical thing that when you ask someone directly about a problem, they're almost embarrassed. I think we're less inhibited in Turkey because everything is out in the open. People will deal more openly with each other. People have a lot more arguments and disagreements in Turkey. It's much more fiery. Not just in families either. There's a lot of arguments in shops, at work and in meetings. Meetings can be very fiery.

Unit 10

2.36

1 What was the crime?
2 Where did it take place?
3 What was the criminal wearing? What did he look like?
4 Were there any witnesses?
5 What were they doing? What did they look like?

2.37

HIROMI Oh, I haven't told you!

FRED What?

H I saw someone breaking into the flat opposite me the other day.

F Really? What happened?

H Well, I was working from home and taking a break ...

F When was this?

H A couple of days ago.

F Really?

H Yeah, so I was having a cup of tea and just staring out of the window when I saw this guy, he was only a boy really, climbing through a window into the ground-floor flat opposite!

F Wow.

H Yeah, and I remember wondering how he got in there. It was during the day and it was on a street, in public, you know. I guess someone must have left the window open. Anyway, he got in. I couldn't see anything after that. I didn't know if anyone was in the flat at the time. I was so surprised, I forgot to phone the police. Anyway, a few minutes later, the boy came out the front door of the block of flats with a bag full of stuff in his arms

and ran off down the street. Then I remembered to pick up the phone.

F That's amazing. Weren't you scared?

H Not really, it all seemed so unreal.

F What did you tell the police?

H Well, I just told them what happened.

F What did he look like?

H Erm, I can't remember what he looked like. But I can remember that he was wearing a rugby shirt. It had a number one on it, I think.

F Did you see his face?

H No, not really. Oh, that reminds me. He had a baseball cap on. I forgot to tell the police that.

F And was there anyone else outside at the time?

H Erm, you know, I've forgotten a lot of what happened. I remember I looked down and I noticed someone crossing the street. A teenager, I think, a young man. But there was nobody else around.

F Did you recognise him?

H Who?

F The guy breaking into the flat.

H No, no. Well, you know, I've only just moved there so I didn't recognise him. I'm sure I've never seen him before. I mean, looking back on it, it's all a bit worrying, really.

F Yeah. It does sound strange.

H Anyway, you'll have to come round and see my new flat.

2.38

TARIQ I lived in France for a few years and they have a very different attitude to complaining than we do in the UK. In the UK if someone goes to the front of a queue without waiting in line, people generally won't complain because they're too embarrassed. They might moan about it to someone they're with but they won't actually say anything directly. I remember when I was first in Paris. Someone walked right up to the front of a queue and three or four people started talking to him. "Hey, you, what are you doing? Get to the back of the queue" they were all saying. Another time, I was on the Metro and a man lit a cigarette, and again, a couple of people immediately said "Put the cigarette out." I'm not sure what would have happened in the UK. I think that maybe nobody would have said anything.

I think that in the UK, though, people do complain. Especially if there's a problem with a business or a service that isn't good. People phone up and complain or write emails. And maybe people are slowly becoming more outspoken in public situations too.

🔊 2.39

RECORDED MESSAGE   Hello and welcome to Anybooks.com customer service helpline. Your call is important to us and we will be with you as soon as we can. …
Hello and welcome to Anybooks.com customer service helpline. Your call is important to us and we will be—

GERRY   Hello, Anybooks.com customer service helpline, Gerry speaking, how may I help you?

MARIAH   Hello. You know, I've been waiting to speak to someone for ten minutes.

G   I apologise for the delay in answering your call today, madam. Monday mornings are often an extremely busy period for us.

M   Yes, I understand that, but I've been trying to contact you for two weeks now and no one has got in touch with me. It's extremely frustrating!

G   I apologise about that. How can I help you today?

M   I bought a book from your website and when I got it in the post, some of the pages were missing and some were torn. It was in terrible condition.

G   OK. We should be able to help you with that. What you need to do is write an email to our …

M   But I've already done that and nothing happened.

G   You've already …

M   I've written two emails, but I haven't received a reply.

G   Well, I'm very sorry about that. That shouldn't happen. What's your order number, please?

M   Yes. Erm, it's 18635PK.

G   Is that 35PK?

M   Yes, that's right.

G   Can you hold the line while I speak to my supervisor?

M   OK.

G   I'll have to put you on hold. Is that OK?

M   How long will that be for?

G   It'll only take a couple of minutes.

M   OK, thank you.

G   Hello?

M   Hello.

G   Sorry to keep you. Yes, that's fine. I've just ordered you a replacement copy.

M   So … I'm getting another copy of the book?

G   Yes, I'll send that out to you today.

M   And when will I get the new book?

G   You should receive it within five working days.

M   OK. Great, thanks.

G   No problem, bye now.

M   Bye.

🔊 2.41

IAN   Hello. How are you?

JAMES   I'm OK, thanks. And you?

I   Er, yes, fine, thanks. Er, yeah, that

reminds me, I've been meaning to talk to you, actually. About your son.

J   Oh, yes?

I   Well, he keeps kicking his ball into our garden.

J   Yes, he's full of energy, isn't he? Such an active kid.

I   It's just that, er, his ball ruins our plants and flowers. It's a bit annoying.

J   Oh, I'm sorry. But, you know, he doesn't mean any harm.

I   I'm sorry but you're missing the point. I've been wanting to speak to you for some time about this.

J   Really? I had no idea. We're just happy he's getting some fresh air, you know?

I   Well, to be honest, we'd like to have a bit of peace and quiet. It's hard to relax when that ball keeps flying over our heads.

J   Oh, he's just a bit high-spirited. He won't do any damage.

I   Well, to be fair, he has kicked the ball quite close to our windows. I'd be grateful if you could have a word with him about it.

J   OK, if you feel that way, I'll speak to him.

I   Thanks for that. If you could ask him to try not to kick the ball into our garden, I'd really appreciate it.

J   I'll see what I can do.

I   Thanks. Have a good day now.

J   Yes, and you.

🔊 2.42

HIROMI   Hello?

GILL   Oh hello. I'm Gill. I live next door. I think you've just moved in?

H   Yes, that's right. I've been here a few days.

G   Well, I just wanted to introduce myself. Erm, I've made you some cakes.

H   Oh, that was very kind of you. They look delicious. I'm Hiromi. Would you like to come in for a coffee?

G   Erm, yes, that would be nice, thanks. Ah … you have children then?

H   Yes, a son, Toshi. He's six.

G   That's the same age as my grandson, Robert. Would Toshi like to come round and play?

H   How thoughtful of you. I'm sure he'd love that.

G   So where were you before?

H   We've just moved here from Japan.

G   Really? That's so brave of you! But your English is so good.

H   Ah well, my husband is Scottish and we've spent quite a lot of time here, you know …

🔊 2.43

1   Can I help you with your bag?
2   You look lovely today.
3   Would you like a lift to work?
4   I've fixed your computer.
5   I've decided to leave my job.

🔊 2.45

RITA   You're late again! You've missed dinner. You've been working late all week and you've been missing dinner every day too. It's not good for you.

HASAN   I know. But I've had lunch with clients three times, so it's not so bad. I'm sorry about the late nights. You know I've been having interviews all week.

R   Yes, but what if you don't get another job? This has been going on for too long now. You need to talk to Tim about your hours.

H   I have. I've had three meetings with him this week.

R   Oh good. You didn't tell me about that.

H   No, I haven't had time. I've been doing other things.

🔊 2.47

1 school	6	souvenir
2 soon	7	prove
3 tooth	8	super
4 soup	9	truth
5 grew	10	drew

Unit 11

🔊 3.1

A

A   Look, the president is a joke! He's weak and indecisive. We need strong leadership in times like these.

B   But he just needs time …

B

A   Did you hear that Alicia and Malcolm have split up?

B   No!

A   It's true. Jan told me. She said they've had problems and that they're splitting up.

B   I can't believe it

C

A   Aah!

B   What's happened?

A   Er, sorry, nothing. I thought I saw a mouse under this cushion, but it's not.

B   What *is* it?

A   It's a toy mouse.

D

A   Are you free this afternoon?

B   Yeah. Shall we go for a coffee?

A   Good idea.

E

A   I cannot believe it's raining again. It's been raining for days now.

B   I know. It's always the same.

F

A   Can someone come and help me? Quick! I'm about to drop everything!

B   Coming. What are you doing with all that stuff?

G

A   I have to travel a lot, you know.

B   Right.

A   Oh, yeah. I've been to three continents this year alone. And the money's pretty good. Do you know how much I earned last year?

3.2

SURESH Meninda, are you still there?

MENINDA Sorry, you took me by surprise, Suresh. I really had no idea!

S Well, what do you think? Do you think I'm doing the right thing?

M Well, er, it's difficult to say right now. To tell you the truth, I'm a bit stunned. Have you told your parents?

S Er, no, not yet. You won't tell them, will you?

M No, no, I won't say anything. Don't worry. But when are you going to tell them?

S I'm not. Well, not yet anyway. I'll call them when I get to Australia.

M What! You can't do that!

S Think about it. How do you think they'll react when I tell them?

M Er, it's hard to say. You know they'll both be upset. Especially your dad.

S Yeah, so you see the problem if I tell them now.

3.3

INDRA Hi Meninda, how are you?

MENINDA Yeah, good, thanks. Listen, have you spoken to Suresh?

I No, not for a while. Is he OK?

M Yeah, he's fine, and we were just chatting, when suddenly he says, "Look, I want to tell you something, but can you keep it quiet?"

I Oh go on, this sounds good ...

M So then he said, "You know I've been offered this great job by that law firm?" So of course I say yeah, and then he says to me, "Well, I said no!"

I What? He's crazy!

M Yeah, I told him that. I said, "You're mad!" Then I said to him, "Have you found something better?" And he goes, "No, I've got a more interesting plan." So, I'm starting to worry about what's going on, and I'm like, "Whoa! You're not going to do anything wild, are you?" So he goes, "No, of course not, but Mum and Dad will go crazy." So I'm like, "Yeah! So what are you going to do?" And he says, "No, no, don't worry. I'm going to go travelling around the world for a year. Maybe longer."

I Wow!

M I told him to slow down a bit. I'm like, "Don't rush into anything here." I was just stunned. Can you imagine what Jhulan and Rahul will say? I mean, he's actually got a job offer, a great job offer to do exactly what he wanted, and he's saying no to go travelling!

I I know! I mean, I'm pleased for him, jealous actually, but how is he going to tell them?

M Well, I asked him that. I was like, "When are you going to tell them?" And this is the really shocking bit. "I'm not," he says. "I'm going to go, and then I'll call and tell them where I am." ...

Exactly! So I told him what I thought. I went, "You can't do that! You've got to tell them! They'll be really upset if you don't." And he's like, "I know, but they'll be upset whenever I tell them, and it'll be so awful, I'll give up on the idea of travelling, and I really want to do this." And I do sort of know what he means.

I Yes, but ... He has to say something to his parents. Don't you think? We should talk to him together.

3.5

SURESH Dad.

RAHUL Yes?

S Erm, there's something I need to tell you.

R Yes?

S I'm not going to take the job with—

R What? I don't believe it! So what do you think you're going to do with your life then?

S It's not the job. It's just that I'm not ready to settle down yet. I want to go travelling, Dad.

R Travelling?

S Yeah. I didn't tell you because I thought you and Mum would try to stop me going. But I'm definitely going. I've bought the tickets and everything.

R Hm, travelling? ... Well, it's good to see the world.

S Really, Dad? You don't mind?

R Well, it could be worse. Where are you planning to go?

S I'm going to start in Sydney, Australia. I'll try and get some work there.

R Hm, I know some people there you could stay with.

S Really? Thanks, Dad. That would be great.

R And what are you going to do about the job?

S I suppose I have to say no to the offer.

R Well, maybe not. You might be able to postpone it for a year.

S Really? Can you do that?

R You can try, at least. Jobs like that don't come along all the time.

3.6

JAMIE Do you think it's ever OK to lie to people?

EMMA Erm, I don't just think it's OK sometimes. I think it's vital on certain occasions.

J I totally agree.

E Erm, there's a ... I think there's a big difference between black lies and white lies.

J Yeah, definitely.

E A white lie is when you're lying for the benefit of the person you're talking to, and I think that sometimes those are necessary. Things like, "Yes, Mum, I was in bed by midnight."

J Yeah.

E You know.

J I mean, yeah, I think white lies, most people would agree that they're fine. Personally, I think I use grey lies and maybe charcoal lies. Er, it's a, it's a big grey area. And I think, it sort of, it depends on the situation. Sometimes you can lie to protect someone. So being honest I don't think is fundamentally good in every situation, but if you can, it's ideal.

3.7

NAOMI How was work?

KYOKO Difficult. I had two people off. That reminds me. You know Simon? My production assistant?

N Yeah, I think so. The new guy?

K Yeah, well, basically he lied about being sick today.

N How do you know?

K Well, Anra said that she saw him in town with someone.

N How do you know he wasn't sick?

K Well, after lunch, I rang him and I told him what Anra said. He said that he wasn't really sick; he told me that he just needed to see his brother. He was really embarrassed and he promised not to do it again.

N Hm, but is that good enough? I mean ...

K Well, he explained why he did it.

N Yeah? Why?

K Oh, his brother was having some personal problems, something came up suddenly.

N Hm, OK.

K So, I asked him to come in for the afternoon and said that if he needs time off for anything in the future, he should ask me. Anyway, I've agreed to let it go this time.

N Sounds reasonable.

K Yes, well, I just hope it doesn't happen again. How's your boy?

N Oh, he's wonderful. He was really funny the other day.

K What happened?

N We were at home and he came into the front room and he had chocolate all over his face. But when I asked him about it, he wouldn't say anything. I mean, I said, "Have you been eating chocolate?" and he just looked at me and shook his head!

K Really?

N Yeah. He clearly didn't realise he had chocolate all around his mouth. I asked him to tell me the truth but he kept saying that he hadn't eaten anything.

K Oh, that's really funny. Poor little guy.

N Yeah. So, anyway, I told him to look in the mirror.

K Oh, that's lovely.

N Yeah, it's really hard to be angry with him sometimes, you know.

K Yeah, I know.

🎧 3.8

MEL Did you hear about Hussein?

URI No.

M Well, you know he was going on holiday? Someone said he missed his flight.

U Oh, that's not what I heard.

M Really?

U Yeah. I heard his plane was cancelled and he was put on another plane. He had to stop over in Amsterdam on his way to Buenos Aires.

M Who told you that?

U Hakim. He said he was really upset, because he was meeting his wife over there and he was going to be late.

M Oh, really? That's horrible.

HAKIM Hi everyone, sorry I'm late.

M Hakim. Hi, how are you?

H I'm OK, thanks.

M Have you spoken to Hussein lately?

H I talked to him yesterday actually. He was only a day late in the end. He sounded really happy and relaxed.

M Oh, that's good. Has anybody heard from Mehmet?

U Someone said he's got a new girlfriend.

M Who said that?

U Erm, I can't remember.

🎧 3.9

PATTY My mum's Scottish and my dad's Italian but we lived in southern Italy, so I was brought up to do things in his way, that is, the southern Italian way. Family units are very close, and children, it doesn't matter how old they are, are expected to take part in most family activities, whereas from my mum's British point of view, children are encouraged to be more independent, and it's OK for them to go off and do what they want more. I think there isn't as much sense of belonging to a community in Britain as in Italy, although I guess the friendship group is often stronger in the UK, almost like a family, in fact.

QUANG In Vietnam, many people continue to live with their elderly parents and if they're not living with them, they're certainly living very close to them. Er, I had a good friend, Xuân, who couldn't get married to his girlfriend because he was forced to spend his time and income supporting his elderly parents. So, he wasn't able to pay for a flat where he could live with a wife, and he was very frustrated by that duty to his family, which was so strong.

ÇIGDEM In modern Turkey, some people live with their partner before getting married, but in some circles it would be unacceptable to live with your partner before you get married.

Typically, people leave their family home when they get married. So, I have a friend in her mid-forties who has never married. She has a boyfriend. She's quite modern, she often goes with him on holiday and stays with him in his flat, but she's not moved in with him. She still lives with her parents because she's not married.

Lots of Turkish friends of mine who have their own families, they live near their parents, they're happy to follow in their parents' footsteps. They go out with their mum's friends, they're basically told by their mothers what to do and how to conduct themselves in society.

Unit 12

🎧 3.11

MIKE Hello, everyone. My name is Mike Caxton and I'm an instructor at the Stunt Training Centre in Vancouver. Today, I'm going to talk about the fire courses at our training centre and what you will learn if you take one of our courses. To start with, there are three things you need to know.

First of all, it's important to remember that when you watch a movie that has a stunt performer on fire, you're seeing exactly that, a body that is fully on fire. This type of stunt work is extremely dangerous and must be done in the safest way possible. The stunt performer must use the highest-quality safety products. But you have to remember one thing: nothing is completely fireproof. Everything will eventually burn if it stays on fire long enough. To perform a fire burn safely, everything must be carefully choreographed, rehearsed, and timed to the second.

Secondly, fire is like wind: if there's an opening, it will find a way in. On our course, students will learn how to keep flames away from the most sensitive areas of the body, how long they can stay on fire and what type of movements to do while they're burning.

And finally, you need to know that the fire course is our most challenging course. Having said that, it's certainly the most exciting course you can do.

I'm going to move on now to talk about the different parts of the course, but first may I just say that copies of our brochure will be available for you to take home at the end of this talk.

🎧 3.12

MIKE Right, the first part of the course will cover everything you need for a fire burn. Students will learn about all the fire products, such as the fire suits,

gloves, hoods and special fire gels you need to protect you from a burn.

The second part of the course will cover the fire burn set-up. Students will learn how to use the fire products properly, for example, how much fire gel to put on the skin, where to put it and when to put it on.

Finally, the third part of the course will allow students to accomplish both a partial and full body burn. A partial burn is where the face stays uncovered, so the audience can still see it, and the performers can deliver lines, if the scene requires it. There will be a medical technician and vehicle on site for this day. All students will be videotaped and photographed, so that they will be able to view and critique their performance.

Before I move on to enrolment, are there any questions?

STUDENT 1 Yes, erm, how long is the course?

M Erm, good question. The initial course is two weeks long and, as I said, it's a very challenging two weeks! Training is six days a week, ten hours a day. Any further questions?

STUDENT 2 Yes, can I ask what qualifications the instructors have?

🎧 3.14

First of all, it's important to remember that when you watch a movie that has a stunt performer on fire, you're seeing exactly that, a body that is fully on fire. This type of stunt work is extremely dangerous and must be done in the safest way possible. The stunt performer must use the highest quality safety products. But you have to remember one thing: nothing is completely fireproof. Everything will eventually burn if it stays on fire long enough. To perform a fire burn safely, everything must be carefully choreographed, rehearsed, and timed to the second.

🎧 3.15

MARIAMA I think it's easier to talk to strangers, say, for example, in Nigeria because people are more open to speaking to you and to asking about how you are or where you're going or if you need anything, so it's not seen as anything particularly strange to talk to somebody on the street or somebody if you're waiting, somebody who's in the queue with you if you're waiting for a, for a taxi. I think what's strange is if you go through a town or a supermarket and not say "hello" or make any eye contact because people would probably think you were ill or that you actually couldn't speak.

🔊 3.16

A

RECEPTIONIST Hello, Hotel Plaza.

CATHY Oh, hello. I was wondering if you could help me. I stayed at your hotel with my husband last weekend and I'm afraid I left my credit card there.

R Oh, OK. Could I take your name?

C Yes, it's Cathy Watson.

R Oh yes, we have that.

C Oh great. Would you mind sending it to me?

R Of course, let me just …

B

LUCIE Would you mind if I opened the window? It's really hot in here.

DAVE No, of course not.

L Actually, could I ask you a favour?

D Yes, of course.

L Could I ask you to look after my case while I go to the toilet?

D No problem.

C

INTERVIEWER Excuse me. Hello, I'm from C.O.S., or Clean Our Streets. Would you mind answering some questions? It won't take a minute.

MARTA No, OK. That's fine.

I Could you tell me how you get rid of your rubbish at the moment?

M Er, well, the local council comes to collect it, er …

I And how often do they come?

M Well, it's supposed to be once a week, but they don't always come on time.

I I see. And how much rubbish do you throw away each week? …

D

INTERVIEWER Could I ask you to do something for me?

ALISTAIR Sure.

I Can you fill that in for me? … OK. I was wondering if you've applied for any other jobs?

A No, no, I haven't.

I OK. So, could you tell me a little bit about your background?

A Yes, of course. Well, I started in …

E

SPEAKER And so we come to the end of the presentation. Thanks very much for listening. I appreciate you all coming. If you have any questions, then please, ask away.

MARCO That was very interesting. Could you tell me what you think about people who say global warming isn't really happening?

S Well, …

M Could you tell me your views on that, please?

S Yes, of course. I think I can best explain it by …

🔊 3.17

MARTIN OK. I'd be happy to answer any questions you may have about treasure hunting. Anyone? Yes, what would you like to know?

QUESTIONER 1 Er, yeah. Could you tell us how you first became interested in treasure hunting?

M That's a good question – for most people there's a story behind the hobby. I was once involved in clearing out an old house. In the attic, hidden underneath some boards, I found a glass jar full of old coins. I also found a rare old magazine and a few other minor treasures.

The important thing to remember is that treasure is not always obviously valuable. Things we pay other people to take away are often sold for a lot of money. My experience made me wonder what else could be 'treasure', and where else I might find it. … Yes?

QUESTIONER 2 I was wondering if you could tell me how much this vase might be worth?

M Er, I'm afraid I can't answer that right now, but I'll find out for you. If you send a photo and anything you know about it to my email address, I'll get back to you as soon as I can.

QUESTIONER 3 Could you tell us about the law on treasure hunting? Is it legal to take things without permission?

M That's an important point. Theft is theft, anywhere, and all responsible treasure hunters have their own rules. If you join a club, we all follow some simple rules, which you can see on our website.

QUESTIONER 4 Where's the best place to begin treasure hunting?

M Well, it depends what you want to find. If you're interested in historical artefacts and you have an old house, you could start in your own home – under floorboards, behind walls, above ceiling tiles. If you're looking for coins or jewellery, take a metal detector to the beach or be there when snow melts. You often find things of value around the edges of snowdrifts as they melt.

QUESTIONER 5 Do you think that anyone who spends enough time looking will find something of value?

M All I can say is that you will definitely find something of interest. It may not be valuable, but you start to get interested in the things you find. Everything has a story, a history.

QUESTIONER 6 Where's the best place to look for gold?

M To be honest, I don't know the answer to that. If I did, I probably wouldn't be here. Personally, I'm not involved in looking for gold. If you're really interested in getting involved, the best advice I can give you is to join a club in your local area. We're a community – it's a very sociable hobby – and we enjoy sharing information about things we find and their locations.

🔊 3.18

KANA Can you believe it? My daughter's learning presentation skills at school.

JUAN CARLOS Actually, I think it's a good idea. It's an important part of learning to communicate.

K Yes, but on the other hand, it's not really a subject, is it? It's not like history or maths.

JC So, in other words, we should only teach academic subjects at school?

K Well, yes. To put it another way, education is about learning how to think and acquiring knowledge.

JC Among other things. What about how to get on in the world of work? Another point is, it teaches kids an important life skill. You have to talk to groups of people and answer questions all the time, in your social life and in your work life. You need to be able to communicate effectively. Another thing is that it builds confidence. Lots of people are scared of talking in public. But if they did it at school, from a young age, then it would just be a normal part of their lives.

K Hm, but it might just put people off. I mean, if a young kid has to give a talk and gets nervous and has a bad experience then they may never want to do it again …

🔊 3.22

1 coin	6	joy
2 poison	7	destroy
3 toilet	8	join
4 loyal	9	ointment
5 annoying	10	toy

Unit 13

🔊 3.23

STEVE Do you remember Ratners – the chain of jewellery shops?

DEBBIE Yeah, it used to be everywhere. Didn't it go bankrupt or something?

S Yes, there's a story about the guy who ran it, Gerald Ratner, here. He's got an autobiography out.

D Yeah? Why now? I mean, it was ages ago, wasn't it?

S Yes, I think he's making a comeback or something. I didn't know this, though. Apparently, his business failed because he made a joke about how rubbish some of his products were in a speech.

D Well, he shouldn't have sold such cheap stuff.

S Hm. I think it was the first time lots of people could actually afford to buy jewellery. He was just saying that you get what you pay for. I think it's a bit harsh, to lose your business just for making a bad joke.

D Well, maybe, but business *is* tough. Anyway, he shouldn't have said it in public.

s Well, I like the fact that he said it. Not many business people are that honest.

D No, there's a reason for that! Look what happens when you're honest.

s Yes, but it's unfair, isn't it? Maybe he could have just apologised, you know, and explained that it was a joke.

D Hm. Once you've done something like that, there's nothing you can do about it.

s Yeah, I know, but to make one silly mistake like that, and it wrecks your life.

D Yeah, but he should have kept his mouth shut! Didn't somebody else do something similar recently?

s Oh yeah, the guy who runs that credit card company. I think he said he doesn't use one because they're too expensive or something.

D That's right. And he wouldn't let his children use credit cards …

3.25

1

KEVIN A couple of years ago I caused a car accident by driving into the car in front, and the driver of that car, a young woman, had to go to hospital. I visited her a couple of times and we got on surprisingly well. A year later we got married.

2

ALISHA When I went to university more than ten years ago, I had a great time, but I didn't take my studies seriously and I didn't get a very good degree. A few years ago, I decided to study law but my degree wasn't good enough. I did carry on but it's taken much longer and been much harder than it needed to be.

3

JÜRGEN About ten years ago I went to see a Mexican film which I really loved. I became really interested in Mexico. I started to learn Spanish and went to Mexico several times on holiday. Now I live in Mexico and I absolutely love it here.

4

HELEN I didn't enjoy school and my teachers didn't like me. But my English teacher was different. She thought I was intelligent and she encouraged me to work hard. Anyway, later I did an English degree at university and then I went on to become a journalist. I'm very grateful to her.

5

YULIA I just got back from the worst holiday in my life. The resort was horrible, the hotel was terrible and the food was awful. Anyway, I was complaining about it to a friend at work, and she told me she went there last year and had a terrible time too. If only I'd known!

6

NEIL I bought a second-hand car a month ago after looking online. I don't know anything about cars, but I really liked the way it looked. Since then it has broken down four times and cost me a lot of money. I really don't know what to do about it.

3.26

STEVE OK, this isn't funny. Where are we?

DEBBIE Well, I recognise this roundabout. We've been here before.

s Turn left, turn left.

D Aah! You could've told me sooner.

s Er, sorry. We shouldn't have done that. It must be the next exit, I think.

D Yeah maybe. Well, we'll have to carry on until we can turn around.

s Yeah, this map just doesn't make sense. It would've been better to bring our own.

D I know. I couldn't find it and we were in a hurry.

s Well, if you'd asked me, I could've told you exactly where it is. It was on the shelf, next to the TV in the hotel room.

D I'm sure I looked there. Anyway, it's too late now. Look, there's a garage. We can turn round here.

s Well, actually, maybe we should ask someone for help.

D How? Do you speak Greek suddenly?

s Very funny. Where's the phrase book?

D Er, don't know. Probably on the shelf with the map.

s You mean we came without the phrase book? I don't believe it.

D Well, if I'd known we were going to get lost, obviously I'd have brought it. And the map.

s We should've known, really. We always get lost.

D Yeah, it would've been sensible to get the more expensive car with satnav.

s Easy to say that now. Look, if you wait here, I'll try to speak to someone in the garage.

3.27

PATRIZIA When I'm asked about life in southern Italy I immediately think of *l'arte d'improvvisare* – the art of improvisation. What this means is that there are rules for what you're supposed to do, but often people don't follow them exactly. So things happen in certain situations which are unexpected and you have to make decisions, in each case, about what to do.

JON So if someone was smoking in a place where they're not allowed to smoke, would people care?

P Yeah, they would care, but say, if a policeman or passer-by approached and said something, they'd start talking and they'd end up having a friendly discussion about it.

J Hm. It seems to me people in the UK make a big fuss if you're doing something you're not supposed to do. I mean, if you were smoking in a non-smoking café or something, they'd make you leave. They don't let you just cycle the wrong way down a street, for example. They feel they have to say something. People are very aware of what they're allowed to do – or not allowed to do – in England. People are really conscious of rules. It sounds like in Italy people let you do what you want more.

P Er, well, in Italy, a law is a law, but laws can be interpreted differently. Traffic is a perfect example of how people improvise and, er, embrace risk taking.

J What do you mean?

P Well, it looks chaotic, but actually it's quite controlled. A driver might break the speed limit or think of ways to get from point A to B by bending the rules, but there is another code.

J Which is?

P It's very much about how you can protect yourself and take a risk without hurting yourself or other people. And everyone is doing the same thing, so it's a kind of controlled anarchy.

Unit 14

3.29

NEWSREADER Here are the news headlines at 10.30:

A large grass fire is sweeping through far North Queensland towards the town of Tolga.

Two officers have been hurt in an incident involving a family of three.

New laws have been introduced into Queensland State Parliament about the clearing of trees.

By 2050, many more of us will be living to see our 100th birthday.

An injured crocodile has been sharing the bathroom of the wildlife carer who rescued it.

Join us for full news and weather at 11.00.

3.30

1

Residents of the town of Tolga are being evacuated from their homes as a large grass fire sweeps through far North Queensland.

The fire is moving quickly towards the town of Tolga on the Atherton Tableland on the Tolga–Kairi Road.

Twenty-eight firefighters in six fire engines are at the scene and more are on their way from Cairns.

Police are asking motorists to stay away from the area. It is not known how the fire started.

2

Two police officers were involved in an incident in Townsville yesterday morning. The two officers suffered cuts and bruises in a shocking attack by a 14-year-old boy and his parents shortly after 8am yesterday.

The family reportedly hit the officers and threw a heavy coffee cup at one of them. Senior Sergeant Tony Melrose said the officers had moved forward to arrest a 14-year-old boy for assault when the child's parents, a 41-year-old man and 37-year-old woman, attacked them. Both officers were taken to the Townsville Hospital for treatment. The family was charged with 10 offences, including three charges of serious assault. Anyone who saw the incident is asked to call Townsville CIB or Crime Stoppers.

3

A new law has been introduced into Queensland State Parliament to ban the clearing of trees.

Premier Anna Bligh says that this will not be a complete ban, however. Landowners with a special permit will still be allowed to clear trees.

The LNP's Jeff Seeney says that his party will not support the new laws. He says landowners were promised four years ago there would be no more changes to tree clearing laws.

Green groups say Queensland's new tree clearing laws will not work. Nick Heath from the World Wildlife Fund says the government has missed an opportunity to protect the environment. Queensland emits more greenhouse gas per head than any other state in Australia.

4

About 4,000 Australians currently live to see their 100th birthday but by 2050 it is estimated that number will rise to around 25,000.

British medical journal *The Lancet* has published a new study that suggests it will become quite common for babies born in 2000 to live to see 100. Paul Murray talks to demographer Bernard Salt about what life might be like for our future centenarians.

5

A wildlife carer in north Queensland is sharing her bathroom with a 1.6 metre crocodile run over by a car in Townsville early this morning.

Lana Allcroft from North Queensland Wildlife Care says the crocodile has a sore eye and is missing a couple of teeth. She says the injured croc has not been as cross as you might expect, but that he did get a little upset when he was moved out of the bathroom so she could have a shower. The trick, she says, is to keep a towel over his head to keep his stress levels down.

The croc will be collected from Lana Allcroft's home by rangers later today.

🔊 3.31

ABBY   How was Tim's birthday party?

JOE   It was a disaster. All these kids he didn't know turned up and trashed the house. We had to call the police.

A   That's awful.

J   Yeah, the thing that makes me angry is that normal kids can't have parties any more. I don't understand kids these days.

A   Oh, I don't know. I think kids have always been the same – most of them are fine.

J   Maybe, but there was a story on the news this morning of a 14-year-old who was arrested for assault.

A   Really? Why?

J   Well, I can't remember the full story but what's interesting is the officers were going to arrest the boy so his parents attacked them!

A   No! The thing that bothers me is the parents' attitude, not the boy!

J   Absolutely.

A   Was anyone hurt?

J   Well, the officers had to go to hospital, but I don't think it was serious.

A   Oh, right. Did you hear about that fire?

J   The one near Tolga?

A   Yeah. It's scary, isn't it? They've evacuated loads of homes.

J   Yes, it's too close for comfort. The thing that worries me is how it started. I mean, it could be deliberate.

A   Yeah, we'll probably never know. What's funny is it's a grass fire, not a forest fire. You don't hear about those so often.

J   That sounds like it should be easier to put out but it probably doesn't make any difference. I guess what's important is no one gets hurt.

A   Yeah, I know, but it must be awful to lose your home like that …

🔊 3.33

2   What's‿important // is no one gets hurt.

3   What's‿interesting // is the officers // were going to arrest the boy, // so his parents‿attacked them.

4   The thing that makes me angry // is that normal kids // can't have parties‿any more.

5   The thing that worries me // is how‿it started.

6   The thing that bothers me // is the parents'‿attitude, // not the boy!

🔊 3.34

MELEK   Did you hear that thing in the news about the twins?

TOM   Er, was it the one about the identical twins?

M   Yeah, two sisters, who were adopted as babies by different families.

T   Oh yeah, I heard something about that. Weren't they from New York?

M   I can't remember, but they didn't find out about each other until they were in their thirties. And when they met, they discovered that they had led practically identical lives!

T   Hm. Oh, I read a similar article a while ago. There was a study into identical twins who were separated at birth and they discovered that in lots of cases, they were amazingly similar. It was talking about whether it's nature that makes us the way we are or nurture – you know, er, how we're brought up.

M   Yeah, that's what this was about too. It actually said these twins were part of an experiment on twins raised in different homes.

T   No!

M   Yes, but apparently, the parents didn't know about it. Anyway, can you imagine meeting someone who is exactly like you, that you never knew existed?

🔊 3.35

NATHAN   Ah, this one looks good. Erm, it's about some kidnappers who copied their idea from a television show.

MELEK   That sounds interesting. So what exactly did they do?

N   Er, well, apparently, four Chinese men kidnapped a Shanghai business executive outside his home. But they used toy guns, so no one was hurt.

RUTH   Yeah, but did they get caught?

N   Yeah, they've been arrested. They asked for a huge ransom.

M   Yes, but what's interesting is they copied the idea from a TV show. What does it say about that?

N   Well, it says the ringleader had watched a programme about a man who kidnapped someone – for the ransom obviously – because he couldn't find a job. It seems to be saying that they got the idea from the plot of this show.

R   Yeah, but it's just a crime story, isn't it?

N   Well, remember it's just a starting point. It could lead on to a report into the influence of TV on real life.

M   Yes, yes, and there are other stories about people who've copied plots from TV shows. I think it's good.

N   Yeah, yeah. OK, so it's got potential. Erm, what's yours about?

R   Oh, it's about a drummer from some band I've never heard of, who's helping researchers investigate the benefits of interactive computer games, you know, things like Guitar Hero, where you play a virtual guitar and actually hear what you're playing. It's good fun, actually.

M Yes, but what are the benefits?

R Well, I don't really get it. Apparently, it can help people with brain injuries.

M Yeah, that makes sense.

R Yes, but it also talks about childhood and adult obesity. What I want to know is: how can Guitar Hero reduce obesity?

N No idea. Erm, I think you have to stand up when you play Guitar Hero so maybe that helps you to lose weight. You have to move around quite a bit, don't you? I think it could make a good programme. Personally, I'd go for this one.

M Yes, maybe.

R Hm, I'm not convinced. What's yours about?

🎵 **3.36**

MENINDA Can you put the news on?

RICHARD You've just missed it. I'll just see if it's on another channel.

M Ah well, don't worry. I'm not really bothered. Do you want to watch that film tonight?

R Yeah, OK. I'll see when it's on. Erm, oh, it's in a few minutes, on Channel 7.

M That's good timing. Can you turn over then?

R No, hang on, I love this advert.

M What?

R It's brilliant, have you seen it?

M Of course I have. It's, erm ... what's it for?

R Oh, I don't know, but it's funny.

M That's ridiculous. I don't see the point.

R I like ads. They're fun. You can see what new stuff to buy, like stuff for the home.

M Yeah, yeah, too much stuff. And I still don't know what that was for.

R Well, you were talking too much.

M There's a new channel with shorter ad breaks, but I can't remember the number.

R If you give me the remote I'll see if I can find it.

M No, not now. We'll miss the beginning of the film. Oh look, there's that actress – Adele something, who lives up the road.

R Oh yeah. Look, she's advertising Tilman's supermarkets.

M Yeah, this is dreadful.

R Hm. I see what you mean, but supermarket ads are always dreadful. We haven't seen her much lately, have we?

M Actually, I saw her drive past here the other day. Oh, and I saw her come out of the supermarket yesterday. And it wasn't Tilman's!

R Hm. She'll be all over the news for being in the wrong supermarket.

M Oh dear. Can we change channels now?

R Yeah, yeah. Oh! We missed the beginning.

M You see? All because of that stupid advert!

🎵 **3.39**

1	sky	6	sight
2	kind	7	shy
3	might	8	apply
4	provide	9	dry
5	wife	10	fright

The sounds of English

Vowels

Short vowels

/ə/	/æ/	/ʊ/	/ɒ/	/ɪ/	/i/	/e/	/ʌ/
teacher ago	married am	book could	on got	in swim	happy easy	wet any	cup under

Long vowels

/ɜː/	/ɑː/	/uː/	/ɔː/	/iː/
her shirt	arm car	blue too	or walk	eat meet

Diphthongs

/eə/	/ɪə/	/ʊə/	/ɔɪ/	/aɪ/	/eɪ/	/əʊ/	/aʊ/
chair where	near we're	tour	boy noisy	nine eye	eight day	go over	out brown

Consonants voiced unvoiced

/b/	/ð/	/v/	/dʒ/	/d/	/z/	/g/	/ʒ/
be bit	mother the	very live	job page	down red	magazine	girl bag	television

/p/	/θ/	/f/	/tʃ/	/t/	/s/	/k/	/ʃ/
park shop	think both	face laugh	chips teach	time white	see rice	cold look	shoe fish

/m/	/n/	/ŋ/	/l/	/r/	/w/	/j/	/h/
me name	now rain	thing drink	late hello	carry write	we white	you yes	hot hand

Irregular verbs

Infinitive	Past simple	Past participle
All forms are the same		
	bet	
	burst	
	cost	
	cut	
	hit	
	hurt	
	let	
	put	
	set	
	shut	
	split	
	spread	

Past simple and past participle are the same	
bend	bent
bring	brought
build	built
burn	burned/burnt
buy	bought
catch	caught
deal	dealt
dig	dug
dream	dreamed/dreamt
feed	fed
feel	felt
fight	fought
find	found
get	got
hang	hung
have	had
hear	heard
hold	held
keep	kept
learn	learned/learnt
leave	left
lend	lent
light	lit
lose	lost
make	made
mean	meant
meet	met
pay	paid
read /riːd/	read /red/
say	said
sell	sold
send	sent
shoot	shot
sit	sat
sleep	slept
smell	smelled/smelt
spell	spelled/spelt
spend	spent
stand	stood
strike	struck
teach	taught
tell	told
think	thought
understand	understood
win	won

Infinitive	Past simple	Past participle
All forms are different		
be	was/were	been
begin	began	begun
blow	blew	blown
break	broke	broken
can	could	been able to
choose	chose	chosen
do	did	done
draw	drew	drawn
drink	drank	drunk
drive	drove	driven
eat	ate	eaten
fall	fell	fallen
fly	flew	flown
forget	forgot	forgotten
forgive	forgave	forgiven
freeze	froze	frozen
give	gave	given
go	went	been/gone
grow	grew	grown
hide	hid	hidden
know	knew	known
lie	lay	lain
ride	rode	ridden
ring	rang	rung
rise	rose	risen
see	saw	seen
shake	shook	shaken
show	showed	shown
sing	sang	sung
sink	sank	sunk
speak	spoke	spoken
steal	stole	stolen
swim	swam	swum
take	took	taken
tear	tore	torn
throw	threw	thrown
wake	woke	woken
wear	wore	worn
write	wrote	written
Infinitive and past participle are the same		
become	became	become
come	came	come
run	ran	run
Infinitive and past simple are the same		
	beat	beaten

Acknowledgements

The authors would like to thank all the team at Cambridge for their ideas, support and commitment to *English Unlimited*, in particular their editors Karen Momber, Greg Sibley, Keith Sands and Liam Guyton, and David Lawton for his work on the cover and page design. They'd also like to thank Adrian Doff for his consistently encouraging and remarkably detailed feedback; and Dave Willis, Jane Willis, Alison Sharpe and Sue Ullstein for their ideas and inspiration in the early days of this project.

Thanks are also due to Çigdem Ford, Patrizia Congedo and Anne Budden for particular ideas and contributions.

Theresa Clementson would like to thank Anthony, Sam and Megan for their ideas, support and unwavering confidence, and Cristina Rimini for her help and advice on all matters TEFL over the years.

David Rea would like to thank the students, teachers, trainers and staff at IH Kraków, IH Heliopolis, IH Buenos Aires, IH Paris and IH London for all the support, development and fun over the years. He'd also like to thank Emma McLachlan: the most beautiful woman in the world.

The authors and publishers would like to thank the following teachers for invaluable feedback they provided when reviewing draft material:

Stephanie Dimond-Bayir, Sarah Greatorex, Philip Dover, Merryn Grimley (UK); Sandra Oddy (UAE); Alexandra Latimer, Gill Hamilton (Spain); Justyna Kubica, Luiza Wójtowicz-Waga, Hayden Berry (Poland); Karen Stewart, Rafael Diazgonzalez (Mexico); Katherine Kolarik (Australia); Rachel Connabeer (Italy); Antoin Eoin Rodgers, Wayne Trotman (Turkey); Jamelea Nader (The Phillipines); and the various members of the Cambridge Adult Panel.

The authors and publishers are also grateful to the following contributors:

Design and page make-up: Stephanie White at Kamae Design
Picture research: Hilary Luckcock
Photography: Gareth Boden
Audio recordings: John Green at Audio Workshop and id-Audio, London

The authors and publishers would like to thank all of those who took part in the authentic recording sessions, especially:

Paula Porroni, Megan Rivers-Moore, Charlie Nurse, Mariama Ifode, Remco Weeda, Fran Disken, Astrid Gonzales-Rabade, Nuria Gonzales-Rabade, Munizha Ahmad-Cooke, Pierre Star, Jamie Matthews, Emma Freeman, Giulia Conto, Alexander Kentikelenis, Mathieu Desruisseaux, Laurence Star.

The authors and publishers acknowledge the following sources of copyright material and are grateful for the permissions granted. While every effort has been made, it has not always been possible to identify the sources of all the material used, or to trace all copyright holders. If any omissions are brought to our notice, we will be happy to include the appropriate acknowledgements on reprinting.

The Guardian for the adapted article on p8 'Can you believe what you read?' from 'The day I downloaded myself' by Mike Scott, *The Guardian* 23.03.2007. Copyright Guardian News & Media Ltd 2007; Daily Telegraph for the adapted article on p16 'Could social networking sites mean the end of lasting friendships' from 'Facebook spells end of lasting friendships, says expert' by Rebecca Smith, *Daily Telegraph* 03.07.08 © Telegraph Media Group Limited 2008; Daily Telegraph for the adapted article on p18 'Email Survival Guide' from 'An email addict's search for life outside the inbox' by Bryony Gordon, *Daily Telegraph* 19.10.07 © Telegraph Media Group Limited 2007; Dr. David McNeill for the adapted article on p22 'Mr Song and Dance Man'. Reproduced with permission; Daily Mail for the adapted article on pp46–47 'How I lived on £1 a day' from 'How a cash strapped teacher beat credit crunch' © *Daily Mail* 06.09.08; The Independent for the adapted article on p54 'The 5-minute interview: Carlos Acosta' by Alice-Azania Jarvis, *The Independent* 13.03.08. Copyright © Independent Newspapers; Daily Telegraph for the adapted article on p56 'Can pets and their owners become more alike over time?' by Nic Fleming, *Daily Telegraph* 27.10.07 © Telegraph Media Group Limited 2007; The Guardian for the adapted article on p62 'Declutter your life!' from 'Dejunk your life' by Maureen Rice, *The Guardian* 23.01.2000. Copyright Guardian News & Media Ltd 2000; Dr Edward de Bono for the text on p72 'Six Thinking Hats™'. Copyright IP Development Corporation 1985; The Sunday Times for the adapted article on p88 'New computer software to catch email liars' by Abul Taher and Dipesh Gadher, *The Sunday Times* 25.02.07. Copyright © The Sunday Times and NI Syndication.com; The Independent for the adapted article on p94 'How to set yourself on fire' from 'What it feels like... to set yourself on fire' by Jack Arnott, *The Independent* on Sunday 13.08.2006. Copyright © Independent Newspapers; Daily Telegraph for the adapted article on p119 'His goal was to make it simple to use and beautiful to look at. The result was the ipod' by David Derbyshire, *Daily Telegraph* 19.11.05 © Telegraph Media Group Limited 2005; Australian Associated Press for the adapted article on p122 'Aussie legend supports drug use'. Reproduced with permission. Copyright © 2002 AAP; Matt Renton for the adapted article on p122 'Is Money in sport out of control' from 'Money in sport is out of control!' by Matt Renton, taken from: http://www.pponline.co.uk/blog/money-sport-out-control-40087 ; Drug Free Sport NZ for the adapted article on p128 'Athletes need to speak out against drugs, says Ulmer' taken from: http://www.drugfreesport.org.nz/Students+Section/Athlete+Views/Sarah+Ulmer.html Reproduced with permission.

The publisher has used its best endeavours to ensure that the URLs for external websites referred to in this book are correct and active at the time of going to press. However, the publisher has no responsibility for the websites and can make no guarantee that a site will remain live or that the content is or will remain appropriate.

The publishers are grateful to the following for permission to reproduce copyright photographs and material:

Key: l = left, c = centre, r = right, t = top, b = bottom

Alamy/©UpperCut Images for p6(tcl), /©Image Source for p6(ccr), /©Hemis for p11(tr), /©Amanda Ahn for p11(b), /©David Frazier Photolibrary Inc for p14(cl), /©Mohamad Itani for p14(br), /©RayArt Graphics for p15(t), /©Steve Hamblin for p15(b), /©Rob Cousins for p25(r), /©Image State Media Partners/ Impact Photos for p25(l), /©Big Cheese Photo LLC for p25(cl), /©Louise Batalla Duran for p27(tl), /©Images and Stories for p33(br), /©Blend Images for p49, /©Lebrecht Music & Arts Photo Library for p54, /©db images for p58(tr), /©Blend Images for p59(tl), /©Dania Delimont for p59(br), /©Elena Elisseva for p59(bl), /©Sue Cunningham for p60(tr), /©Radius Images for p64(t), /©Afripics.com for p68(r), /©PhotoAlto for p75(br), /©Image Source for p87(tr), /©Photos12 for p88(l), /©Ron Chapple Stock for p90(t), /©Radius Images for p90(b), /©Scottygo for p97, /©Image Source for p99, /©Phototake Inc for p100, /©Alexander Caminada for p111r, /©Alex Ardenti for p112(l)(bicep), /©Rob Rayworth for p125; Art Directors & TRIP for p6(cr), 6 (bl), 6(tcr), 6(ccl), 6(tl), 8(t), 18(background), 18(t), 50(l), 63, 67, 98(background), 102(br), 102(bl); BAA Photo Library/©David Hares for p39(b); Bubbles Photo Library/©John Powell for p26(background); Corbis/©Image Source for p6(cl), /©Nisar Ahmed/Reuters for p32(l), /©Daniel Aguilar/Reuters for p33(tr), /©Vladimir Godnik/moodboard for p55(r), /©Chris Carroll for p60(tl), /©Peter Harholdt for p68(c), /beyond for p74(background), /©Dean Lewins for p110(tl), /©Corbis for p114(background), /©Radius Images for p116; Getty Images/©Blend Images/Jose Luis Pelaez for p22(tr), /©AFP for p22(b), /©Eri Morita for p44, /©Digital Vision for p56(t), /©Zubin Shroff for p91(crt), /©Nivek Neslo for p98(t), /©Jerry Driendl for p107(t); HarperCollins.com for p10(tl); Hodder & Stoughton Publishers for p10(cr); istockphoto/©onebluelight for p9(l), /©Eduardo Jose Bernardino for p11(tl), /Christian Pound for p19(t), /©livjam for p28, /©Ryerson Clark for p32(r), /©Julien Grondin for p33(l), /©Scott Leigh for p34(background), /©Keith Wheatley for p46(r), /©Jodi Matthews for p55(l), /©Karl Barrett for p56(b)(a), /©Eric Isselee for p56(b)(e), /©Joshua Hodge Photography for p59(tr), /©Dean Mitchell for p59(cr), /©Klaas Lingbeek-van Kranen for p60(b), /©Sergey Lavrentev for p89, /©Rob Friedman for p95(tr), /©Matej Michelizza for p120, /©Koch Valerie for p121, /©Andrey Prokhorov for p131; Masterfile/©Chad Johnston for p56(b)(d), /©Alfo Sport for p58(background), /©Jerzyworks for p75(bc), /©Mattias Kulka for p78(t), 79, /©Image Source for p81, /©Hill Street Studios for p82, /©Photos India for p87(tc), /©Blend Images (RM) for p96(b), /©Cultura RM for p108, Newspix/©NewsLtd/Lindsay Moller for p110(r); Michelle Passoff for p62; Photolibrary/©Cultura for p6(tr), /©Arnaldur Halldorsson for p9(b), /©Brenan O'Sullivan for p16(t), /©Walter Hodges for p22(tl), /©Simon Charlton for p42, /©4x5 Coll-PR Productions 1995 for p51(b), /©fotosearch value for p56(b)(c), /©Creatas for p75(bl), /©Ghislain & Marie David de Lossy for p91(cl), /©fancy for p95(tl), /©Rubberball for p105, /©Ghislain & Marie David Lossy for p107(b), /©Steven Puetzer for p129; Reinitz Asset Liquidations for p68(l); Rex Features for p66(r); Rex Features/©NBCUPHOTOBANK for p10(tr), /©David Lomax/Robert Harding for p32(c), /©Alex Segre for p96(t); Rocky Taylor for p94(t); Science Photo Library/©TEK Image for p88(r), /©PASIEKA for p112(l) (DNA), Shutterstock/©RT Images for p40(t), /©Krasowit for p56(b)(b), /©Rohit Seth for p87(tl), /©mypokcik for p92, /©jocicalek for p119; South West News Service for p47; TNR.com for p8(b); Topfoto.co.uk for p10(cl); Dr Himanshu Tyagi for p16(b); Wiley Blackwell for **The Rise and Fall...and Rise Again** by Gerald Ratner for p102(t); www.greekboston.com for p106(background).

The following photographs were taken on commission by Gareth Boden for CUP:

14(cr), 18(b), 20, 26(r), 36(l,r), 38, 39(b), 50(r), 51(t), 52(t,b), 64(b), 71, 73, 76, 78(b), 80, 84, 103(t), 106(t).

We are grateful to the following for their help with the commissioned photography:

Claire Butler; Crest Nicholson plc; First Capital Connect; Grand Arcade, Cambridge; Great Northern Kitchen, Cambridge; Linda Matthews; The Hertford Tea Room; University of Hertfordshire, Hatfield.

Illustrations by Kathy Baxendale, Kate Charlesworth, Maxwell Dorsey, Mark Duffin, Julian Mosedale, Sean Simms, Ben Swift, Dan Taylor, Lucy Truman.